The Man Who C[reated]
STAR TREK
Gene Roddenberry

By James Van Hise

Designed and Edited by Hal Schuster

JAMES VAN HISE writes about film, television and comic book history. He has written numerous books on these subjects, including BAT-MANIA, 25th ANNIVERSARY TREK TRIBUTE BOOK, STEPHEN KING & CLIVE BARKER: THE ILLUSTRATED GUIDE TO THE MASTERS OF THE MACABRE, CHEERS and HOW TO DRAW ART FOR COMIC BOOKS: LESSONS FROM THE MASTERS. He is the publisher of MIDNIGHT GRAFFITI, in which he has run previously un-published stories by Stephen King and Harlan Ellison. Van Hise resides in San Diego along with his wife, horses and various other animals and writes comic books.

OTHER PIONEER BOOKS

Library of Congress Cataloging-in-Publication Data
James Van Hise, 1949—
    The Man Who Created Star Trek: Gene Roddenberry

    1.   The Man Who Created Star Trek: Gene Roddenberry (television)
I. Title

Published by Pioneer Books, Inc., 5715 N. Balsam Rd., Las Vegas, NV, 89130.

First Printing, 1992

INTRODUCTION:
The Worlds Of
Gene Roddenberry

If any one name is synonymous with STAR TREK, it is that of Gene Roddenberry. STAR TREK's creator maintained his integrity as a dedicated and idealistic writer/producer in the vast, Philistine-infested wasteland of 1960s television. Now Roddenberry, sadly, is gone, but he has left an enduring legacy, a legacy that continues to enthrall and inspire millions throughout the world.

Roddenberry was always a dreamer, a visionary. Long before STAR TREK reached the screen, he fought to bring quality and intelligence to television in such shows as HAVE GUN, WILL TRAVEL (for which he served as head writer for several seasons) and THE LIEUTENANT (his first series as creator/producer).

It seemed that he should gravitate towards science fiction, perhaps the only genre in which he might be free to slip in pointed commentary on current events. Playing close to the vest, he pitched his proposed series as a "Wagon Train to The Stars," speaking the language the networks understood in order to get the go-ahead.

After two years, he succeeded. STAR TREK's first pilot was rejected as "too cerebral." Roddenberry was then given an unprecedented chance, the green light for a second pilot. The rest is history of almost mythical proportions: the fight to keep the show alive; its cancellation; resurrection in syndication; the years of struggle to revive the show; the phoenix of six movies; and the offspring of a next generation.

Through it all, Roddenberry kept busy, developing new series which, unfortunately, never found a place on any network. The pilots (SPECTRE, THE QUESTOR TAPES, GENESIS II) stand as intriguing glimpses into worlds that could have been. The seventies were a difficult time for Roddenberry, but he persevered. Fees from public speaking kept him afloat much of the time.

Finally, STAR TREK's resurrection came to pass, and Roddenberry's vision once again shined for all to see. The trials of the past behind him, he steered his Trek universe to new glories, both on the silver screen and on television. By creating STAR TREK: THE NEXT GENERATION, he beat the odds again, achieving the allegedly impossible. He proved you can't keep a good man down. The triumph of STAR TREK's twenty-fifth year, highlighted by the appearance of Spock on THE NEXT GENERATION and the immensely successful STAR TREK VI: THE UNDISCOVERED COUNTRY, has been dimmed by Gene Roddenberry's passing, but the continuing sagas prove he was right all along. After all, how many men truly create something of world renown that will live on after them? Gene Roddenberry did. His spirit and vision shall never be forgotten.

—James Van Hise, January 1992

I In The Beginning

"I have a terrible hunger for ideas." —G.R.

Eugene Wesley Roddenberry, the creator of STAR TREK, was born in El Paso, Texas on August 19, 1921. The young Roddenberry spent his formative years in Los Angeles, a science fiction aficionado from the word go. It started with a battered copy of ASTOUNDING STORIES magazine, and took off from there. Of course, he never considered writing in any genre or medium until much later in life, after college.

When he did, there would be no denying that he had a certain knack for it! Young Gene was a sickly boy whose parents often worried about his developmental problems. They failed to realize he had a vividly active imagination which made the trials of reality easier to bear. His discovery of science fiction, including Edgar Rice Burroughs' John Carter of Mars books, actually led him back to reality, demonstrating the possibilities of existence. Adolescence brought improvement in Gene's health, and he soon became a highly active youth. "I was somewhat handicapped as a child," Gene freely admitted. "I had the good fortune to lose most of it. "I was a science fiction reader from the time I was about eleven years old. Since the age of four I've been reading everything in sight. I suspect if you gave me a telephone book I would read it. At the age of fourteen I read DAYS OF OUR YEARS by Pierre Van Paussant, which is a story that is sort of outmoded now but it was the first statement I read about the evil of war and that wars are often manipulated for reasons other than the ones offered. I should say the whole range of reading through school, I could think of fifty-five writers, but not [only] one or two [that have influenced him.]"

As a child, Gene had radio (the home entertainment system of the day), but television didn't exist yet. He became a reader. He'd go to the library every week on the W-Line streetcar and then home again. "I remember getting some peanut butter and crackers and falling into the dream world of books."

His mother didn't share Gene's interest in books. She openly wondered if he planned to read every book in the library, something the boy would have been happy to have accomplished.

"I have a terrible hunger for ideas," Gene recounted. "I've had it since my early years. In my youth, I realized I had this terrible hunger for knowledge—like an addict for knowledge. I remember that I just couldn't sit down without my mind working, without reading something, some experience. It seemed that this was more a flaw, this terrible hunger."

This pursuit of knowledge would continue all his life. As an adult he would often wake up at five o'clock in the morning so that he could read for two hours before the normal distractions of the day began. Gene read omnivorously in both fiction and non-fiction.

He noted, "If something comes out by Arthur C. Clarke, I grab it immediately. The science fiction people are good enough to send me proofs of almost everything that's being published and I just really pick and choose on that. But you don't read just science fiction. This is a big, big world.

"The other morning my wife came by my bed," Gene continued, "and there was a copy of THE BATTLE OF THE NORTH SEA, and she said, 'What do you expect, to be an admiral some day?' No, that's not it. Everything you read helps you grow. Science fiction is not enough to read alone."

Gene's father was a Los Angeles street cop. A third grade dropout, the elder Roddenberry was proud he had taught himself to read and write. Later Gene would recall that his father was a very intelligent man, who obtained his high school diploma while working for the Los Angeles Police Department. Gene believed he had received some of the beliefs that would serve him throughout his life from his father. Years later, when STAR TREK was first on television, Gene received a letter from two elderly women in Florida who thought the show was created by the elder Roddenberry; he had met these ladies while on his way to fight in World War One, and had impressed them with his talk of the future.

The elder Roddenberry did not go to church, but Mrs. Roddenberry took her children every week to the Baptist church. "A great deal of my early training was due to my father who, mysteriously, never showed up in church," Gene recounted. "I can remember now what things he had to say. He did not think the church was particularly the guidance that he would have pushed me to have. He felt that it was good for me to go to church but be damned careful of what the preachers say!"

Gene didn't think much of the proceedings. At about the age of fourteen, he started paying attention to what was said in the sermons, and came to the conclusion, which he kept to himself, that it was nonsense. He became a good deal more interested in the deacon's daughter then the gospel.

"My Baptist background offered images of streets of gold and repossessing our present bodies and personalities—all sorts of similar nonsense," he said. "I would certainly never buy a script from a science fiction writer whose imagination was that limited. It seems the more religion tries to answer such questions, the more nonsensical it becomes." Gene went on to point out, "They said God was on high and he controlled the world and therefore we must pray against Satan. Well, if God controls the world, he controls Satan. For me, religion was full of misstatements and reaches of logic that I just couldn't agree with. "

The concept of communion, of eating the body of Christ and drinking his blood, made him wonder if Christianity hadn't been created by cannibals. The supernatural, magical nature of religion eluded Gene Roddenberry, bringing him to conclude it had no place in his life.

He didn't make waves, but continued to attend church. He sang in the choir, but made up "cowboy lyrics" instead of singing about Jesus.

"How can I take seriously a god-image that requires that I prostrate myself every seven days and praise it? That sounds to me like a very insecure personality," Gene once said, by way of explaining his belief system. "Yet, there can hardly be any subject more important to us than what we are, our purpose, our relationship to the universe. Science is strangely silent on the subject. There's a tradition of avoiding that area. I find it frightening that scientists, our best chance for a logical examination of the subject, refuse to consider it. And yet, we have an abundance of theories about the Big Bang and black holes and all that, but almost no scientific thought considering the purpose of the universe."

Gene never looked down on the religious any more than he scorned a child's need for Santa Claus. He only felt humankind had outgrown the need for such cherished delusions.

"As the human race moves into adolescence and adulthood, it can no longer afford to guide its affairs via those simple myths," he said. "Our human ancestors thought long and hard on who and what they were and came up with the best explanations they could make. The frightening thing is that we—almost at the end of the 20th century, entering the space age, becoming a society based on knowledge—are still hanging on to those explanations, which date back to our Stone Age. I think we need a more fruitful way to analyze these questions. We need exciting philosophical thought. I don't dislike religion, but I am in considerable fear of what today's brand of it can lead to."

As a child, Gene kept his private thoughts to himself, regarding them as nobody's business but his own. Earlier, he had realized such dissimulation was sometimes necessary to get along with others.

When a fourth grade teacher erroneously accused him of skipping a stair (apparently a serious offense), she would not accept his protestations of innocence. Concluding that honesty was useless, Gene caved in and admitted he probably had skipped the stair without realizing it. The teacher was satisfied and Gene came to believe we are all two people anyway: the inner and the outer self. As long as the inner self is true to what it believes, the outer self can fudge things a bit— within limits.

Gene learned tolerance from his father. Although the elder Roddenberry was not religious, he never made an issue of it in the family, and sometimes took relatives to church when they came to visit. On one occasion in 1933, the elder Roddenberry's irreligiousness was strangely confirmed when an earthquake struck Long Beach during the service!

Gene came to realize, in looking back, that his father had a great deal of foresight. Once in the 1930s, Gene's father took the boy out in front of their Monte Vista Street home and explained that one day entire blocks of the city would be ripped out to make room for huge highways—what in years to come would be called freeways.

Although Gene would, for a time, follow in his father's footsteps and become a policeman, he became much the same kind of policeman his father had been. Gene believed his father was embarrassed by the excesses that police were commonly guilty of in the Thirties and Forties. His father never talked about his police work. Gene knew his father had been attacked once in the line of duty and slightly wounded when a man shot at him. "He was never a macho police officer," Gene said. "He was more interested in the types of things we talked about—how would the city change. He was a very thoughtful man."

While his father was not well-educated, Gene believed that his own personal philosophy about ordinary people and his optimism for humanity was inspired by him. Gene believed that his tolerance for other races was also learned from his parents; they never taught him that one race was superior to another. Because of this Gene found other ethnic groups interesting rather than strange.

Gene's father died in December 1969. His mother was still living at the time of Gene's death in October 1991.

Gene found that his mother's religious ardor soon faded. It was replaced, perhaps, with a keen instinct for playing poker, a game Gene much enjoyed throughout his life. He would quote Somerset Maugham, who viewed poker as a test of an individual's intelligence.

As children, he and his brother, Robert, learned math with cards and learned to calculate with cards, particularly for cribbage. Card playing was a major family activity for the Roddenberry clan while Gene was growing up. Gene also developed an enthusiasm for golf, which his second wife, Majel, shared.

His brother and sister drifted away from religion as they grew older. What had outwardly been a religious family faded as the children grew into their twenties.

Gene's grandmother was also a moral influence in his life, teaching him that a person should always keep true to their own beliefs. Years later Gene came to understand just how much his grandmother cared about them.

As an adult he learned that when he used to go swimming in the river near her home, she'd allow the children to rinse themselves off with her garden hose. What he didn't realize as a child was that this was during the Depression, and people had a water ration. Their grandmother used up much of hers letting her grandchildren rinse off with that garden hose. It's one of those adult realizations that adds meaning to otherwise average childhood events.

Gene Roddenberry studied pre-law at Los Angeles City College, then aeronautical engineering at UCLA. During World War Two, he served as a fighter pilot at the helm of a B-17, flying eighty-nine missions in the South Pacific.

Gene's military decorations included the Distinguished Flying Cross and the Air Medal. Later, he would build his renowned character of Captain Kirk around the personal attributes he believed made up a top-notch pilot.

While stationed in the South Pacific, he began to write, and made his first sales to magazines for flying aficionados. He also wrote poetry, some of which was accepted and published by the NEW YORK TIMES.

After his combat duty ended, Gene stayed with the Air Force for the duration of the war. He was assigned to lead investigations into the causes of aircraft crashes.

When the war ended in 1945, he took his aeronautic skills into the private sector, becoming an international airline pilot for Pan American World Airways. In 1948, on a night flight from Calcutta, India, Gene's plane crashed in the Syrian desert. He was one of eight survivors. Gene led his companions through an incredible ordeal that included driving away desert nomads intent on robbing the corpses of those not fortunate enough to have survived the crash.

This didn't deter him from continuing to fly, but it may well have contributed to his declining interest in it as a career. As he once observed, "Being a pilot is taking off from strange airports and countries and not sleeping regularly. It's good if you want to build an image. Nice to drop in on a cocktail party and say, 'Ah, yes, London—I was there two days ago,' or even more exotic places. But writing is an exciting life. It introduces you constantly to new subjects and makes you think in new and different ways."

While working as a pilot he lived in New York and studied literature at Columbia University. His writing professor gave him an interesting piece of advice which he never hesitated to pass along to people who wanted to be writers. "He used to look at the class, assume we were above average intelligence (which if we weren't, we had no business being there), that we were omnivorous readers (which we should have been), and he would say, 'Anyone in this class willing to write three million words free of charge can probably begin to sell something.' He would then finish off by saying, 'Fortunately, thirty out of the forty of you will give up. I say fortunately because otherwise we'd be up to our neck in writers.'"

Throughout the late 1940s Gene continued to write for flying magazines. In 1949 the writing bug led him to quit his airline job and move to Los Angeles, "where I knew television eventually would be based. But I was a little early, and to make ends meet I joined the Los Angeles police department." He had come out from New York in 1949, "to see my dear and old friend, who was then Inspector William Parker in the Wilshire Division. He wasn't very enthusiastic about my plans. In fact, he did his best to talk me out of it." But Gene disregarded Parker's advice and joined the LAPD, following in his father's footsteps.

The job provided him with insights no office job could have offered. The next year, Parker, who had become chief by then, proposed that Gene do "normal police stuff" six months out of the year, and work for him the rest of the time. The curious partnership lasted almost five years.

Politically Gene was considerably to the left of Parker, but the two enjoyed long philosophical talks. He remembers the legendary hard-line chief as almost Liberal on some subjects.

The special duties included writing speeches for his friend, and Gene even ghosted most of Parker's book, PARKER ON POLICE, still regarded as a classic of police philosophy. In a 1990 interview with THE HUMANIST magazine, Gene recalled, "I was Parker's speech writer, writing his philosophical beliefs. I had to justify for him many of the things he did. These were things of rare honesty. I was close to him in the days when he dreamed of building a better police department and when he was engaged in putting his dreams into action. We exchanged a lot of confidences as our relationship went beyond that of a chief of police and one of his sergeants. He used me as a philosophical sounding board, and I used him the same way. Our relationship was such that we were capable of intimate thought and philosophical exchanges."

Gene was impressed by Parker's openness to new ideas and his diverse intellectual interests. He would fall back on this in 1964-65 when he created Mr. Spock and the Vulcan philosophy of "infinite diversity in infinite combinations." (IDIC).

"The only thing that ever corrupted him," Gene continued, "was that mysterious thing of believing in something so strongly [that] you believe what you said. He had the strength to do that. He was an honest cop. I wrote some good speeches for him. It's as close as I've come to writing pure philosophy.

"It is rare that a person can be everything you want them to be. At various moments, all of us are capable of depth of soul and profound honesty. Many people who only knew Parker in his latter years don't believe he was capable of that sort of self-examination and deep philosophical expression."

Gene managed to slip a bit of his own more Liberal views into the right-wing Parker's texts. Parker was often perplexed when people he regarded as left-wingers enthusiastically applauded his Gene-penned speeches.

Looking back on that time, Gene stated that he didn't think he made a very good policeman himself because he hated writing tickets. He was probably the only policeman in Los Angeles who was a card-carrying member of the American Civil Liberties Union. Yet he never regretted the five and a half years he spent with the Los Angeles Police Department. "It gave me a good look at life and death. Policemen see things that you just don't ordinarily run into during your life. In a few years in police work you see life really stripped bare. It's awfully good experience for a writer."

Since he had come to Los Angeles to write for television, he knew he needed an agent and soon hatched a scheme to secure one. Gene also knew that a well-known writer's agent drove through his beat each day, so he just patiently waited until the man committed a traffic violation. Instead of writing a ticket, he got the agent to arrange an interview at Four Star Productions.

Gene dressed casually for the interview, and as he became more involved in disclosing his concepts and story ideas, he removed his sports coat. After that the executives were really hanging on his every word. It was only later that he realized that under his coat, he'd been wearing his shoulder holster and .38 police special.

"First of all, forget about having to sell the first show you ever write," Gene explained, recalling his earliest days in the business. "I went to an agent and he said that if you're willing to write four or five shows, complete scripts, and send them out, you will sell the fourth or the fifth script. I thought to myself, well, he doesn't know me! I sold the fifth. I spent long hours writing these shows. Writers today don't seem to be willing to do this."

He sold his first script to television in 1951. At the time he wrote under the name "Robert Wesley" (a combination of his brother's first name and his own middle name) because the Los Angeles Police Department frowned on its officers moonlighting.

In 1953 Gene sold his first science fiction story, "The Secret Defense of 117." The 117 referred to in the title was the planet Earth. "It was bought by Four Star Theatre for Chevron's show," Gene recalled. "In those days Four Star was astonished to get it and astonished that they liked it. They considered it one of those odd things that happens, and it never occurred to them that science fiction might have a life of its own. U.S. Steel wanted it, too, and everyone was startled than an interesting story could be made out of science fiction elements.

"I went on from that to do other non-science fiction things like HAVE GUN WILL TRAVEL and THE LIEUTENANT because it was obvious to me that no one was looking for science fiction at that time. And as I found out when I was trying to sell STAR TREK, they still weren't!"

While working as a cop, Gene continued to write, and submit his writings, which, as any writer will tell you, is the pre-eminent requirement for success. It would only be a matter of time before Gene Roddenberry would change careers once more.

Television

"Writing is pap and useless talk unless there is an idea in your script." —G.R.

Falling back on his ongoing experience as a police officer, Gene Roddenberry sold a script to DRAGNET. He also applied his experience to scripts for such shows as MR. DISTRICT ATTORNEY.

Gene said, "Then one day my wife, Eilene, said, 'Look, Gene, your job as a policeman brings you $435 a month but your writing hobby is earning $1100 a month. Why don't you stick to your hobby?' We went to dinner, to a Chinese restaurant, to talk it over. I opened a fortune cookie and it read: 'A change of name will bring you fame.'"

Gene had been selling his scripts under the name Robert Wesley. "I opened another one and it read, 'Tomorrow is an excellent time to change jobs.' Intrigued and amazed, I opened still another one and this message read, 'You may be sure of it.'

"That did it!" he recalled. "I quit as a policeman the next day. I still have those fortune cookies framed and on my desk."

When Gene quit his job with the L.A. Police Department, he was already writing for U.S. STEEL HOUR, PLAYHOUSE 90, KAISER ALUMINUM HOUR, FOUR STAR THEATRE, GOODYEAR THEATRE, THE JANE WYMAN THEATRE, DRAGNET, "And also in Hollywood some very bad shows like MR. DISTRICT ATTORNEY and so on, but I was learning to write. As I began to master my profession a little better then I moved on to better and better shows."

After freelancing for a variety of series, including WEST POINT STORY, BOOTS & SADDLES, HARBOR COMMAND, NAKED CITY and DR. KILDARE, Gene became a story editor for the Richard Boone Western series, HAVE GUN, WILL TRAVEL. The show aired from 1957 to 1963 on the CBS television network.

He contributed, in part, to that series by having the philosophical gunslinger Paladin frequently quote from the works of the ancient philosopher Erodius the Second. When the network began to receive viewer queries about this personage, an executive was dispatched to learn more about Erodius from the seemingly erudite Roddenberry. Gene promptly confessed he'd been making up such quotes as "The sweetest sugar is after you have tasted bile," and that Erodius, too, was his own invention. [Erodius being derived from E. (for Eugene) Rod-enberry.]

Gene soon became head writer for the series. His script for the HAVE GUN, WILL TRAVEL episode entitled "Helen of Abajnian" was awarded the coveted Writer's Guild Award.

Writing for television presented a variety of challenges to Roddenberry, and sometimes he chose not to confront them. Gene said, "I used religion several times in HAVE GUN WILL TRAVEL. Once in a penitentiary where a pastor was trying to keep a fellow from being hung, I wrote that the pastor grabbed a hacksaw blade, was cut by it, and was bleeding. I had him make some comment about blood and salvation. It's not that I actually believed in blood and salvation being connected, but that was the way the audience believed and I can remember going out of my way not to deal directly with what my thoughts were for several reasons."

Gene admitted that he just didn't want to take on the system. He went along with what was expected of him, but bit by bit found it more and more difficult.

One common aspect of many early TV shows was violence. "Television got off to a very bad start regarding violence," Gene recalled. "They had pretty much unthinking writers. The Western with the man who was fast with a gun is a good example. I've been puzzled for many years why people who should know better, including philosophers, incorporate that in their thinking—that violence is an answer to many things—because we know in life it isn't. Violence begets violence. Everything that is supposedly wrong with television is part of what a writer puts in and reaps."

While HAVE GUN, WILL TRAVEL featured Paladin, who often relied on his wits more than his gun, Gene admitted that sometimes his writing took the easy way out. "I'm not pleased with the scripts where I fell off the wagon and created a crafty fast gun who was evil—without questioning very much why he was evil—and had Paladin slay him," Gene said. "But I am pleased with the times I didn't. Violence has always been a part of American television. It seems to me that it is so easily arguable that violence is not the key or important ingredient in television drama."

Gene lived through interesting experiences as a writer, some of which brought him face to face with situations he couldn't in good conscience back down from. He recalled, "I remember once when I was a freelance writer and I was sent out to a place and they said, 'We've got a show called RIVERBOAT—would you like to write it?' The price was right and it was adventure, so I went out and it was Mississippi—1850s, and I talked a story and they said, 'Fine, you've got an assignment. Oh, uh, just one thing. No Negroes.' Mississippi? 1860?? We got into an argument and I lost the assignment."

Gene simply couldn't go along with the lie. He explained, "That is patently false. That is lying; that is lying both to children and adults, and I think things like that are immoral. It's those immoralities that are my principal fight with the networks. Within the limits of their commercial system where television exists only to sell products, they probably do the best they can. I, for one, am waiting for the whole system to be changed so that when we make a show directly for the audience. If the audience doesn't watch it, then fine, I goofed and I'm willing to admit my blame. It is this present strange system where you never get an appeal to the audience, you go through so many committees and agencies and vice presidents that make the decisions that most of us, most dramatists, object to so strongly."

That is just one example of the censorship rampant in the early days of television. "I once wrote into a script that the newspapers on this corner were held down in the wind by a tire iron. I needed that because someone was going to grab a heavy object there as a weapon in a scene," Gene said. "I was called in and they said, 'Please take the tire iron out and make it a brick.' I said I sort of like the tire iron. And they said, 'Yes, but it really conjures up the failure of an advertised product—tires—and we'd rather not have that.' It actually reached that far.

"In those days you couldn't, in a Western, have your people 'ford' a river because you might be trying to get Chevrolet as sponsor."

THE MAN WHO CREATED STAR TREK

In the same interview in which Gene recalled the early days of television for the March 1976 PENTHOUSE, he didn't feel attitudes among network personnel were had changed over the years. He said, "No, in some areas it's gotten worse. If I wanted to write a show saying I believed organized religion was evil, I couldn't. No matter how entertaining a drama I wrote, I couldn't get it on television.

"I couldn't get a show on television questioning whether the United States was a mistake. I cannot write a television drama commenting seriously on unions or management, or on the armament sales that we're involved in. I couldn't write, assuming I wanted to, a pro-Arab, anti-Israeli drama.

"Now, the answers that you get are that, 'Yes, but we do brave things in news and public affairs programming.' What they miss is the fact that fiction affects people more strongly than news and public affairs. Drama makes you identify with what's happening. If a good writer, or many good writers, during the Vietnamese conflict had been permitted to write fictional tales of what was happening in Vietnam, making you identify and become a Vietnamese peasant whose daughter has just been burned to death by napalm; or had we been able to write fiction so you could feel the horrible changing of a man that produced a Calley and made you become that man and wrench your guts as it happened, I'm absolutely certain that the war would have been over two years earlier."

As far back as 1968, when he gave a talk on the Berkeley campus, Gene believed in the future of television and the people, like himself, who were working in it. "As bad as television is," he insisted. "I think they'll look back and see many good things they did, too. I think the audience becomes more sophisticated every year. I can remember at the beginning of television fifteen years ago, and many of us were working as screenwriters on even the bad shows that we started with. MR DISTRICT ATTORNEY—you can't get much worse than stuff like that—and we would always insert in our scripts that to be of a different color or a different creed does not make you bad. Lessons of tolerance and things like that.

"You had to do it very carefully, the network didn't want any preaching in it, but I think these things had an effect. I don't think these things could play every night in Mississippi and places like that around the country and not have an effect on the society and on the people growing up. I think TV has done some good. I just think it's a damn shame that we've had to do it as saboteurs and not with the support of the studios and the network."

Gene felt that it was important for a writer to do the best job they could. "I think that all serious writing is valuable," he said. "It is the duty of the writer to speculate on things of importance to us, and to give us new insights into ourselves, who we are, what our society is, what its pitfalls are—what its joys should truly be. In that sense I think STAR TREK was valuable, and that all serious and entertaining writing is valuable."

"I'm very concerned about the way television is going and what it can become," he said in a 1977 interview. "We are beginning to realize now with certain studies coming out of UCLA, Harvard and other places that television has an enormous impact on people—much stronger than was ever before recognized. If over the next twenty-five years it remains merely the tool of merchandising people, that would worry me. I'm worried about the future of a country which is being bombarded with sound and image in which the sole basis of whether it gets on the air is will it or will it not sell toothpaste, soap, beer and so on. I think we are going to have to protect ourselves from public TV by going to some kind of pay TV, not that we don't have it now. We pay a tax on television with every bar of soap we buy. Probably the phoniest cry you'll ever hear is, 'Don't pay for what you're getting free now.' You have pay TV now except you're paying for a lot of stuff you don't want."

Gene realized that freelancing left the final product of his mind in the hands of others. To retain control, and earn greater profits, he became a producer. His first few pilots failed to result in a series.

In 1959 he produced a pilot for a police show called THE NIGHT STICK. It didn't get picked up for a series, nor was it ever even aired on any of the networks.

In 1960, he produced a pilot entitled 333 MONTGOMERY, about a famous San Francisco lawyer named Jake Ehrlich, portrayed by DeForest Kelley. Kelley said the pilot didn't sell because "the pilot material was too strong and the network didn't like the idea at all that my character had defended a guilty man that the audience knew had committed this crime—but he got him off with a prison sentence. And in the end, he said something like, 'I don't like you but I just did what I had to do,' or something like that." Kelley felt the show was just slightly ahead of its time as just a couple years later THE DEFENDERS became a hit doing similar hard-edged storylines.

Kelley also appeared (but did not star) in Gene's 1964 unsold pilot, POLICE STORY, which bore no relation to the much later series of the same title. In 1962 Gene wrote two more unsold pilots, APO-923 and DEFIANCE COUNTY (a thinly disguised reworking of 333 MONTGOMERY).

APO-923 was a World War II adventure show which starred James Stacy, Pat Harrington Jr. and Ralph Traeger as three members of the American military fighting the Japanese in the South Pacific. A sixty minute show based on a seemingly simple idea, according to Lee Goldberg's book UNSOLD PILOTS, it was criticized by the Leo Burnett Agency for being "in extremely bad taste....badly written and conceived."

Persevering once more, Gene came up with yet another pilot. He was frustrated watching too many pilots filmed but left unpurchased by the networks and wanted to see a series all the way through to completion.

His first series to air was THE LIEUTENANT, which ran for the 1963-64 television season. Starring Gary Lockwood as a newly-commissioned officer in the peacetime Marine Corps, and co-starring Robert Vaughn, this was an intelligent, drama which unfortunately failed to draw much of an audience.

Gene recalled, "It lasted a year but it had a reputation around Hollywood for high quality. I wrote a lot of them and got into great trouble with the Marine Corps. They felt that if I was going to do a story about a young Marine it should be John Wayne coming over the hill every week."

Gene described the misadventures explaining, "THE LIEUTENANT was not a Marine Corps picture. It was the story of a young man growing up. I just picked the Marine Corps because a lot of the decisions he has to make are very dramatic. He's in charge of a platoon of men and all that, but I could have easily put him in a stockbroker's office and told the same stories. We did stories about his first unfair boss, his first ideals which were shattered, his first designing woman—all of the firsts that happen in any young man's life. His growth, as he does those things and deals with those things. And his first moral thing that he has to stand up for even though it may cost him something. It was kind of a fun show to do."

The USMC allowed them to shoot on military facilities so they were obliged to submit scripts for approval. "But the Marine Corps got mad at us finally because we insisted on doing this script, based on a true story, where a young Sergeant was up for officer candidate school [and] he was denied because his mother was in the Communist Party. They didn't want us to do that, but we insisted on doing it," Gene said.

He continued, "The thing I remember best about THE LIEUTENANT was an episode we did which had Dennis Hopper, who was still unknown, in it. Lieutenants have platoons, in the military, and in my lieutenant's platoon there was this black soldier, this black Marine, [who] rather disliked this white Marine, and was highly intolerant of the white. Don Marshall played a southern boy who really the whole thing focused on.

"Many don't know, but those were in the days when television was finally allowed to show its first blacks on screen. Until then, it hadn't happened.

"We were sort of pushing at the envelope, as we had this black Marine at a time in which, if you had a shoeshine boy, he had to be white. The preferred occupation for a black was a brain surgeon. But I thought it was a great theme, a black who was prejudiced, and so we made a show of it.

"My problem was not the Marine Corps, here, it was NBC, who turned down the show flat. The studio, MGM, said, 'you'll spend a hundred and seventeen thousand dollars which you won't be able to recover, and we take this very seriously.'

"I had only one thing I could do," Gene continued. "I went out to [the] NAACP, and an organization named CORE, and they lowered the boom on NBC. They said, 'Prejudice is prejudice, whatever the color.' And so we were able to show the show.

"I was trying to make the point that prejudice is prejudice. I want to examine prejudice from every angle, and that particular angle was a black prejudice against whites.

"One thing I remember [about] that show particularly, though, [is that] after the lieutenant had tried to bring about tolerance through common sense, and failed miserably, his captain called him in, and his captain was played by Robert Vaughn. The captain pointed out that he had failed, but he said, 'I'm curious about one thing, lieutenant. Had you succeeded, what would your next move have been? Attempt to walk on water?'"

Gene explained, "About this time, a war in Asia began shaping up, and we made some early protests about this, and we didn't get a second year on the air. Again, I probably think that that was more NBC than the United States Marine Corps."

Ironically, another Marine-centered series premiered the following year and was successful enough to last through the rest of the decade. GOMER PYLE was not, however, noted for its intelligence!

One episode of THE LIEUTENANT featured an actor named Leonard Nimoy as a flamboyant Hollywood director. Majel Barrett, Walter Koenig and Nichele Nichols also appeared on the show. Gene would soon employ all four performers in a new series he was creating.

According to press releases, he was working on a "turn-of-the-century adventure-comedy-drama." What became of this project is unknown, but it is difficult to imagine its story would have survived in the way his next concept to find its way to network television would.

"Prior to THE LIEUTENANT I had written some other pilots," Gene stated. "They were produced by other people, and none of them sold. I began to see that to create a program idea and write a script simply wasn't enough. The story is not 'told' until it's on celluloid.

"Telling that final story involved sound, music, casting, costumes, sets, and all the things that a producer is responsible for. Therefore it became apparent to me that if you want the film to reflect accurately what you felt when you wrote the script, then you have to produce it, too. This is why television writers tend to become producers.

"Producing in television is like storytelling. The choice of the actor, picking the right costumes, getting the right flavor, the right pace—these are as much a part of storytelling as writing out that same description of a character in a novel.

"Although the director plays an important role in this, the director in television comes on a show to prepare for a week, shoots for a week, and then goes on to another show. Unlike the producer, he is neither there at the beginning of the script nor rarely there for long after you end up with some 25,000 feet of film which now has to be cut and pasted together into something unified. There is immense creative challenge and pleasure in taking all of these things and putting them together into something that works."

Following the cancellation of THE LIEUTENANT in 1964 Gene worked on two more pilots, one as writer/producer and the other as just the producer. THE LONG HUNT OF APRIL SAVAGE was a Western starring Robert Lansing, but not a comedy. The plot revolved around Lansing searching for the desperadoes who had murdered his family. Created and written by Sam Rolfe, this thirty minute pilot didn't attract any attention. There is no listing of any air date for the show.

POLICE STORY was written and produced by Gene in 1964 but didn't air until September 1967. Starring Steve Ihnat, Gary Clarke (as a policeman named Questor), Rafer Johnson and Malachi Throne, the thirty minute pilot also featured brief appearances by DeForest Kelley and Grace Lee Whitney. This aired on NBC during the opening month of the second season of STAR TREK, but any tenuous connection didn't benefit the show.

POLICE STORY suffered from a poor write-up in the September 13, 1967 issue of DAILY VARIETY: "If inexplicably there should be an insane demand this year for still another half-hour police show and NBC just had to act hastily, it might choose to fill the order by reviving this Gene Roddenberry project. Otherwise, there's absolutely no reason why the network should have given its rejection a second thought, assuming it ever really did. POLICE STORY doesn't have a lot of things—originality, dramatic tension, character interest or good writing—but chiefly what it lacks is that ineffable chemistry in a pilot that conveys a sense of all the elements working together, whatever their individual worth. The two leads, Steve Ihnat and Gary Clarke, are good looking fellows who don't for a minute convince that they're on a police force, and only convention gives them presumed regard for each other. They're somehow an unsuited pair, and while their relationship to the detective lieutenant is at least not cliche, it's not much else, either. This is a cold pilot. The people in it don't seem to feel a thing for each other, and needless to say, the viewer maintains his own aloofness all the way."

In 1964, as THE LIEUTENANT was winding down, Gene was developing ideas for another pilot—something he called STAR TREK.

III Creating Trek Frontier)

"The primary purpose of television is not to entertain people or amuse them. The primary purpose is to sell deodorants." —G.R.

By the time THE LIEUTENANT went off the air, Gene had already submitted a proposed STAR TREK format to MGM, the studio behind THE LIEUTENANT. Gene said, "Although I never thought of myself as a science fiction writer, I was appalled by what had been done in most motion pictures and in practically all television, so I thought that I would try to do science fiction the same way we had done PLAYHOUSE 90, NAKED CITY and other shows with high emphasis on people and believability. I felt science fiction was a rich body of literature that was being ignored. People didn't know science fiction when they saw it. They thought science fiction meant monsters. It seemed to me, as a dramatic writer, they were making a major mistake.

"Once they got their hands on science fiction, they were treating it as if it were an entirely different form of writing. They were putting in cardboard characters and just not worrying too much about believability and all those things. I thought, hey, why not do science fiction, write it and produce it the same way you do a PLAYHOUSE 90 where characters are important, believability is important and all of that. And so that started me thinking of science fiction."

Gene thought he could use science fiction to bypass the censorship restrictions which hamstrung so much of television. He said, "I guess it was the thought that under the terrible restrictions of television it might be a way I could infiltrate my ideas, and that's what it's been all the time. You see, it's difficult for people to understand that even in the barren vineyards of television you might do these things. Actually you can do them better there because you reach more people with more impact. You don't do it by each of your episodes being a fine HALLMARK HALL OF FAME, or those great shows that are meaningful and deep and advertised as such. The power you have in a show like STAR TREK, which is considered by many people to be a frothy little action-adventure—unimportant, unbelievable, and yet watched by a lot of people. You just slip ideas into it.

"I've been very much heartened by the fact that some key people like the Smithsonian Institute take a look at STAR TREK, and they understand. They don't expect it to be more than it is because what it is is a lot. Other shows can be the same thing. We do love America to be turning out things that are deep and meaningful and sending people staggering out of the theatre and away from the television set, but those are special-occasion-type shows. What you need is for the small mills of television drama to do these things."

Gene believed censorship existed on television because the networks didn't want to offend anyone who might tune in and see the commercials. Programs exist to sell products for sponsors. That's where networks make their money. Gene noted, "The primary purpose of television is not to entertain people or amuse them or educate them. The primary purpose is to sell deodorants, beer, soap, automobiles and so on. As a result, the sole question behind what gets on the air is 'Will it attract a mass audience and hold them sufficiently long to get the commercial messages over to them?' "Censorship then comes along because the people who want to sell products feel no obligation to have anything in their programs that offends people. Anger may be transferred against the product. They don't censor programs because networks are dull or stupid or evil; they censor because networks are products salesmen.

"I know that if I had gone to John W. Campbell, the great science fiction editor in the days when he was bringing up [Isaac] Asimov and [Arthur C.] Clarke and people like that before TV, and said: 'And on this planet the way they judge what gets on the air is by how much beer it sells,' he would have thrown me out of the office! He'd say, 'No society could be that crazy!' The power of sound and image— it is tremendous!"

The original premise for STAR TREK Gene submitted to MGM was the one now familiar to millions, but the characters were radically different. There was a starship and a crew, but other aspects would be fine tuned before it finally went before a camera. The Captain was Robert T. April, his executive officer the logical female Number One, and the navigator José Tyler. The doctor character was nicknamed "Bones" but otherwise an older, completely different character. Mr. Spock was in the proposal, but described as having "a red-hued satanic look" and, according to one source, he absorbed energy through a red plate in his navel!

Sam Peeples, who wrote the second STAR TREK pilot, remembered this early Spock quite clearly, "Spock was a red-skinned creature with fiery ears, who had a plate in the middle of his stomach. He didn't eat or drink, but he fed upon any form of energy that struck this plate in his stomach. I told Gene that I thought this very effectively destroyed him as an interesting character because he was no longer human, and that he should be at least half-human and have the problems of both sides."

Only the Enterprise and its mission made it to the screen unchanged from this original format. Gene also insisted the science fiction in the show be ordered and logical, presenting the story with the same techniques used in other drama, without resorting to convenient fantasy resolutions with no basis in reality. The initial STAR TREK proposal Gene Roddenberry created was dated March 11, 1964. Gene revised it again and again before the version we know came to be. [See Appendix Two]

The earliest influences on the STAR TREK premise have always been a bit hazy, but Sam Peeples revealed that he helped provide Roddenberry with research materials during the development of the initial STAR TREK outline. He explained, "I remember he borrowed a copy of ODD JOHN by Olaf Stapledon. Then he came out to my house. I have a collection of science fiction magazines, probably one of the most complete around. He and I waded through them, and photographed some of the covers, and we discussed every element of what he was doing.

"I thought it was fascinating and fun, because he was going to try to do what I considered to be science fiction, which is not often done in Hollywood. Most so-called science fiction movies are horror plays, and similar stuff that dated back to the silent days.

"Gene actually had an idea, a plan, a dream of making a genuine science fiction series that would be very much like the better science fiction magazines," Peeples continued. "I think he wanted to do a more realistic, a more earthy version of Olaf Stapledon's concepts that were so enormous and staggering, especially the idea of pursuing a far-flung empire in space. It's space opera, which is I think exactly what he had in mind, and of course they are sort of a perfect Western. I wrote enough Westerns, I should know."

Roddenberry discussed his views of the science fiction of Olaf Stapledon once and stated, "I think the type of thing he did, the traveler through space and imagination and so on, really doesn't work for mass-audience weekly shows. You've got to put the ideas he talks about into the heads of more ordinary characters who merely fly a starship that goes places faster than the speed of light."

In 1963 MGM told Gene they were uncertain whether THE LIEUTENANT would be renewed after its first season. They also asked him to create another series idea as a replacement. He created the initial series premise for STAR TREK.

When he told MGM what he was working on, they expressed interest. Then, after it was submitted, weeks went by with no reply. It became obvious the studio wasn't interested in the science fiction. Gene submitted it to other studios including Warner Brothers and Columbia, but they also rejected it as too unusual and too expensive to produce weekly.

Then Gene learned that Desilu Studios was looking for series ideas. Desilu, named after Desi Arnez and Lucille Ball, was hurting financially; Lucy was their only viable property. They frequently rented out their facilities to other studios to pay the monthly overhead.

The studio was impressed with Gene and his ideas, including the STAR TREK proposal. They signed him to a three-year pilot development deal.

"It was the only studio that would take it," Gene admitted. "The reason Desilu took it was because they had gone five years without selling a pilot and they were desperate. They said, 'We'll even try Roddenberry's crazy idea!'"

"I think we would have had an easier time with it if we'd been at a bigger studio with more special effects departments and so on, but it probably wouldn't have ended up much different. We'd have added a few years to our lives, would've been all."

Momentum built almost immediately. Gene pitched STAR TREK to an assembly of CBS's highest ranking executives on behalf of the studio. The execs listened intently for two hours; Gene was convinced he'd sold them.

They were fascinated by his thoughts on saving costs and designing ships, but their questions turned out to have another motive entirely. When he finished, they thanked him politely, but passed on the proposal. They already had a science fiction series of their own in the works, LOST IN SPACE.

Roddenberry was furious. He felt used, an unpaid consultant for CBS' new show. He may very well have inadvertently helped launch LOST IN SPACE, which even, by some coincidence, had the Robinson family embarking on a five-year mission of exploration. The CBS show premiered in 1965, a year before STAR TREK, and, like STAR TREK, ran for three seasons.

Although disheartened by CBS' cavalier treatment, Gene kept on trying. In May of 1964, Desilu's Oscar Katz submitted the STAR TREK outline to Mort Werner at NBC. NBC was interested but wanted to see more.

The network offered $20,000 in story development money. Gene was to develop three story ideas for a STAR TREK pilot, then write a pilot script based on the idea chosen by the network.

He hired Dorothy Fontana as his assistant. She had previously worked for Samuel A. Peeples when he was producing the series FRONTIER CIRCUS and she'd sold her first story to that series. Fontana had previously worked for Gene on THE LIEUTENANT and had garnered eight television script credits by this time.

GENE RODDENBERRY

Gene completed three story outlines to NBC by the end of June 1964. The network questioned whether a small studio such as Desilu could produce a series of the calibre they promised, and whether Gene possessed sufficient experience as he had only one previous series to his credit.

They decided to go with "The Cage," which still featured Robert April as the starship captain, although the Yorktown had been renamed the Enterprise by this time. Gene set to work on a shooting script.

In a story datelined July 7, 1964, DAILY VARIETY announced the birth of a new television series: "Desilu 'Star Trek' As NBC-TV Pilot — Desilu Productions has made the first co-production deal in its history with NBC-TV, on an hour long sci-fi series, STAR TREK, created by Gene Roddenberry, for the 1965-66 season. It would be the first sci-fi series with regular characters. Roddenberry, who recently joined Desilu after a tenure with MGM-TV, will produce the series via his Norway Productions, with Desilu. Deal with the net was set by Desilu production veepee Oscar Katz. Roddenberry has a multiple deal with Desilu, and other projects in his deal include ASSIGNMENT 100, an adventure-police show, an oater, and a historical adventure series. All are hourlong."

When STAR TREK went to series in 1966 (rather than 1965 as originally intended), Roddenberry's other possible series ideas went by the wayside. The "adventure-police show" may well have been an early version of THE TRIBUNES that Roddenberry and Sam Peeples later soldin 1972. It was never filmed.

In September of 1964, the script for "The Cage" was approved. The first STAR TREK episode received the green light.

Although at this time most television shows were still being filmed in black and white, NBC wanted STAR TREK to be in color. There was an interesting commercial reason for this. Roddenberry once explained, "You see, NBC is part of RCA which had great interest in selling color TV's at that time. So realizing that they had science fiction, probably with a host of strange and myriad colors, they decided to use our show as a color sales show."

Gene had already started laying the groundwork for the show. Of primary importance was the starship Enterprise, which he hoped would avoid all previous spaceship clichés. While he knew he wanted to avoid the standard cigar-shaped spacecraft, he didn't know what would work.

"No, I hadn't the slightest idea," Gene recalled. "I just had the art directors keep coming in bringing me shapes. We went through thousands of old sci-fi magazines looking for shapes—couldn't find 'em. Finally, one day, Matt Jeffries brought in a shape that looked something like near right. He'd threatened to quit several times by then. He said, 'What do you want?' I said I'll know when you bring it in. Then we just kept improving on it and it just emerged."

The final design of the U.S.S. Enterprise was largely the work of assistant art director Jeffries. He had a strong background in aviation. Like Gene, Jeffries had flown B-17 missions during World War Two (over Africa, in his case), and later devoted much of his spare time to restoring vintage airplanes. The starship and its various sets emerged from Jeffries' own familiarity with aeronautics.

As a member of the Aviation Writer's association, Jeffries was able to collate a large number of designs from NASA and the defense industry. . . as examples of what not to do. Previous science fiction spaceship designs were also held as things to be avoided.

The design of the Enterprise slowly grew from a pile of hundreds of sketches; the main hull was, at one point, going to be spherical, and even the now-familiar final design almost wound up being shot upside down. Admittedly, this wouldn't make much difference in space.

As a final touch of authenticity, red and green lights were added on the port and starboard sides, a time-honored nautical practice. A three foot, and then a large fourteen-foot, model of the Enterprise, were constructed.

THE MAN WHO CREATED STAR TREK

Matt Jeffries' Air Force engineering background again came in handy in the design of the sets. The U.S. Navy was so impressed by the bridge design that they supposedly used it as a basis for one of their own communications centers.

Another seemingly insurmountable problem grew from Gene's desire to feature a green-skinned woman in the pilot. For some reason, all the make-up department's experiments failed to show up on the test footage shot for this purpose. (The test footage was not of Oliver, but of stand-in, Majel Barrett.)

No matter how dark they made the green, their model always looked perfectly normal. Eventually, they discovered that someone at the photo lab, perplexed by the pictures, was color-correcting what he thought was a flaw in the photography. When this was discovered, the desired effect was achieved with minimum fuss.

"The Cage" began shooting with a cast of characters drawn from the original format, although the captain was now named Christopher Pike. Pike was portrayed by Jeffrey Hunter, who had the rare distinction of having once played Jesus Christ, in KING OF KINGS.

Shortly after NBC had first expressed interest in STAR TREK but before the first script was written, Gene had approached Lloyd Bridges as the lead. Bridges was a television actor in the Sixties who had starred in four years and 156 episodes of the popular adventure series SEA HUNT. In 1950 he had appeared in the low-budget science fiction film ROCKETSHIP X-M.

Gene recalled, "Lloyd Bridges was very much under consideration, except when I approached him with it he said, 'Gene, I like you, I've worked with you before in the past, but I've seen science fiction and I don't want to be within a hundred miles of it.'

"I understood what he meant then. I tried to convince him that I could do it differently, but at the time I wasn't that sure that I would treat it differently. I wasn't sure I could manage it."

Roddenberry's first wife, whom he'd later divorce while STAR TREK was on the air, suggested James Coburn for the lead. "I said to her something I've heard over and over for many years since," he said. "'No sex appeal.' That was a monster of a goof and I came to realize, though, that there just weren't a lot of actors who would do it. I was talking about what was, in many people's eyes, a silly show."

Most of the rest of the cast was set by the time Roddenberry signed Jeffrey Hunter. John Hoyt played the ship's doctor, Philip Boyce. Leonard Nimoy appeared as Spock, but the character was different; the logical aspect of his future personality still belonged to Number One, portrayed by Majel Barrett.

When Gene first called Leonard Nimoy regarding his new project, Nimoy assumed he would be trying out for the part of Spock. He didn't realize he was already Gene's choice for the role.

Gene had other choices in case Leonard turned the part down. He said, "I probably would've gotten Marty [Martin] Landau. I'd worked with him. I had him in mind as a possibility."

When he was still working out exactly who and what Spock would be like (the early series premise described Spock as a red-skinned Martian), Roddenberry had toyed with going for a very otherworldly look. He even considered casting Michael Dunn, the dwarf actor who had played Dr. Lovelace in THE WILD WILD WEST.

"I wanted Spock to look different and be different, and yes, to make a statement about being an outsider looking in," Gene recalled. "I did finally pick the way we went because I was dealing in weekly mass-audience television, and I needed Spock to be attractive even though he was different. I'm afraid Michael Dunn might not have been.

"Dunn was a serious second choice because of his being a dwarf. That seemed certainly to put the stamp of being from another place on it, but as I said I was also dealing in a mass audience, and Spock had to have an attractive look then. It was the right choice for the time."

Ever since Gene had seen Leonard when he cast him in an episode of THE LIEU-TENANT, he'd wanted to have the actor play an alien, he just didn't yet know in what. Then came STAR TREK. The prospect of a regular series excited the actor, who, despite frequent guest appearances on television, didn't yet have a stable income.

Nimoy had misgivings. He feared that if the show was an unmitigated flop, he would become a laughing stock, forever derided for those silly-looking pointed ears.

"As we tried them on [him] and began doing camera tests," Gene recalled, "the crew began chuckling and calling him 'jackrabbit,' and so on, and he finally started to get a little upset."

In conference with his friend Vic Morrow, Nimoy even pondered the possibility of developing makeup that would completely conceal his true face. Fortunately for his future recognizability, he thought better of the idea.

One obstacle remained. The makeup department had to develop a painless means of applying the ears. Nimoy's ears hurt where the glue was applied. In fact, one reason for Spock's general stiffness was that even slight facial movement increased the physical discomfort.

Matters were confounded due to contractual obligations; the ears had to be made by the props department, not the makeup department. Considerable variation in the shape of the ears—as well as in Spock's general appearance—can be seen in the two pilot episodes. Nimoy expressed dissatisfaction to his producer. Gene could tell Nimoy's anguish was real— but what could he do?

"I tried to talk him out of the pointed ears one day," Nimoy recalled. "because we were having trouble with it physically. They weren't looking good; they weren't being made right. The company that was making them was incapable of making them. Then we switched companies and it was okay.

"But in the meantime the start date was approaching and they were looking like hell. They were looking ludicrous and I was scared! I thought I'm going to look ludicrous! They didn't look like my ears—they looked like something junked on there.

"I went to him and I said, 'Gene, it's not working. We've got the haircut, we've got the skin color, we've got the eyebrows—the ears are not working. I'm worried about it.' He said, 'We're going to keep doing it, keep chipping away at it, because if you don't, if you start to give up pieces of the vision, then you end up with something homogeneous and what's the point? There's no point.' And he was right.

"There really was the classic joke—he said, 'We'll do thirteen shows and if you're not happy with the ears, we'll get you an ear job!' " When Leonard pondered this and broke into laughter, the fate of the ears was sealed.

Robert Butler, who had previously directed episodes of THE LIEUTENANT for Gene, recalled the experience of directing "The Cage". "He liked my work on THE LIEUTENANT very much," Butler said, "and I suppose that at that green point I was beginning to formulate stuff that I've done since: very real, very dry, and very naturalistic, and I suppose he liked that and responded to it. He was a cop, you know, and he must have a feeling about naturalism in spite of his enthusiasm for science fiction.

"So he must have thought I was good casting because of my kind of true touch in the science fiction zone, and I got along with him. I enjoyed working with him, and vice versa."

In spite of Butler's excellent job directing the pilot (which ultimately cost $630,000 due to constructing all the sets in anticipation of a series coming out of the deal), he felt "The Cage" was too wild. He said, "I do remember beginning to try to suggest to Gene that the stuff was impossible. I remember trying to get Gene into a conversation like that, and as a 'hired gun' director one is careful at such points because the producer-writer is usually pretty blind in terms of seeing the forest for the trees.

"I remember trying to suggest to Gene that we ought to do some straightening out, or that at least we should discuss it, and I remember thinking that Gene was too far into it, so I just gave up. It seems to me we had a conversation as I was considering taking the job, and from my perspective the conversation was, 'Are we going to go with this, or would you consider any minor surgery?' and he said in so many words, 'No, I wouldn't consider any minor surgery,' and the conditions under which he said that were such that he just couldn't see any minor surgery. He was too close to it.

"It taught me always to speak out, subsequently, but anyway that's the way I remember it. I don't think Gene might remember such a scene. I was political and I was careful about it, because what does it get you to start yelling at the producer-writer about the obscurity of his script?" Filming on "The Cage" began December 12, 1964. Shortly before filming began, the main character's named underwent two revisions, first from Capt. April to Capt. Winter, and then at last to Capt. Christopher Pike.

"The Cage" introduces viewers to Gene's nascent version of the Enterprise crew as it is headed towards a Starbase after a disastrous first contact with an alien culture. The captain and his crew are tired and in great need of rest when they are distracted by a distress signal from a nearby planet. When they investigate, they find a colony of scientists who survived a crash nearly twenty years earlier and a beautiful young girl.

She lures Captain Pike away from the encampment and into abduction. He finds himself part of an alien zoo, held prisoner by telepathic beings who mentally project him into a bewildering variety of scenarios.

He wonders if the girl is an illusion or another captive as she tries to get him to accept his situation. Instead Pike is freed after resisting mind control and it is revealed that the woman was the only survivor of the crash. Not truly young, disfigured by the crash, she elects to stay and live the rest of her life in illusionary happiness.

NBC was overwhelmingly enthusiastic when they viewed it in February 1965. In intelligence and appearance, the pilot surpassed anything previously done for television. In fact it looked better than the majority of theatrical science fiction films. No one uttered a bad word.

NBC rejected it anyway.

The network feared the story would go over the heads of the audience. They wanted something more action-oriented. Gene couldn't blame the network, but came to realize it was his own fault.

"I told the network in order to get the show sold, okay, look I'm going to give you space opera," he said. "and then when I did 'The Cage' I really got involved trying to do something a little deeper than that and I shouldn't have. The first time I should have given them an action adventure, such as we did when we made 'Where No Man Has Gone Before.' "

In an unprecedented move, NBC gave Gene a second shot at a pilot. There was a catch; the network wanted him to get rid of the guy with the pointed ears. They feared religious groups might be offended by a demonic-looking character.

Gene set out to revamp the entire show, but was determined to keep Spock. An alien presence on the ship was, he felt, a vital part of the concept. He discarded Number One and promoted Spock to second-in-command, bringing him closer to the forefront. Regarding Number One, Roddenbery explained, "NBC made us throw her out. Even the women in the test audience group said, 'Who does she think *she* is?' We've come a *long way* since those days."

In Gene's words, "It seemed to me that we were having so many arguments at this time that I couldn't save both of them [Spock and Number One] and so I decided to save the alien character. And it was at this time that we gave Mister Spock the woman's logical, unemotional qualities and kept him on the show, created the Vulcan background, and Leonard Nimoy stayed on the show.

"I then married the woman [Majel Barrett married Roddenberry in 1969], but obviously, I could not have legally done it the other way around."

This time NBC wanted three complete scripts. Work started in March and they were presented to NBC in June 1965. All three—"Mudd's Women" by Stephen Kandel, "Omega Glory" by Gene, and "Where No Man Has Gone Before" by Samuel A. Peeples—had plenty of action.

The network chose the Peeples script; the second STAR TREK pilot was soon underway.

"What actually happened," Peeples recalled, "was that Gene had produced 'The Cage' and he wanted me to see it. I went down and saw it at one of the very first screenings down at Desilu-Culver, the old RKO Studios. I liked it, but I thought it was too much of a fantasy and not enough science fiction, which is what we originally talked about his doing, and he said he thought so, too.

"My understanding was when it was submitted to NBC they felt much the same way, that it should be more hardcore science fiction than fantasy. Gene told me that he had an okay from NBC to do three more scripts and from those three, if they liked them, they would pick a second pilot to be shot. Mine was the one that NBC picked, so technically I wrote the pilot script that sold the show.

"There was a lot of rewriting on it, and with my blessings." The title of the script, which was incorporated into the prologue of the television series, was conceived by Peeples. "That was the original title of the very first copy of the very first version of the story that was submitted to Gene Roddenberry."

In addition to holding on to Spock, Gene was determined to maintain the Enterprise's multi-ethnic crew. This despite the network's fears it might effect ratings, especially in the South.

"We put on a multi-racial crew in the days when television networks and advertisers were very much against that. We were cautioned that we might lose participation in the show in big hunks of the nation. We didn't believe this would happen. All of us on the show shared one feeling, that the television audience is much brighter than the mass infantile mind the networks seem to think exists out there."

Discarding Number One left a vacancy for a new second-in-command. Spock fit the bill perfectly. He inherited Number One's cold, dispassionate logic. Gene explained, "I guess because I've screwed up in my own life so many times because of emotion, I thought it'd be nice to write a character that didn't have that problem." The character gelled into a fascinating amalgam of intelligence, restraint and mystery, admirably brought to life by the highly capable Leonard Nimoy.

Gene had to give in on one aspect of the crew of the Enterprise—the division of men and women. "I would have liked to have the crew fifty percent men, fifty percent women," Gene explained, "but you must attract and hold a minimum of eighteen million people.

"There's no point in striking a great blow for women's lib, or for any other thing, and not getting the show on the air. So what you do is you go as far as you can go and then you try to infiltrate the rest.

"Now, this doesn't mean that you give in on everything. There are certain principles that I have and that other writers have that they will not violate even to get a show on the air.

"I don't like too much violence. I refuse to have the future run by the United States of America because I don't think that's the way it will be. I refuse to have an all lili-white, Anglo-Saxon crew. And I think if they had said, 'This ship has to be an instrument of the CIA of the future, of keeping the galaxies safe for democracy,' I certainly would have said, 'You can shelve the whole project."

Although Gene approached Jeffrey Hunter about continuing his character in the second pilot, Hunter's wife convinced the actor that science fiction was beneath him. In the same year he made "The Cage," Hunter had also starred in a low-budget science fiction film called DIMENSION 5 which did nothing to advance his career.

With Nimoy the sole holdover from "The Cage" pilot, Gene created an entirely new cast from scratch. Of course the most important character on any ship is the captain. Inspired by C.S. Forrester's heroic Horatio Hornblower, Gene created a new leader for the Enterprise, James T. Kirk.

Kirk, a Midwesterner, is a confident and driven officer, unafraid to take a stand. Apart from his senior officers, he confides in few, internalizing full responsibility for his command. Yet he is not without humor and possesses a highly developed sense of adventure.

For this all-important lead role, Gene cast Canadian actor William Shatner. Gene recalled, "Bill had just come off a series and I'd known him from 'Susie Wong' on Broadway and so he was easy to cast."

William Shatner remembered, "I was in New York and he called me. I didn't know him and I met him. We talked about what we would do to make changes in the second pilot and we made the second pilot. And then for several months in the beginning of that first year he was involved very closely in the making of STAR TREK and he and I were very closely involved and he and I had a very good professional relationship. A wonderful working relationship."

Since Kirk would command the crew, Gene created chief engineer Montgomery Scott to run the ship. A regular shirt-sleeves kind of guy, with an unbending devotion to his captain superseded only by his love of his ship, Scott would often be called upon to do the impossible, in as little time as he could manage.

His ethnic background was suggested by the actor who signed on to play him, a man gifted in dialects. Since there was a long tradition of Scotsmen in nautical and military engineering, he suggested they continue the tradition into space. The actor is James Doohan, who, like Shatner, began his career in his native Canada. "Jimmy Doohan I had never worked with," Gene said, "but a director brought him in and asked him if he could do a Scottish accent and he did like an hour and a half of accents and had us falling on the floor laughing, so there was never any doubt that he had the job."

For the helmsman who doubles as weapons officer, Gene crafted a character of Asian background. Sulu, primarily Japanese with Filipino blood, is portrayed by George Takei.

At a time when the networks were dubious of black characters (Bill Cosby's equal billing with Robert Culp on I SPY was the exception), Gene pushed the envelope. He made the communications officer black. In the second pilot, the Communications Officer was played by a man, Lloyd Haynes.

With the new cast ready to go, "Where No Man Has Gone Before" started shooting on July 21, 1965. Although filming took eight days, postproduction lasted several months, finishing in January 1966. The pilot cost 330 thousand dollars. Needless to say, the network was eager to see what they'd bought.

Although Gene didn't like excessive violence, he wasn't against using physical confrontation when it served the demands of a story. He felt most comments on violence were too simplistic.

He explained, "I think violence is a part of our life and our world. I'm against its being used for violence's sake, improperly motivated and improperly depicted. I am not against depicting a fight between two men in which one man gets hit in the mouth by the other man because that is part of the life we lead and that is a dramatic subject and it can be a part of a statement you're making.

"What I am against is the fact that in a typical Western a guy gets hit in the mouth and he reels back and he hits the other guy in the mouth and they go at it. I know from my own life, when a large man hits another man full in the mouth with his fist, teeth are going to break, lips are going to be cut open, and I think if this happened the ugliness of it would tend to eliminate violence.

"I think that if our war movies for the past 25 or 30 years had shown violence as it really is in war, where you don't clutch your breast and die cleanly but you lay out there screaming your guts out, there would have been a lot less people anxious for running the war. I think it depends on how you use violence."

Gene used it in "Where No Man Has Gone Before." He was sensitive to NBC and felt pressure from all sides, so he gave them what they wanted in his rewrite of Samuel Peeples' script. "One thing that was put in that I didn't particularly like," Peeples stated, "was the fight at the end. Although I thought it was staged very well, I was opposed to it because I felt that an all-powerful man like Mitchell wouldn't have to resort to physical violence. Gene wanted this physical action at the end of the script, and that's the way it worked out."

Gene and his team were on tenterhooks. Would NBC reject this effort, too?

In February, word came through. STAR TREK would debut in December, with the network committed to sixteen episodes. It was time to start producing the series.

With a budget of roughly 180 thousand dollars an episode, it was going to be quite a ride. Early on, the idea of incorporating the rejected "Cage" pilot into a two-part episode was put forward as a means of relieving the expected time and budget crunch. Set building, prop design, and, of course, scripts, filled this preparation period.

Gene showed "Where No Man Has Gone Before" to a suitably impressed audience of five hundred die-hard science fiction fans at the World Science Fiction Convention in Cleveland, Ohio on September 4, 1966. Without him, they would have had to settle for an episode of Irwin Allen's TIME TUNNEL, which was shown first and which Roddenberry watched the audience hoot and jeer.

Gene said, "I was nervous, particularly when I saw them watching other films that were shown before, and booing, and stomping, and laughing at things. I walked out thinking, 'They're finally going to show this one.'

"There was a rather loud gentlemen surrounded by other people, discussing something at the time my show was starting, and upset already, I turned on him: 'For Christ's sake, could you be quiet? My show is on now.' And Isaac Asimov said, 'Yes, you're perfectly right. We will tone it down.' And someone said, 'You're dead, you just insulted Isaac Asimov.' Well, it turned out that I had not, and over the years we became fast friends. He understood. Then I watched how they accepted this show. "

"Where No Man Has Gone Before" was different from the STAR TREK that would follow. Uhura had not yet joined the roster; nor had Yeoman Janice Rand. The ship's doctor, Dr. Piper, was portrayed by Paul Fix; Sulu was a physicist, not the helmsman. Several key characters would appear only in the pilot. What the Worldcon audience saw was the story of how the Enterprise tried to penetrate a mysterious purple energy barrier in space.

During this attempt, strange radiations effect the crew; Lieutenant Commander Gary Mitchell seems normal, but his eyes begin to glow silver. It soon becomes apparent that the radiation has boosted his latent extrasensory perceptions to a previously undreamed-of level.

Spock becomes convinced Mitchell is a threat to the Enterprise. He prompts Kirk to kill him. The Captain cannot bring himself to terminate an old friend from the Academy.

Ultimately, Kirk and Mitchell battle to the death in a harsh landscape altered by Mitchell's godlike powers. At one point Mitchell produces a tombstone bearing the name of James R. Kirk, proving that even a nearly omnipotent being can get someone's middle initial wrong. Finally, Kirk destroys Mitchell, but it is a hollow triumph, as he has killed his friend.

The audience gave Gene a standing ovation. He knew he was on the right track.

"I didn't know how people were going to react," Gene recalled. "I think I finally got to my feet and said, 'Is anybody going to say whether they liked it or not?' and it was only afterward that the applause began.

"I remember calling up the studio and saying, 'I really think we have something here,' and the studio's reaction was, 'Well, so a thousand goofs who go to a science fiction convention like it? That means nothing in television.' And they were almost right, because we did get low ratings.

"I said to myself, 'Yes, there *are* people, if we go this way and try these things, who are going to appreciate them.' I realized then that we should have fans of some sort and, of course, where that went is insanity.

"Who expects to have millions of fans? At that time I realized that we'd reached some people. I didn't think it would be anything like it was, but I did realize at that time if I did the show I would be approached by people now and then who would say, 'I saw the thing you did years ago, and I liked it.' That's enough."

IV Classic Trek

"I don't consider STAR TREK to be a work of genius."
—G.R.

NBC had committed themselves to an initial order of sixteen episodes of STAR TREK for which the network would pay $180,000 per show. The debut was set for September 1966, a year after originally announced due to the rejection of the first pilot. Despite the heroic effort of creating two pilots, now the real work would begin.

Robert Justman was hired as assistant director for "The Cage" partially based on his experience on THE OUTER LIMITS. He worked so well for the first STAR TREK pilot that he'd been promoted to Associate Producer on "Where No Man Has Gone Before." Staffing STAR TREK would be a demanding task due to the unique skills the people would need.

"I realized that we had an impossible production job," Gene explained, "and a lot of the people we chose were assistant department heads who wanted a chance at the top. Matt Jefferies, for instance, was a draftsman, not an art director, and we had to cover for him until he got his ticket. We also did similar things in a lot of other areas: set decorators, editors.

"Our people turned out to be good because we looked for young, bright, malleable people, but they did not necessarily come to us with long, shining reputations. I figured older people who were solid in their trade worked at a certain pace, and it might be difficult to change that pace. However, I knew that we would get more creativity and work and imagination out of assistants because it would have been their only big chance, and indeed it turned out like that.

"It's easy to look back now and say, 'Oh, well, of course you had a proven crew.' No. We had some names and recommendations, but it was far from being a proven crew. It became a proven crew because of the way we operated. We gave credit to people when they did good work, and cheered, and we very quickly created a family feeling for STAR TREK."

This family feeling was very strong. As producer, Gene became a father figure and came to be dubbed "The Great Bird of the Galaxy."

At a press conference held January 23, 1975 at Florida State University in Tallahassee, Gene explained that the creation of STAR TREK was a group effort. In so doing he diminished his own credit for the effort while enhancing that of many others, something he would do less and less as years went by.

"Although they have the title in the show 'Created by Gene Roddenberry,'" he said, "this means that I created the format. I laid out the skeletons of a lot of characters and things.

"What I principally take credit for is [that] I surrounded myself with a group of very talented creative individuals, from the art director, the costume, wardrobe designer, [and the] actors who took my 'skeletons' of Spock and Kirk and really put flesh on the skeleton and made 'em work. If you watch the first ten shows, you can see the characters really forming and becoming things. And so television sort of is the exception to the rule that a committee never created anything. The committee in this case does need leadership, but it is a group effort."

In the March 1976 issue of PENTHOUSE, Gene said, "I made STAR TREK for two reasons. One was that I thought science fiction hadn't been done well on television and it seemed to me, from a purely selfish career point of view, that if I did it well I would be remembered. I suppose if a Western or a police story hadn't been done to my satisfaction I might have done that, too.

"The second reason is that I thought with science fiction I might do what Jonathan Swift did when he wrote GULLIVER'S TRAVELS. He lives in a time when you could lose your head for making religious and political comments. I was working in a medium, television, which is heavily censored, and in contemporary shows I found I couldn't talk about sex, politics, religion and all the other things I wanted to talk about. It seemed to me that if I had things happen to little polka-dotted people on a far-off planet I might get past the network censors, as Swift did in his day. And that's indeed what we did."

Gene often compared what he did on STAR TREK with the work of Jonathan Swift. He said, "He wrote a number of charming things so that a child can read it and enjoy it as a marvelous fairy tale, and as you know later on, when you're in college, you read it and understand that it was also a marvelous satire on the political and religious systems of his time. And that's what we tried to do in STAR TREK—we tried to write it so that more thoughtful people would see it in the other things we were talking about."

In preparing STAR TREK as a series, Gene made more change. He replaced Paul Fix with a younger actor, DeForest Kelley. He had worked with Kelley before, having cast him in the lead of the unsold pilot 333 MONTGOMERY.

Kelley was eternally grateful to Gene for casting him in this role, and as early as 1968 said publicly that Gene "went out on a limb for me. The town had forgotten the actor I used to be. I feel very lucky to have this role."

Gene had originally wanted Kelley for the doctor in the first pilot but the networks wouldn't go along with the choice because they felt Kelley was typecast playing villains. After they saw Kelley's work in Gene's POLICE STORY pilot, they changed their mind.

"When I saw John Hoyt do it [play the doctor in the pilot], he had this one scene with Jeffrey Hunter and I was very fascinated," Kelley recalled. "I thought that if this character is developed well it could be very meaningful. So I was pretty excited about it, but outside of the fact that it was seven weeks work, I thought that was that. It probably never will go any farther than that, and here I am twenty-five years later!"

Majel Barrett, whose role as Number One had been deleted after "The Cage" was made, was returned to the series as a blonde nurse Chapel. With the exception of a good role in "What Are Little Girls Made Of?" in the first season, and a good scene in "The Naked Time," Chapel became an often seen but little used character on the series.

Taking his concept of a multi-racial crew to even further limits, when Lloyd Haynes wasn't available for the series, Gene changed the character to a woman and hired Nichelle Nichols. She had previously worked for him on THE LIEUTENANT.

Even after the loss of Number One, Gene was determined to have a woman in a responsible position on the Enterprise bridge. Uhura, whose name is based on the

Swahili word "uhuru" which means freedom, was proof changes in Earth society would be achieved in Gene's hopeful vision of the future.

Gene said, "One of the reasons the show succeeded was that it was one of the rare shows that told the young-minded audience that there was not only hope for a better tomorrow, but that tomorrow would be here—that they weren't going to be bombed out of existence. I stated that mankind was on the brink of the greatest challenge of all time and that they would be able to take part in these challenges. The fans wanted to hear this. They didn't get encouraging philosophy like this from other programs."

Gene did not believe STAR TREK actually depicts the 23rd Century. He explained, "It depicts us, now—things we need to understand about that."

Using drama to reach people was always uppermost in Gene's mind, particularly when he gained the position of producer of a television series and could direct the areas the show explored.

"I think that the purpose of all writing is to reach people and say something you believe in and think is important," he said. "You may do it as a scientific or philosophical tract, but with fiction and drama and a certain amount of adventure you reach them easier and you reach more of them, and you can infiltrate your messages into them.

"I think people forget too often that literature—usually fiction—is responsible for more changes in public opinion than new articles or sermons. An excellent example of this is UNCLE TOM'S CABIN—actually it's not a very good book—which probably did more to propel us into the Civil War than any other writing of the time.

"So historically this has been true of literature and whether we like it or not, television is literature. It may not be very good literature usually, but of course not everything that is printed is very good, either."

Gene gave an example of just what he was doing on STAR TREK when he appeared on a Seattle radio station in January 1983. He said, "I was down in South Carolina a couple of years ago and they put me at a table to eat lunch with what you would call a Southern Cop, and coming from the South, there is such a thing. I was in sort of a decorated Hollywood outfit and he's giving me a strange look, and I said, 'Don't let this bother you, I used to be a police officer myself.'

"'What do you do now?' he demanded. And I said, 'Well, I sort of work in the future.' 'Hey!' he says, 'have you seen that there show called STAR TREK? I'll tell ya', they got something in that just 'cause something's different don't mean that it's bad, or that if you think different don't mean. . . '

"This guy gives me a fifteen minute lecture on tolerance. I tell you, you can reach them and it's a pity more television doesn't try to do it."

In an interview published in 1968, during the second season of STAR TREK, Gene stated, "So-called entertainment shows on TV misrepresent by omission. The great majority bear little resemblance to real problems of today. Kids who watch TV could grow up believing no problems exist if they were to derive their values from this sort of current television fare. They'd be in for a rude awakening when they got out in the world."

During early 1966, Gene met with many writers about working on the show. They included writers familiar with the genre of science fiction such as Robert Bloch, George Clayton Johnson, Harlan Ellison, Richard Matheson and Theodore Sturgeon, all of whom later wrote for the series.

"You know," Gene said, "science fiction is quite a lovely form of writing, and done well it can be very exciting. Of course, there's been a lot of crap in science fiction.

"I always remember Ted Sturgeon's statement when he joined us here to write for STAR TREK. Some friend of his said, 'Ted, how can you possibly write for television? Don't you know that ninety percent of television is crap?' Ted looked back at him and said, 'Ninety percent of everything is crap.' "

In launching the series, Gene felt it necessary to rewrite many episodes the first year in order to maintain continuity. So he didn't try to have giants of science fiction such as Ray Bradbury or Isaac Asimov write for the show.

"I would not have wanted Isaac Asimov or Ray Bradbury or people like that to have penned a script for us," Gene explained. "Would I want to be known as the guy who rewrote *them*? Their scripts may have been brilliant but I couldn't use them and keep my characters the same way. Rewriting is often the name of the game in writing, but a series has got to have unity."

Among the many problems Gene contended with was the urging of NBC to have characters on the series smoke cigarettes. Gene said, "They came to me and said they were going to advertise cigarettes and since we all smoked, could you get it in there?

"I said, listen, in that time they're not going to smoke.

"And they said, oh, you can use some square science-fiction cigarettes. Can you imagine STAR TREK reruns with 'ol Kirk sitting there smoking a square cigarette?"

Strangely enough, even though no one ever smoked on the series, a single publicity photo exists of William Shatner as Captain Kirk holding a cigarette in his hand in a way which emphasizes the cigarette. Although this exists as a still photograph, it is not believed to have ever been published.

That wasn't the only request NBC made. They also thought there should be a chaplain on the Enterprise.

"Presumably, each one of the worlds we were dealing with was very much like Earth in that several religions must have arisen over time," Gene said. "Contending religions. How could you have a chaplain if you've got that many people of different and alien beliefs on your ship? With as many planets as we were visiting, every person on the ship would have to be a chaplain!"

Of course, it is common practice in our time for a chaplain on a ship or within a military unit to provide for the needs of people of different religions from that in which they are ordained. For example, a Catholic priest may minister to a person of Jewish faith.

Gene learned not to argue. He explained, "So I would just nod sagely and pretend to go along with them, and I would keep my own thoughts."

By seeming to agree, all he had to say was that the ship had a chaplain and then never use the character. The network would periodically pressure him on this point.

"It came and went because I think that the people of intelligence realized it was an impossible situation to rationalize," Gene said. "A couple of times we had a prayer or a ceremony when someone got married." An example is the episode "Balance of Terror" which actually mentions that the Enterprise has a chapel.

Finally, on September 8, 1966, STAR TREK premiered on NBC. (Actually, the first broadcast was two days earlier, on Canadian television.) The episode aired was not the pilot (that was shown two weeks later) but the sixth episode filmed, "Man Trap" by George Clayton Johnson. The show is perhaps best known for its Salt Vampire.

VARIETY insisted the series wouldn't work. Their published review in the September 14, 1966 issue read in part: "STAR TREK obviously solicits allout suspension of disbelief, but it won't work. Even within its sci-fi frame of reference it was an incredible and dreary mess of confusion and complexities at the kickoff. The interplanetary spaceship trudged on for a long hour with hardly any relief from violence, killings, hypnotic stuff and a distasteful, ugly monster."

If that wasn't bad enough, the review went on to say, "By a generous stretch of the imagination, it could lure a small coterie of the smallfry, though not happily time slotted in that direction. It's better suited to the Saturday morning kidvid bloc."

It was a depressing day on the Desilu lot when that review appeared, and that was after only one episode. If only hardcore science fiction fans could understand the show, while the average person was left as perplexed as the VARIETY reviewer, they would all soon be looking for new jobs.

"Man Trap" introduced a new character who quickly become an indispensable part of the mythos, Dr. Leonard "Bones" McCoy. The seemingly cynical but strongly compassionate humanitarian provided a counterpoint to the cold logic of Spock. Their running battle of wits soon became the stuff of legend.

The good doctor was technically introduced in the first episode filmed, "The Corbomite Maneuver," which is why that show has so many character scenes for him. Unfortunately, the more than normally complicated special effects of that episode caused longer post-production time so it actually aired tenth although it filmed first.

George Clayton Johnson explained that while his dealings with Gene were sometimes strained, he respected the man. Gene could be just as single-minded as George. Johnson recalled, "I remember having an argument with Gene Roddenberry, the great speckled bird of the universe himself, in which I said to him, 'I'm unhappy about this.' And he said to me, 'Look, George, it may well be, and I don't argue with you. You know one hell of a lot more about science fiction than I do,' and that is true. This is damn true.

"So he says, 'You know one hell of a lot more about science fiction than I do; however, I know more about this show because I created this show.' Whereupon I started to remind him that he created this show by reading CAPTAIN FUTURE." CAPTAIN FUTURE featured a handsome hero with three sidekicks, one of whom was an android, another a robot, and a third a brilliant emotionless scientist, Simon Wright, who existed only as a brain in a transparent floating case. George felt that elements of these characters were ancestral influences on STAR TREK.

This may be true. CAPTAIN FUTURE was very popular in the 1940s in a vein of science fiction very similar to E.E. Smith, another science fiction writer whom Gene named as a definite influence on his own work.

Johnson only wrote the one episode. Producer Gene Coon turned down an idea Johnson was enthusiastic about and soured him on working for the show again, something he now regrets.

Johnson said, "I really am glad I worked on the show, but it is a damn shame that something went wrong between me and Gene because I could have written a dozen episodes. I had ideas for plots for that show that just spill out of me. I can't talk to anybody for three minutes without coming up with some new angle on it. I'm glad to see it succeeding. I can see what an icon it has become.

"I also have to admire Gene on another level, which has to do with the man's character and training. One night we were both at the Writer's Guild, and there was a little flare-up: one person threatened another. I was talking to Roddenberry and it was amazing how quickly and quietly he interposed himself between these two guys—how fast he had them quieted down. He just knew what he was doing there, even though he was in a situation where he could have gotten brained. That was one moment in which I looked at Roddenberry and said, 'You know, this guy is not an overgrown boy, which he seems to be sometimes."

The next episode aired, "Charlie X" features Robert Walker, Jr. as a space foundling. His hidden psychic powers are ill matched with an adolescent need for attention and approval in a story about loneliness and alienation. In hindsight, the story is notable because it contains more than passing similarities to the central character in Robert Heinlein's 1961 novel STRANGER IN A STRANGE LAND. Gene was certainly familiar with Heinlein's work and said so when asked to name his favorite science fiction writers.

"Heinlein, Asimov—if I said one favorite I would lose the friendship of about five other writers. I guess I was influenced by the works of E.E. Smith," he said in the magazine TRAPEZE. "But as to what SF I like, Heinlein's STRANGER IN A STRANGE LAND left me stunned for days after I read it. That was quite a book."

"Where No Man Has Gone Before" was the third episode broadcast. Then things really hit their stride with "The Naked Time."

"The Enemy Within" allowed Shatner to strut his stuff when a transporter malfunction divided him into two diametrically opposed selves. This episode originated the much-abused concept of the "evil twin," and is perhaps the only time on TV it was explored with thought and imagination.

"Mudd's Women," one of the three scripts proposed for the second pilot submission, introduced Roger C. Carmel as the rascally space swindler Harry Mudd. The story marks the first time the Enterprise is in dire need of fresh dilithium crystals. Mudd actually gives someone a pleasure drug, a fact somehow overlooked by the network censor! The script was written by Stephen J. Kandel, who went on to become a successful writer/producer of action-adventure shows.

In describing how he came to write "Mudd's Women", Kandel stated, "My first involvement with Gene was when he first called me. We had a meeting and got along famously, and it went on from there. It was really very uncomplicated and very pleasant while it lasted."

"What Are Little Girls Made Of?" again features two Kirks. His brother George is mentioned. "Miri" followed, then "Dagger Of The Mind" introduced the Vulcan mind meld as well as the Vulcan neck pinch because Nimoy felt Spock wouldn't do something as crude as punch someone out.

"The Corbomite Maneuver" was followed by a two-parter, "The Menagerie." It incorporated much of the footage from the first pilot, "The Cage."

With the key elements in place and the show on the air, STAR TREK was now more than a dream. It was a reality. But by the end of 1966, STAR TREK was in trouble.

NBC was dissatisfied with the Nielsen ratings and uncertain how to categorize the series. The show generated positive response in the science fiction subculture so Gene turned to Harlan Ellison for help.

Perhaps if the network knew just how large an audience science fiction fandom represented, they might see the show in a new light. Ellison sent out five thousand letters urging fans to press NBC with a letter-writing campaign. Dated December 1, 1966, Ellison's missive bore the letterhead of "The Committee," an impressive roster of personalities which included Poul Anderson, Robert Bloch, Lester Del Rey, Ellison himself, Philip José Farmer, Frank Herbert, Richard Matheson, Theodore Sturgeon and A.E. Van Vogt. Thus, Ellison, who would later be less than keen on his involvement with STAR TREK ("The City on the Edge of Forever" had yet to be filmed), was responsible for the very first letter campaign launched to benefit the series.

This was in the days when the Nielsen ratings presupposed a bland, uniform TV viewer. In those pre-demographics days, the variety of American viewers wasn't taken into consideration, and the Nielsen ratings were the voice of God as far as the networks were concerned. Those were the numbers that measured a show's advertising value, regardless of contrary evidence.

And evidence there was. The stars of STAR TREK had become wildly popular with the public. . . almost, if not quite, overnight. The ratings seem odd held up against this.

In 1966, Leonard Nimoy and William Shatner appeared in Hollywood's annual Christmas parade. This newfound fame was no guarantee of respect, for while the parade announcer got Shatner's name correct, he introduced the other STAR TREK star as "Leonard Nimsy."

Despite this gaffe, Nimoy was, for the first time in his life, frequently recognized on the street, and constantly besieged for autographs. He took it all in good humor, although he soon became weary of fans asking him where he'd left his ears. Fan mail began to pour in, much of it from younger viewers.

Early in STAR TREK's run, NBC arranged for Leonard Nimoy to be Grand Marshall of Medford, Oregon's annual Pear Blossom Festival, his first real promotional trip. He was unprepared for the chaos.

The parade went without a hitch—but it was announced Nimoy would sign autographs in a small park at the end of the route. A crowd followed Nimoy. By the time he reached the park, it was swarming with immense numbers of people, many of them young and enthusiastic. The lone park employee was swamped and traffic was completely fouled up. In the end, Medford police had to "rescue" Nimoy from the friendly mob.

Eventually people turned down the chance for a Spock/Nimoy appearance. Macy's, the famous New York department store, declined to have Nimoy appear to promote one of his record albums. They honestly admitted they couldn't handle the crowds.

The episodes continued. "The Conscience of the King" was followed by "Balance of Terror" which introduced the Romulans. Mark Lenard, later to assay the role of Spock's father, Sarek, played the Romulan commander.

"Shore Leave" marked the first time a leading STAR TREK character died, only to return intact. That time it was McCoy.

"Probably the most exciting shows were not the best shows," Gene admitted. "We tried to make the equivalent of half a science-fiction motion picture every week and often it was just a miracle that we got the show into the can by Friday with a beginning, a middle and an end. I recall that on one of the shows, 'Shore Leave,' I was rewriting the show sitting in a camper while the actors were acting it. That was a pretty exciting and harrowing and nervous thing."

"The Galileo Seven" brought Spock to the forefront as he commands a shuttlecraft which crashes, leaving him, Scotty and Dr. McCoy stranded on a hostile planet. This was the first episode to really spotlight Spock, but it took several weeks to happen because NBC still had mixed feelings about the character. In fact, the brochure the network sent out that summer of 1966 to their affiliate stations to promote the new series STAR TREK had airbrushed out the points on the ears in all the photos of Mr. Spock.

Gene recalled, "I thought people would identify more closely with Spock than the other characters because in a very real sense we all feel like strangers on a strange planet, hoping that some day we're going to reach someone. If we're fortunate in our lives, we'll make contact with three or four of these strange beings we find ourselves plunked down among. And indeed the audience did identify with him, so I was proved right. But the network people I was working with at the time would not accept this reasoning. We had a great fight and they said, 'All right, you can keep the guy with the ears, but keep him well in the background.

"After we had about ten episodes on the air, I got a call from the new program vice-president out there and went to his office. He said to me, 'You know, Roddenberry, I really don't understand what you're doing on this show because you're supposed to be a good producer and here you've got a hit with this Spock character and you've always got him in the background.' I told him what his predecessor had demanded and he said, 'I don't believe that anyone could be so foolish.' From then on, of course, Spock became a primary character."

"Squire of Gothos" and "Arena" followed. Then "Tomorrow Is Yesterday" brought the first solid time-travel story to STAR TREK when The Enterprise is hurled back to the 20th Century by the gravitational field of a black hole.

"Court-Martial", "The Return of the Archons" and "Space Seed" offer three very different episodes. The last introduced Ricardo Montalban as Khan, who, of course, reappeared in the second feature film.

"A Taste of Armageddon" and "This Side of Paradise" aired next. Then Spock has his emotions liberated in "The Naked Time" when he falls in love with a young botanist who he had known before. He is also referred to as a Vulcanian on the show for the first and last time, since the terminology still hadn't been standardized! "The Devil In The Dark," "Errand of Mercy" and "The Alternative Factor" were then broadcast.

Gene was pleased with what they were accomplishing. He had been rewriting the first dozen scripts himself to make sure everything stayed in line with his vision. This didn't mean he thought it was perfect.

"I don't consider STAR TREK to be a work of genius," he said in a 1986 interview. "We hit some things people were hungry for when we suggested that the human race might be greater than we suspect, or that conformity is not so great. Just because something is different doesn't mean it's ugly."

He liked citing the episode "Devil In The Dark" as a prime example of his philosophy. "Don't forget that our monsters were never the monsters of bad sci-fi," he noted. "They were always motivated beings who might be ugly, but had beauty inside of them. We were constantly saying 'Because something looks different doesn't mean that it's bad, or because other people have a different lifestyle doesn't mean they're wrong.'

"If there was one theme in all of STAR TREK it was that the glory of our universe is its infinite combinations of diversity—that all beauty comes out of its diversity."

"The City on the Edge of Forever" is regarded as one of the best STAR TREK episodes. It's also the episode with the most interesting background history.

Harlan Ellison's original script was rewritten by Gene, unnecessarily as far as Ellison is concerned,. It became a long-standing source of annoyance for the writer.

Gene's reasons have become clouded with the passage of time. He once claimed that Ellison's script included huge crowd scenes and other factors which would have exceeded the show's budget and that the script had Scotty dealing drugs! Ellison's original draft did hinge on a low ranking crew member dealing illegal drugs, but it was not Scotty. Perhaps Gene was simply aghast that someone might show a seamy underside to his perfect human civilization of the future.

Samuel A. Peeples, a friend and frequent collaborator of Gene's, disliked the rewrite. "I thought his version of his script that won the Writer's Guild Award was far better than the script that was shot. So here, Gene and I disagree," Peeples said. "But I think Gene, in thinking back, would probably agree with what I've just said. When you produce a series there are circumstances—hundreds of reasons why you may have to change a script. The original writer of that script is not aware of these, and even if you tell him he doesn't necessarily believe you because he likes what he did, and he wants to see exactly what he wrote.

"I've felt the same way as a writer, and I feel the other side of the hat as a producer, so in my opinion there is no blame attached to the fact that 'City On The Edge Of Forever' was shot from a script much inferior to Harlan's."

The script as written by Ellison was published in the now-out-of-print SIX SCIENCE FICTION PLAYS, edited by Roger Ellwood, and is due to be released again soon by Borderlands Press as a limited edition hardcover with an extensive introduction by Ellison detailing the controversy from his point of view. Ellison's original script won a Writer's Guild Award; the filmed version won a Hugo.

Gene recalled, "Harlan got a chance on the first show and wrote a $350,000 estimated budget show when I only had, in those days, $186,000. And when I told him to cut the budget, he sent me back the script saying in parenthesis to do it with special effects. He then submitted it to the Writer's Guild which gave him the Writer's Guild prize which he deserved for the script, except that many people would get prizes if they wrote scripts that budgeted out to three times the show's cost. I rewrote that script for Harlan, and it won the Nebula Award, which he rushed up on stage and took credit for, too!"

Ellison denied Gene's recollection of events. He resented the claim he didn't write an episode in budget.

Controversy aside, "The City On The Edge of Forever" became DeForest Kelley's favorite episode. According to him, the catalytic character was originally a guest star but was altered to accommodate McCoy. Fans rank the episode as among the series' top ten.

Interestingly enough, it's one of Gene's favorites as well. He said, "I think my favorites among the stories are probably 'City On The Edge of Forever,' which was a sort of romantic tale where we went back to the Thirties. Also, I think, pilot number two, which finally sold the series, and I enjoyed doing 'The Menagerie,' which was a two-parter."

The first season ended with the broadcast of "Operation: Annihilate," which featured the dead body of Kirk's older brother George. The season had been long and hard, resulting in twenty-nine episodes completed and aired.

"Let me tell you what working on it was like," Gene once wearily recalled. "We did STAR TREK twelve hours a day, six days a week, and on Sunday I stayed in bed reading new scripts. Everybody in my office, once a year, would spend time in the hospital from something associated with physical and emotional exhaustion. Out of five of us, we had four neuroses.

"I also took years away from my growing family that I bitterly resent. We finally became friends again."

Gene said he had a five-year-old daughter at the time whom he never saw because he was working so much. It was around this time that his marriage to his first wife, Eilene, broke up.

During the summer of 1967, Desilu and Paramount were acquired by Gulf & Western. Gene saw STAR TREK acquire a new owner, but the rules of the game didn't allow him to share the wealth. He admitted he felt "A little envious of them selling the property and getting several million extra for it and not seeing any of it myself." The situation would not improve under Gulf & Western.

During the spring and summer of 1967, while the first season of STAR TREK was in reruns, word began to spread that the next season would feature a visit to Spock's home planet, Vulcan. Speculation was rife. That year in New York, World Science Fiction Convention attendees were the first to see the promised episode, "Amok Time," as well as the first blooper reel.

Gene was popular with his staff. This is best expressed by an anecdote related by writer Jerry Sohl regarding a birthday Gene had, and the surprise he got. "It was his birthday and so he had no idea what was going to happen," Sohl recalled., "but the door opened and this naked woman came in, and of course he was absolutely flabbergasted! I don't know who she was, but she came in and sat on his lap and gave him a big kiss. And his face was all red. But everybody really enjoyed and liked him and he loved this kind of thing. He said, 'That's the best birthday present I ever had!' and the woman left."

The second season of STAR TREK began on September 15, 1967 with "Amok Time." The episode also marked the first time DeForest Kelley received billing in the opening credits.

The cast was altered to include a new character. The network had been pressing for a character to rope in the "youth" market, something along the lines of Davey Jones of The Monkees. A press release, later revealed to have exaggerated the truth by fabricating the incident, claimed the show was criticized by the Russian Communist newspaper PRAVDA.

Supposedly, among other complaints, they lamented the show's lack of a Russian character in the Enterprise's otherwise multinational crew. To kill two birds with one stone, Gene supposedly created the character of Ensign Pavel Chekov, a young officer with a heavy Russian accent, to satisfy the Soviets. Signing on as Chekov was Walter Koenig.

Keying in on the interest in Spock's emotional chinks, the story of "Amok Time," penned by Theodore Sturgeon, opened with the Vulcan officer acting decidedly strange and sulky. McCoy determines that Spock will die if something is not done about the physical changes he's undergoing. Spock admits, not to the doctor but to Kirk, that he is undergoing pon farr, the Vulcan mating cycle. It will indeed be fatal if he doesn't get to Vulcan and undergo the proper rituals.

Kirk bucks orders and reroutes the Enterprise to Vulcan and the story offers tantalizing looks at local culture. The rituals are remnants of Vulcan's barbaric past. T'Pau, a dignified Vulcan leader, appears, as does the first use of the Vulcan ritual greeting "Live long and prosper." Nimoy provided the accompanying hand gesture, which he 'borrowed' from a Jewish religious ceremony.

Vulcan is presented in sparse but effective visual terms. T'Pau, portrayed by Peter Lorre's one-time wife Celia Lovsky, carries the entire implied culture in her bearing. Author Theodore Sturgeon provided many small but telling touches regarding ethics and customs of the planet; photography and music added immensely.

"Who Mourns for Adonis?" gives Scotty a romantic interest. In James Blish's adaptation of this episode, a final epilogue note from the original script is retained which never actually aired.

"The Changeling" was followed by "Mirror, Mirror," which cast Kirk, McCoy, Scotty and Uhura into an alternate universe in which the Federation developed along bloodthirsty, Klingonesque lines. "Mirror, Mirror," written by Jerome Bixby, was awarded the Hugo Award by science fiction fandom.

"The Apple," "The Doomsday Machine" and "Catspaw" followed. "I, Mudd" brings back Roger C. Carmel as Harry Mudd. Then "Metamorphosis" introduces Zephram Cochrane as the inventor of the warp drive.

"Journey to Babel" introduced Spock's parents, the Vulcan Sarek (Mark Lenard) and his human wife Amanda (Jane Wyatt). The occasion is a diplomatic mission during which Spock and his father achieve a rapprochement after nearly twenty years of estrangement.

In December 1967, another letter campaign came to the rescue of the again-beleaguered series. This one, orchestrated by fan Bjo Trimble and her husband John, was even more successful than the first. Inspired by NBC's decision to cancel the show, it generated an unprecedented number of letters, and proved instrumental in winning the show a third season.

"I was amazed," said Gene at the time. "I think there were a few executives at NBC who thought that I was behind the whole campaign, as if I have a secret telephone somewhere from which I manipulate fans and organizations! I tried to explain to them that if could bring out Cal Tech on a torchlight parade at NBC, if I could have MIT picket Rockefeller Center and do other things like that, I would get out of show business and into politics.

"During MIT's march against NBC in New York, I understand they snuck into the executive garage and put Save STAR TREK bumper stickers on all the executive limousines!"

New Year's Day, 1968, saw the STAR TREK season's continuation with a perhaps unintentional Christmas touch: an episode, "Friday's Child", wherein a child is born in a cave. The child is named 'Leonard James' after McCoy and Kirk, but Spock, not much for children it seems, gets short shrift.

"The Deadly Years" rated as one of DeForest Kelley's favorite episodes. Speaking to Joe Gulick in 1974, he observed, "I enjoyed doing ["The Deadly Years"] because it gave me an opportunity to do something that I would never be called upon to do."

As his character aged, Kelley had him become more and more the old-fashioned country doctor McCoy really envisioned himself as. Kelley said, "Yes, I began to fall back. I had that in mind from the beginning, that the older he became, the more he would fall back into what he really had a feeling in his heart for. Fortunately, it worked very well. There was a great disturbance at the studio at the time because they felt I should have been nominated for that show, but I was not. They were very upset about it."

Nimoy, however, would again receive an Emmy nomination for the second season.

"Obsession" and "Wolf in the Fold" were followed by "The Trouble With Tribbles," perhaps the most comical episode in sSTAR TREK history. Klingons and furry little creatures that reproduce at an alarming rate threaten the peace on the Enterprise.

Gene knew about the write-in campaign but as he approached the end of the second year of producing STAR TREK, the long hours were taking their toll. He had mixed feelings about the show returning.

In a newspaper column published February 1, 1968, he was quoted as saying, "There is a 50-50 chance that it will continue for the next season. I am rooting hard for the show to be renewed. Sometimes I wonder why.

"If I win I will be faced with continuing a 14-hour-a-day work schedule, seven days a week. There are easier ways of making a living and a more profitable one. Like what? Motion pictures. A good writer can earn as much and more in six months that way as he can in a year in television—and be home with the wife and kids every night, too."

"The Gamesters of Triskelion," "A Piece of the Action," "The Immunity Syndrome," "A Private Little War," "Return to Tomorrow," "Patterns of Force," and "By Any Other Name" aired next. Although STAR TREK was in trouble again, good news came at the conclusion of a Gene-penned episode of STAR TREK, "Omega Glory."

This episode featured yet another parallel history. The warring Kohms and Yangs parallel the Communists and Yankees of the Vietnam War era in one of the more heavy-handed episodes of STAR TREK. Gene was candid in admitting what went wrong with this one. He explained, "It was not one of my favorites. I wrote it, and I'm not satisfied with what I wrote. Really, it came out of a visit I'd made to the Library of Congress and looked at the Constitution and was really struck by those three words—'We the people.' It was not planned as a jingoistic, overly-patriotic show. I think those three words, 'We the people' are highly significant, exciting words that will be important wherever there are life forms, and that was what we tried to do. It didn't come off as well as we hoped. It came off rather a little over-patriotic, I think."

Gene admitted that STAR TREK also had other mistakes. He said, "Oh my God, yes. I remember one night we were watching that week's episode and Captain Kirk said a line about something being one to the tenth power. Well the tenth power of one is still one. And I thought, 'How did we let that get by? There'll be a hundred letters!' And indeed there were."

The offending line occurs in the first season episode "Court Martial." Gene went on to explain, "We're just happy we made as few errors as we did. It was twelve hours a day, six days a week to make the show and sometimes stuff got by you. It was not the finest produced show ever made—you can't do it in that time. We just happened to catch a chemistry, and people ready to believe humans are good—ready to believe our philosophy that because something is different doesn't mean that it's bad or wrong and we caught America ready to think about those things, and that's what really helped us."

The fans were willing to forgive the lapses, though, as the second season had also produced such classy shows as Jerome Bixby's "Mirror, Mirror." By this time, the volume of mail provoked by Bjo Trimble's letter campaign led the network to announce on the air after the March 1, 1968 broadcast of "Omega Glory" that STAR TREK would, indeed, be returning in the Fall.

A press release soon followed:

UNPRECEDENTED VIEWER REACTION IN SUPPORT OF "STAR TREK" LEADS TO ON-AIR ANNOUNCEMENT OF SERIES' SCHEDULING FOR 1968-69.

In response to unprecedented viewer reaction in support of the continuation of the NBC Television Network's STAR TREK series, plans for continuing the series in the Fall were announced on NBC-TV immediately following last Friday night's episode of the space adventure series. The announcement will be repeated following next Friday's program. From early December to date, NBC has received 114,667 pieces of mail in support of STAR TREK, and 52,151 in the month of February alone. Immediately after last Friday night's program, the following announcement was made: "And now an announcement of interest to all viewers of STAR TREK. We are pleased to tell you that STAR TREK will continue to be seen on NBC Television. We know you will be looking forward to seeing the weekly adventure in space on STAR TREK."

Gene felt it necessary to personally acknowledge what the fans of the show had accomplished. On March 16, 1968, he issued a statement. He said, "This season, some 1,200 viewers nearly scuttled the spaceship Enterprise. Then more than a million enthusiasts of STAR TREK made their feelings known to NBC. As a result, the show will remain in orbit for another season. "Those 1,200 viewers are, of course, the folks with Nielsen meters attached to their TV sets. What they watch determines the 'ratings.' And the ratings, as a guideline for sponsors, ad agencies and networks, determine which shows live and which die. From September through December of 1967, the ratings of the once-popular STAR TREK were—let's face it—lackluster. And while NBC did not officially tell us we were through, the word trickled back that the network had a phaser gun aimed at our vitals. It was just a matter of time, the grapevine intimated, before the execution order went out.

"News of STAR TREK's plight reached the press and almost immediately complaints poured in from scientists, astronomers, government officials and just plain viewers. A petition to keep us on the air was signed by a majority of the scientists at the Los Alamos Proving Grounds. One hundred graduate students at Cornell fired an angry protest to the network. Five hundred California Institute of Technology undergraduates staged a torchlight parade from their campus to NBC's front door. At the University of California at Berkeley a collection was taken to hire the Goodyear blimp to fly over the city, denouncing television ratings. Representative George P. Miller, Chairman of the House Committee on Science and Astronautics, voiced his objection, as did members of NASA and the National Space Club.

"When a young man threatened to hire a helicopter to drop rolls of toilet paper on NBC's West Coast headquarters, we persuaded him to use the U.S. mails instead. It was a marvelous, spontaneous display of affection which, initially at least, NBC misinterpreted.

"They wondered aloud how I had organized and manipulated this groundswell. I thanked them for the compliment but pointed out that if I could foment such an avalanche of public feelings, I was in the wrong business. I should get out of television in favor of politics.

"By the time NBC stopped counting our mail—around the million mark—a new trend had developed. Several fans, including some top names in the field of computer programming, were questioning the ratings themselves. Using the most modern electronic brains available, these researchers came to the same conclusion: while it is quite possible to project an accurate 'rating' from a small sampling, ideal controls are needed, and these controls simply don't exist when it comes to measuring TV audiences.

"As one expert put it, the ratings are so 'vague and haphazard as to be scientifically ludicrous.' Another technologist added, 'it would be laughable, if it weren't so sad to see a billion-dollar industry base its fate on this sort of nonsense.'

"These comments opened my eyes. I had always looked at the ratings pragmatically. If a show I produced made the top ten, the ratings were irrefutable. If we were scoring badly with the pollsters, the numbers became suspect. Now, even though we have climbed to a respectable rating of between 18 and 20, I no longer read the reports as avidly.

"One thing ratings, valid or otherwise, have never proven is the loyalty of one series' viewers against another's. STAR TREK, I discovered, has as devoted a group of followers as any show in history. It is also an intelligent and vocal audience who resent the bland sameness of most TV entertainment, and who are fed up with seeing television's rare attempts to be different guillotined by a statistical machete.

"What is it they like about STAR TREK? (And here, I'm speaking not so much as the series produce, but as one who spent long delightful hours reading viewers' comments.) They appreciate the fact that basic scientific principles are the seed for each exercise in adventure and derring-do unreel. Take the basic matter of travelling to other planets in other solar systems, where some form of life is present. Illogical? Not at all, according to a Duke University study which disclosed that within our galaxy, circling other suns, it is estimated that there are some three million planets capable of sustaining life. To reach these planets, however, would necessitate a means of travel exceeding the speed of light, an apparent violation of one of Einstein's basic laws. Again, we found scientific evidence—new studies regarding the warping of time and space through use of excessive power—which legitimized these flights of fancy.

"Given these principles, we have a perfect vehicle (no pun intended) for adventure, satire and social comment. Next season, for example, we will travel to a planet which closely parallels earth, with one difference. The police are the best educated, and most highly respected citizens of the land, the equivalent of scientists and educators here. If this raises any questions about our own society, so be it.

"Another episode will deal with medical research and brain transplants. Yes, I said next season. It is apparent that the series will be renewed, and the network has even provided the money to pay for new scripts (an expensive decision if they mean to cancel the series.)"

Gene then went on to thank everyone involved with saving the show. He said, "So, on behalf of the entire crew of the Enterprise I'll take this opportunity to thank all of you whose letters and telegrams have provided the power for our future journeys into space."

Bjo Trimble, who had orchestrated the letter writing campaign, also helped set up Lincoln Enterprises (then called Star Trek Enterprises) wherein scripts and other souvenirs from STAR TREK could be sold legally to the fans. After Bjo had the business up and running, Majel Barrett stepped in and took it over. While Bjo remained friendly with Gene, she was never again entirely friendly towards Majel.

Majel continues to own and operate Lincoln Enterprises. She often attends major STAR TREK conventions where she sells a huge line of exclusive STAR TREK

THE MAN WHO CREATED STAR TREK

merchandise, including scripts from both of the television series as well as an array of posters and other items.

With the series future seemingly secure, the fans were able to sit back and enjoy the rest of the second season. "The Ultimate Computer" and "Bread and Circuses" were followed by "Assignment Earth," which incorporated the script of a pilot proposed by Gene into the STAR TREK continuity.

Once again, the Enterprise travels through time, now to 1968. Here they meet Gary Seven (Robert Lansing), a human (supposedly) trained by aliens to defend Earth. Kirk and Spock follow him to New York. Seven's mission is to prevent the launching of a Star-Wars type orbiting defense system that will actually prove disastrous to humanity. The story ends with a hint that Seven and his secretary Roberta (Teri Garr) will have more adventures, but a spin-off series never materialized.

So ended the second season of STAR TREK with nothing but promises of fine things ahead. After all, NBC knew the following the show had now—they'd have to finally show it respect.

Gene had big plans for the third year of STAR TREK. He believed NBC when they promised him a prime Monday night slot. In a story which ran in July 1968, the writer-producer stated that the network had approached him and suggested that STAR TREK, "should this year deal in even greater depth with drama themes of contemporary meaning to man and his society. Although STAR TREK will and should remain action-adventure entertainment, they have urged us to continue and intensify speculation on any exciting aspect of law, religion, comment on the insanity of warfare, on bacteriological and other horror weapons, on the promises and problems of human organ transplants, on varied or even exotic forms of law enforcement, and on any other matter of current public debate and interest."

The Fall Preview of TV GUIDE came out with an item about STAR TREK including the following: "More hazardous than all their encounters in outer space for the Star Trekkers are those Nielsen ratings, and they just barely eked by with a renewal for this season. Last term, their future was in considerable doubt, and only a heavy mail campaign from avid viewers played an important part in keeping the show on. Executive producer Gene Roddenberry still was on the verge of quitting the show because they changed its time slot to 10 P.M. Fridays, a time he thinks bodes no good for the future of his series, since it slots the show opposite the movies on CBS and JUDD on ABC. But he did agree to remain with it, despite his unhappiness at the change. Roddenberry tells us that this season the only change is to expose the secondary characters more fully, to give viewers a better idea of their personalities. He remarks of the gang in Trek, 'We have the truly multi-racial cast, and in two years we've had only three crank letters.' In one of the stories this season, the Trekkers land on a planet identical in physical makeup to Earth. On that planet, police are selected as carefully as we select scientists, and the question is posed: Could our police be better? 'We are using science fiction to show the police as they could or should be if they had support from the public, and scientific support,' explains ex-cop Roddenberry."

The item was more than a bit premature. Gene did quit as producer, and, as suspected, NBC was sneakily shifting its stance. They announced that the show would be aired in a 7:30 PM, prime time slot on Mondays. . . only to turn around and stick STAR TREK on at 10:00 PM on Friday, a time slot reeking with the stench of certain death. It seemed Rowan and Martin's LAUGH-IN had a prior claim on that time slot. To further compound their infamy, the network only contracted for thirteen episodes instead of a full season. In the end, the series did run one last full season.

Gene planned to put Gene L. Coon in his place, but illness and other commitments kept this from happening. OUTER LIMITS producer Joseph Stefano was invited to step in but declined. Gene was forced to choose someone untested in this kind of series.

Although Fred Freiberger came highly recommended, he was not familiar with the basic ideas and relationships within the series. He was destined to oversee a number of episodes in which the basic integrity of STAR TREK and its characters were sadly undermined.

Freiberger had most recently produced the very successful first season of THE WILD WILD WEST, and despite claims to the contrary, he did have some background in celluloid science fiction. In 1953 he had co-written (with Lou Morheim) the movie THE BEAST FROM 20,000 FATHOMS (which was stolen from a Ray Bradbury short story—Bradbury got screen credit after he was shown the screenplay by his friend Ray Harryhausen). Freiberger also wrote the low-budget 1957 film BEGINNING OF THE END about giant grasshoppers.

Freiberger liked STAR TREK. He felt that the show should be more like the first pilot, "The Cage," which the network had deemed too cerebral.

Gene recalled his departure, saying, "I had been told by the network that we would get a 7:30 time slot, early in the week, and I said, on that basis I'll come back and become line producer. By that time we'd lost Gene Coon, who we'd all admired, and I would line produce the show.

"Then they put us, [at the] last moment, into Friday night at ten, and I told them that—using the only leverage I had—that if they did that, I would not produce the show as promised. And I couldn't get them to back down, and I felt, at the time, I had to stick by my statement, since I would have to bargain with them again at other times.

"I think there was a little rationalization in that on my part. I think also what was affecting me at that time was an enormous fatigue. I think maybe I was looking for an excuse to get out from under the fight that I had been having, not just for two years, but really for four. . ."

Some years later, DeForest Kelley would reflect on the series' final season. "The third year was not a good year because there was too much going on," he recalled. "Problems with the network, thinking we were going to be dropped, put into bad time slots. A kind of internal revolution took place, so to speak, and it began to show, which we were all very concerned about.

"[Gene Roddenberry] began to slack off in the latter part of the second season because other things enter into what then was thought to be a successful show. Demands began to be put upon his time in other directions and he then, in turn, brought in other people to assist him. The third year he began to battle with NBC over the time slot and he became terribly upset and told them he would not produce the show personally if it were place in a ten o'clock time slot on Friday night. We had a tremendous university audience and school audience and it would lose viewers if it were on at that time. NBC went ahead and did it and Gene pulled out. They brought another producer in who was not familiar with the show and it began to go downhill."

Gene was somewhat more diplomatic, saying, "Obviously, when you bring a producer in, and you're going to let him produce it, you've got to let him do it his way, and I think his way, or their way, was somewhat different than our way. So it did look different. As long as the original creator stays with the show, it gives it a certain unity. When other minds become involved, it's not that they are lesser minds or not as clever writers, but you lose the unity of that one driving force."

Indeed, on September 20, 1968, a very different STAR TREK began its third and final season with what may rightly be considered its single worst episode, "Spock's Brain." Fans were incensed by what they saw as the new production team's deviation from the true nature of STAR TREK.

Strangely enough, VARIETY gave this episode a better review than it had "Man Trap" two years earlier. In the September 25, 1968 issue, the review opened by stating: "STAR TREK has drifted far demographically since its days as kid fare and has now made the transition complete with a move into the late hours. It retains its vigor and spatial spookiness, although it chief characters are largely caricatures and the dialogue tends to turgidity. However, for males of all ages at least, it also retains a bevy of shapely femmes in tight and revealing space suits and enough conflict to accommodate the action-happy."

If the series were really no more than the review stated, NBC never would have cancelled it since this reviewer describes *exactly* the kind of show the networks love to put on the air! What the VARIETY reviewer really liked about STAR TREK says more about the state of TV at that time than anything else could: "The best part of the show continues to be the sets and special effects, an impressive array of blinking and beeping gadgets."

Even as the season yielded some good episodes without Gene at the helm, it faltered. It was cancelled again, with the last episode filmed being "Turnabout Intruder." There had been a chance that NBC would order three more episodes, and William Shatner had been promised that he'd be able to direct one of those, but he never had the opportunity as the network did not make the final order.

It was over. Visitors to the STAR TREK set during the last week of filming included O.J. Simpson and Gene Roddenberry.

In 1976, seven years after the end of STAR TREK, Gene was asked if he had seen any good science fiction on television since the end of his series. He replied, "I regret to say that I haven't, and this is not a selfish feeling. I have no feeling that I want all other SF to fail so that my efforts in STAR TREK would stand above them. I would like to see good SF on television. I think that it's a marvelous vehicle, and nothing would please me more than to see good shows come on, and I think they will. But you still, today, even after STAR TREK, have to fight past the studio and network attitudes that SF is really just zap guns and lots of flashing lights."

V | After Star Trek... Sex, Marriage & Tarzan

"My dreams were going downhill because I could not get work after the original series was cancelled."
—G.R.

When Gene stepped down as line producer during the third season of STAR TREK, he continued working, but on something completely different. It was a screenplay based on a character Gene had read much about in his youth—Tarzan.

Gene discussed his feelings about the project in a talk he gave at Berkeley in 1968. He told the gathered campus community, "I always felt similar about Burroughs and Tarzan as I did about science fiction at the beginning of STAR TREK. That I'd seen all of the Tarzan films, but I'd never seen Tarzan on the screen.

"So among the new projects will be that of writing and producing a new Tarzan in which my aim and my commitment I have made to myself and to the company is to try and do Tarzan as Edgar Rice Burroughs conceived him. There will, of course, be some changes. The screen inherently has certain limitations.

"Obviously it is a different medium from a novel, but what you aim to do as we do on STAR TREK is with the limitations—in our case time, budget, and those other things—is to do a visual science fiction as close as possible, to prove that visual science fiction will work. I've never boasted or pretended that STAR TREK was all things to all men. We make a few errors on it. We make a few episodes we wish to God we could bury. We now and then make one we're very proud of. And this will be the case with Burroughs.

"You hope for something like 85% and if you get that—why I don't think they ever got 7% before—so if I get 50% it'll be very satisfying. I will try and do my damndest for my own satisfaction, and I hope you enjoy it, too. A writer basically writes for himself. I'll try to do it so it pleases me, and I hope that one pleases you, too, when it is done."

In 1968, at the behest of producer Sy Weintraub, Gene thought about a Tarzan motion picture, and considered the problems of a new Tarzan television series. His main interest lay in the full theatrical motion picture treatment of the lord of the jungle.

Gene described his approach to adapting the character for modern audiences in a letter to producer Weintraub dated June 7, 1968. His insights into Tarzan make for interesting reading, and stand as a guide for any producer tackling the character for either the large or the small screen. Certainly none of the versions produced in the last twenty years thought it through so well.

A lifelong Burroughs aficionado, Gene began with the original Tarzan novels. He cautioned against setting the character in modern times, saying, "The spectacular growth rate of modern technology is rapidly making any modern Tarzan more and more unbelievable. The sheer weight and efficiency of modern transportation, weaponry, and communications available to almost anyone, makes it more and more incredible that any problem could be solved better, if at all, by a half-naked man armed with knife and vine-lariat."

Gene notes that Burroughs himself distanced the original novel from the time of its writing (1912) by setting it in the 1880s, a period when Africa was more mysterious and unknown. He wrote, "It would be possible, of course, to create a 'time cushion' and encourage some suspension of disbelief by now taking Tarzan back to the 1920s or 1930s. However, I think it well demonstrated that these 'half modern' eras hold little romantic attraction to the mass audience, except in very specialized cases such as a Bonnie and Clyde.

"The 1880s era will work best for us," he continued. "It gives sufficient civilization for almost any type of story, but without the advantages previously listed. And the 1880s have a certain romantic appeal. . . interesting male and female costumes, horses and carriages, incredibly difficult safari conditions, the jeopardy limitations of single shot firearms, acceptable paternal colonialism, the colorful contrast of the over-polite manners of 1880 versus our apeman's essential simplicity, the believable existence of Arab slave traders, ad infinitum. This whole new Tarzan spectrum will inevitably give a new Tarzan film and television format a completely new look.

"It has an additional 'extra'— the opening up of totally new story areas for future Tarzan features, one which no film distributor need fear will be 'retread' of any of the features produced in the past."

Gene had a few things to say about Tarzan's treatment in previous films. For example, he said, "We tend to forget that the [in] the Tarzan motion pictures of the Thirties, a half-clad 'topless' man was highly unusual. . . and a mini-skirt-size loin-cloth on a woman was little short of a sensation. The 'strip-tease' element in them, i.e., a fully clad young female gradually having her garments torn into knee-length shreds by jungle thorns, actually created a greater stir and more comment than many current 'erotic' films."

His main criticism of previous Tarzan films was of their believability. He said movie Tarzans had a tendency to leap into a nearby body of water, and swim to the rescue and noted that "The youngest child knows that a man can run faster than he can swim. In one of various screenings at my home to a fairly average audience of children and adults, comments and even derisive laughter accompanied this and similar scenes.

"In other films— after showing some expertise with a junglecraft, Tarzan would then let himself be clumsily ambushed by a white hunter for plot convenience or commit some similar gross error totally unbelievable in a jungle trained animal-man. In another film, having relieved an enemy of an automatic rifle, Tarzan tossed it aside and went after a group of heavily armed men with a knife alone. [This] led to children commenting that this hero was patently feeble-minded in throwing away a superior weapon, the use of which he had already seen demonstrated. It was especially puzzling when a few scenes later he demonstrated himself fully capable of operating a short-wave radio."

In short, Gene proposed bringing the same attention to believable behavior to Tarzan that he insisted on in Star Trek. Although this must remain a dream project, it is interesting to speculate on what his Tarzan would have been like.

He actually wrote a 170 page script, a copy of which is on file in the Edgar Rice Burroughs Collection of the University of Louisville. An examination of the script shows that Gene brought his own sensibilities to the story, including an interest in writing about sex.

Tarzan films over the decades have failed to include even the most passing references to overt sex, with only one exception which appeared after this time. Gene's version would have been ground-breaking.

He followed familiar patterns found in the original novels by Burroughs, adopting a couple of the more familiar ones from the twenty-four book series—his villains were Arabs and the plot involved a search for an ancient lost civilization.

Gene created the unique concept of Tarzan being Lord John Greystoke's secret identity! While Greystoke lives on an African estate, few know that he is really the legendary "white ape," Tarzan.

This didn't protect him when the villainous El Kal attacked the estate some years before as a reprisal for Tarzan's smashing of the slave trade in the region. Jane was carried off by El Kal's warriors and killed. Only later is it learned that Jane's body was never found. El Kal even drops a hint that even though Tarzan learned of her death by torturing two men, what men say under torture isn't always reliable. Yet Gene never picks up on this plot thread, leaving it, perhaps, for a later film.

With Jane dead, Tarzan is romantically unencumbered, freeing him to have an affair with the female lead, Helena Vichay. Helena has come to Africa to search for her fiance, who disappeared into the interior more than two years before.

A note was brought from her brother by a native. Along the way El Kal had intercepted it, keeping the strange metal object accompanying it as proof Richard Templeton had found what he was searching for. The object is a short length of pipe which fires a powerful heat ray.

El Kal uses it to lay waste nearly all of Tarzan's faithful Wazuri warriors in the opening of the story. This quickly sets up events and introduces science fiction overtones.

El Kal soon exhausts the power of the weapon, reducing his conflicts with Tarzan for most of the rest of the story to more commonplace levels. Interest has been piqued that a vast and powerful secret awaits in the mountains.

Gene's first hint of erotica in the screenplay occurs when Lady Helena surprises two Arabs searching her room. They tie her to her bed. Then they search her clothes for the map they think she has and finally start cutting her dress off as they threaten to rob her of her virginity if she doesn't reveal the location of the map. Tarzan arrives in the nick of time, of course.

Gene's long, drawn-out sequence of the Arabs menacing Helena in this manner is weirdly erotic as they cut away her dress, slowly, a piece at a time, carefully avoiding touching her skin with the knife. The following exchange of dialogue from page 38 gives an idea of the tone:

EL KAL

No fear? It is my trade to know females. I say thee are virgin.

HELENA

(hesitates)

I did not. . . expect to remain so forever.

Gene inserts unexpected strangeness throughout the script. A man named Flemming is determined to team up with El Kal and find the treasure he believes Helena has come to search for. He has helped El Kal before and even attempted to murder Tarzan. On page 62 the following bizarre incident transpires:

EL KAL

(seems to consider it)

An English partner might have an advantage. Would thee accept Allah and be circumsized as our faith requires?

FLEMMING

Gladly.

El Kal nods to D'Jin who scabbards his rifle and draws his curved dagger. As he moves his horse in alongside Flemming, the Englishman protests in surprise:

FLEMMING

You mean here? You must be. . .

EL KAL

A test of thy word . . . and thy worthiness.

D'JIN

A simple thing. Does pain frighten thee, Englishman?

ANOTHER ANGLE - INCLUDING MED. SHOT OF FLEMMING

Keeping his pistol aimed at El Kal, hesitating. He knows El Kal would prefer not to die, nor does Flemming want to die immediately afterwards. And the stakes are undoubtedly large; worth a little pain. Finally, he nods. Keeping the pistol trained, he moves his free hand down out of SCENE to prepare himself. D'Jin leans over, moving his knife down OUT OF FRAME, too. Flemming tightens his teeth, preparing for the pain. Then a look of paralyzed astonishment on his face; he GROANS and begins to sink out of saddle.

WIDER ANGLE

The Englishman toppling dying to the ground. D'Jin dismounts, withdraws his knife with a show of apology to El Kal.

D'JIN

A slip of my blade, master.

EL KAL

(smiles)

It might have gone worse for him. Thee were always clumsy with a knife.

Helena goes to Lord Greystoke at his jungle estate, wanting him to help her find her brother. He describes Tarzan to her and the differences between the two of them, and then on page 73 he shows her Tarzan as she's staring at twenty screaming Wazuri warriors who have just appeared on the scene. Behind her, Greystoke begins to undress.

REAR ANGLE

past Tarzan (Greystoke), his back to us, totally naked and reaching for the loin cloth as the Wazuri Chieftain, Tu'in, proffers it. Helena turns to see Tarzan standing there in his splendidly muscled nakedness. She SHRIEKS, leaps to her feet and backs away.

HELENA

shocked, both by the unexpected nakedness and by the new expression which was not on that face a moment ago.

ANGLE ON TARZAN

pulling his loin cloth tight about him, watching her as he hangs the knife into place. CAMERA DOLLIES INTO CLOSE SHOT, emphasizing the expression which says this is a totally different man. Then he whirls OUT OF SHOT.

By page 110, after some adventures, Helena has warmed up to the ape man. The jungle has brought out the primitive in her as she goes swimming with Tarzan in the nude. Things progress until on page 115 and 116 she explains there's always been something different about her, a wildness inside that prevents her from lying down with a man until she's certain he will not be harmed by what is inside her. She's decided Tarzan is the one she's saved herself for.

HELENA

(rolls, facing him; pleads)

Please stay Greystoke! I'm afraid. I've waited so long for an equal. . . a man as strong as I. . .

TARZAN

Eyes say. . . you not want Greystoke here. . .

Helena's eyes are becoming wild. She edges closer as if drawn by something beyond her control. She moves closer to him, still pleading:

HELENA

Please! Please go. Leave me. . . quickly. . .

(still closer; begins to caress him)

Tarzan. . . darling, please! If I'm wrong. . . if you're not that strong. . .

(beginning to shudder; rises over him)

Darling. . . darling. . . help me!

SCREAMS, throws herself across him wildly seeking his lips.

ANOTHER ANGLE

finding his lips, pressing eagerly, trembling hard as her arms seek out an embrace. Then suddenly and with surprising strength she actually lifts his huge form rolling over onto her. Then she rolls him onto his back again. She pulls away to kneel over him, eyes wild, her chest heaving with excitement, her body trembling violently, making strange and wild MOANING sounds. Then she SHRIEKS words in a strange tongue which seem torn from her.

HELENA

Ba' al inat t' eta Ba' al!

She lashes out, clawing at his face.

ANGLE - EMPHASIZING TARZAN

Her nails drawing fine lines of blood at his cheek. Totally ignored by Tarzan. Without understanding what it means or what has happened to her, the half animal male of him recognizes he is being challenged and welcomes it, answering with a RUMBLING GROWL.

Again, the words screamed:

HELENA

Ba' al inat t' eta Ba' al!

Tarzan grabs her, throwing her THUMBING hard to the ground.

STOCK FILM - ANGLE ON MONKEYS

We hear her SCREAM again. The monkeys, screeching in excitement, are fleeing away through the trees.

STOCK FILM - ANGLE ON JUNGLE BIRDS

leaving the trees above in sudden flight.

STOCK FILM - AFRICAN HAWK OR EAGLE

From Helena a long ECHOING SCREAM as the bird of prey plummets down SCREECHING to make a kill. It and its prey falling, interlocking in a frenzied struggle, as we:

DISSOLVE

Tarzan and Helena find their way into a hidden cave in the mountains. Inside they discover a small room with metal walls—which close before the room hurtles upwards!

It's an ancient elevator. They emerge into an ancient city with an Egyptian-style temple and a number of warriors commanded by the long-missing Richard Templeton. He's now a high priest of the ancient religion.

Helena is a descendent of these people. They were visited thousands of years ago by alien beings from space who found they could successfully have sex *only* with the women of this lost race.

When the aliens left, one named Ba'al remained behind in suspended animation. He is now awakened by Templeton after Helena has been prepared.

Tarzan is marched off and locked up in the Hall of Women. There women chained to platforms live only to have sex with imprisoned men.

Tarzan meets La of Opar, a character from three of Burroughs' Tarzan novels. She likes Tarzan.

The screenplay has lots of sex. The screenplay chronicles the tale that Helena is a throwback born to have sex with an ancient alien. Left to his own devices, Gene invariably adds sexual undertones to his stories.

In GENESIS II, Dylan Hunt conducts an affair with Lyra-a after waking from suspended animation. The pretext is that the sexual center of his brain had to be stimulated to assure his well being. Even in context of the story, that seems to come from left field.

In SPECTRE, scantinly clad women populate the mansion of Sir Geoffrey Cyon; two are presented to Ham to enjoy as he pleases. Ham declines.

Overt sex never appeared in the STAR TREK television series only because of the network censors. Gene reshot part of one episode because a scantily clad woman's navel was showing, so he knew the penalty for stepping over the line.

In 1982, asked which subjects he'd been unable to deal with on the original STAR TREK, Gene replied, "I would have liked to have some shows about the sexual differences—unisex, homosexuality." Needless to say, prime time television in 1967 wasn't ready for that.

In Gene's Tarzan screenplay, when the eight foot alien Ba'al is resurrected, he carries Helena screaming into the night. Tarzan doesn't find her until the next morning. On page 152, an unexpected twist enters the proceedings.

PANNING TARZAN

As he drops to the ground running, CAMERA ANGLING with him to reveal the figure of Helena! She lies by a small stream in the area where tall grass has been crushed flat. Tarzan runs in.

TARZAN

Helena.

Helena opens her eyes, looking up at Tarzan who runs anxiously into TWO SHOT. He's not prepared for what he sees next — Helena smiling up at him, her face radiantly happy.

HELENA

Yes, Tarzan?

Even the voice reflects happy contentment and Tarzan hesitates, puzzled. Helena smiling, understands his look.

HELENA

(continuing)

No, I'm not demented. Please try to understand. . . this is what I was born for. I was frightened only because I didn't understand.

(lays back in grass, arms out stretching)

He may seem strange and alien to you, but to me he's become beautiful. He wants me so, needs me, cares so.

Tarzan destroys Ba'al and takes Helena back to civilization, but she isn't happy. In fact, it's obvious she misses Ba'al and regrets his destruction. Definitely a different kind of Tarzan movie script.

Ultimately the story is about sexual reawakening. The story focuses on the sexual rebirth of Tarzan following the apparent death of Jane, and the sexual awakening of Helena, who will never be satisfied by mortal man again.

In a newspaper column dated August 16, 1968, Bill Diehl stated that Gene had announced that filming on a new Tarzan movie would begin. Shooting was scheduled to start in Kenya on November 1; a talent search was under way for a new actor to play Tarzan.

"What we are looking for is not only a man with a good physique, but also one who can act," Gene said. "This film will not be a 'me Tarzan' picture. I think it will be great escapism because we're in an era of such films as 2001: A SPACE ODYSSEY and PLANET OF THE APES, both of which have done extraordinarily well at the boxoffice." [Unfortunately, Gene was incorrect. It took 2001 seven years to break even. It received a lot of attention when released, but it was no blockbuster.]

In a letter dated January 14, 1969, published in ERB-dom #26 (a famous fanzine devoted to Burroughs in the Seventies), Gene stated, "As you probably know by now, the TARZAN feature died at birth. It turned out in the end that National General really never had a serious interest in a motion picture box office TARZAN film, but rather this seemed to be their way of exploring whether or not a new TARZAN television series could get on the air. As you know, this was not my interest.."

He continued, "I wanted to do a first class motion picture, not a 'television featurette.' When they kept cutting the budget they eventually reached the point where I could see that a quality film was impossible, and at that point, I killed the project."

Free of the restrictions of television, Gene had created a very liberated Tarzan story, one which he knew would be gutted and emasculated if translated into a TV series.

Women don't have sex with eight foot non-human space aliens on television, and they certainly never enjoy it if it happens. He had brought his interest in exploring the sexual side of the Tarzan myth to full flower in the screenplay, but that was where it would forever remain.

This had to have come as a surprise to producer Sy Weintraub. At no point in Gene's lengthy letter of June 1968 does he mention the sexual subtext of the story, or that this was the real reason he would have Tarzan unencumbered by Jane.

Although both STAR TREK and TARZAN seemed to have lapsed into oblivion in the same year, no such fate befell Gene Roddenberry. In 1969, he took the big step, and married Majel Barrett.

While scouting locations in Japan for an MGM project, Gene recalled, "I discovered I missed Majel a lot. Now, an American bachelor on an MGM expense account in Japan. . . this can be heaven. But I found myself with these pretty little girls in silk kimonos [and] I found myself talking to them about Majel.

"One night I realized what I was doing. I paid the girl, went back to my hotel and called up Majel to ask her if she would do me the honor of becoming my wife.

"We wanted to get married in Japan, but Majel didn't have a passport and was told it took a minimum of three days. Luckily, she's a good actress. She went down to the Federal Building, crying, 'I know him! The bastard won't wait that long!!'"

She got her passport in twenty-four hours.

Gene felt "it seemed sacrilegious to hire an American minister in Japan. Majel had to carry a dagger so she could kill herself if I dishonored her! She also had to carry a purse of coins so she could get home in case I changed my mind, and she had to wear a hat that hid the woman's horns of jealousy. All I had to do was carry a fan to keep cool."

They were married in Tokyo in a traditional Shinto ceremony.

Gene had two daughters, Darleen and Dawn, from a previous marriage. Majel had three miscarriages before giving birth to a son, Eugene Roddenberry Jr., known as Rod, in February 1974.

Rod didn't discover his parents were involved with STAR TREK until he was six, and later bought a SPACE: 1999 lunchbox. Gene remarked once that he hoped his son would be a writer, but figured that Rod wouldn't just because it was what his dad wanted him to be.

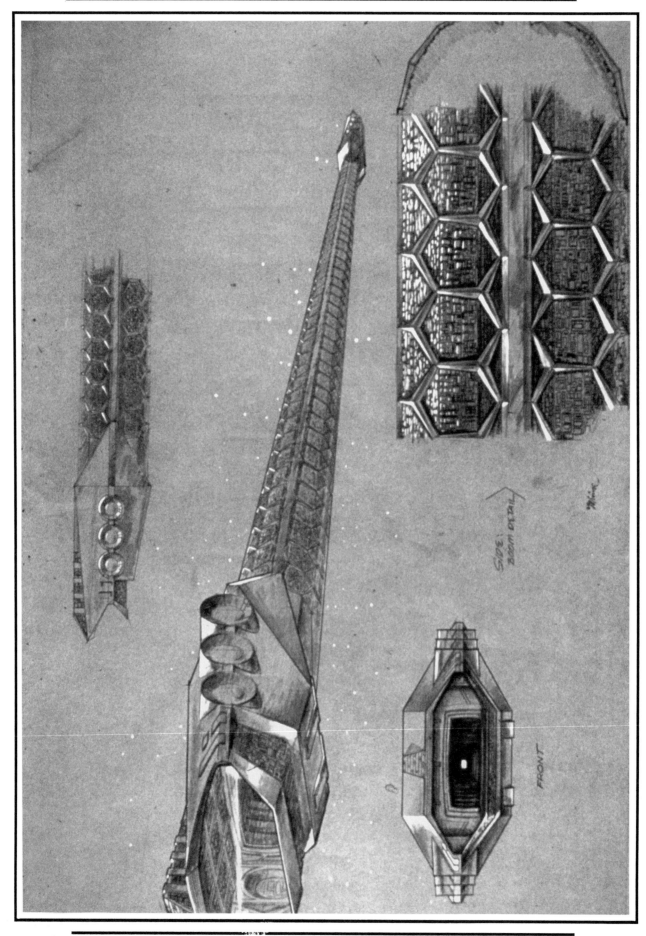

Production art by Mike Minor for the never produced 1977 STAR TREK II television series. Scenes are taken from the same script which was re-written to become STAR TREK: THE MOTION PICTURE.

Gene Roddenberry on the set of the TV pilot movie GENESIS II (1973).

From PLANET EARTH (1974) the ill-fated sequel to GENESIS II. The two pilots dealt with the same characters and futuristic setting but didn't excite enough interest to become a regular series.

VI Pilots and Projects

"The greatest science fiction in the world is written in accounting offices! "—G.R.

Gene had many ideas for projects in the late Sixties and early Seventies. Not all went as far as a pilot. During the last year STAR TREK was on the air, he discussed his post-series plans. He could already see the handwriting on the wall.

Gene knew NBC wouldn't be coerced into renewing the series again. "I don't intend to hold only to science fiction," he maintained. "I would like to exercise in all mediums. I love science fiction dearly, but as a dramatist a person wants to get good properties first. I would rather do a good cops-and-robbers than a bad science fiction, though I would hope I never have to make choices like that."

The early Seventies weren't a creative period for Gene until his pilots started getting aired. He wrote and produced a movie called PRETTY MAIDS ALL IN A ROW, directed by Roger Vadim and released in 1971 to quickly disappear. Made by MGM, the film stars Rock Hudson, Angie Dickinson, Telly Savalas, John David Carson, Roddy McDowall and James Doohan.

Leonard Maltin's TV MOVIES AND VIDEO GUIDE describes the film as a "silly but enjoyable black comedy; high school guidance counselor/coach Hudson advises frustrated Carson in sexual matters, while school is plagued with murders of pretty female students."

As STAR TREK popularity grew in the Seventies, Gene became depressed as he had sold his interest after the series was cancelled. Part of the agreement entitled him to one-third of the profit the series would make in the future.

At the time, it seemed the show would have no future in syndication. While it started slowly in the Fall of 1969 (except to Canada), it soon gathered steam, not that Roddenberry benefited.

In a 1982 interview, Gene stated, "Paramount is basically the owner of STAR TREK, and I'm supposed to get one-third of the profits. You want to talk about science fiction writing? The greatest science fiction in the world is written in accounting offices! You know, Paramount accountants say that this show that has played all over the world is now half a million dollars in the hole."

"It's true. But I think they deserve praise," he added sarcastically. "Despite losing money, they have shown STAR TREK consistently for sixteen years all over the world. That's decency."

During this period Gene wrote a little known script called "The Nine." It's about a fictional writer of a science fiction series which is making a lot of money in syndication while he must earn a living making personal appearances at science fiction conventions. It's a bitter tale delving into the character's intimate personal life.

Years later, when Harold Livingston was working on STAR TREK: THE MOTION PICTURE, he read a copy of the script for "The Nine" that Gene lent him. Livingston said that "The hair on my neck stood up. Gene was writing about himself."

This disturbing script is virtually unknown to all but Gene's closest friends and associates. Copies have never been circulated.

In a 1979 interview in the ST. LOUIS POST-DISPATCH, Roddenberry admitted that the early Seventies, following the cancellation of STAR TREK, were not as exciting as he'd tried to make them appear earlier in the decade.

"I went through a lot of bad times after it went off the air," he said. "I was stereotyped as a science fiction writer, and sometimes it was tough to pay the mortgage. They said, 'You're a science fiction type.' I said, 'Hey, wait a minute, I used to write Westerns; I wrote police stories,' and they said, 'No, you're now science fiction.'

"I don't feel bitter about that. That's the way Hollywood is, and that's the way mediocre people think. It's an easy way to think and television, like movies, like plays, like everything in the world, is staffed by mediocre people with, thank God, a few other people who do make things happen. They make the big changes."

After the failure of PRETTY MAIDS ALL IN A ROW, Gene chose to return to television. At the time he was very glib about it, explaining that, "I discovered, to my absolute consternation, that playing golf seven days a week wasn't really as much fun as sitting behind a desk."

He went on to say, "I tried features and they were fun, but I guess there's something perverse in me that misses the afternoon crisis of television. I think it's also common sense. How can a writer ignore a medium that hits fifty million people? You just can't."

Roddenberry would have a love/hate with the medium over the years. At times he condemned it; at other times he praised its potential, recognizing where the future would take it.

In 1973 Gene, flushed with success, claimed to have sold four series ideas. The deals were for SPECTRE, QUESTOR, THE TRIBUNES and GENESIS II.

Explaining his good fortune, he stated, "I don't credit super talent. There is an imaginative shift in the business, and I picked the right time to come back. In the face of some of the gloom, I've never been more optimistic about what's going to happen in TV in the next ten years.

"There is more willingness by studios and networks to take a shot if something is new. Part of this is due to the quality of the executives. Something has happened in TV in the last three years. ALL IN THE FAMILY talks about menopause, racial hatreds, unions, and it's broadly accepted by the public. STAR TREK had the same appeal.

"There is a new respect for the audience. The idea that the audience has a 14-year-old mind is gone. I think this will happen more and more."

The 90 minute pilot for GENESIS II aired Friday, March 23, 1973. Gene Roddenberry wrote it and put the lie to the claim he never penned anything good after "The Menagerie" episode of STAR TREK.

Directed by John Llewellyn Moxey, it was produced for Warner Brothers Television by Gene. It told the story of Dylan Hunt, a NASA scientist who goes into suspended animation in 1979 and awakens 154 years later in the year 2133. Gene repeated himself at one point here, as he did from time to time. Elements of STAR TREK often pop up in his pilots.

In GENESIS II, when Dylan Hunt awakens from suspended animation, he croaked out the words "how long," the exact phrase Khan utters when awakened from suspended animation in STAR TREK's "Space Seed."

Dylan Hunt finds that civilization collapsed while he slept but has begun to rise again, aided by a peace-loving group named PAX. They seek to preserve the best of the past, whether the treasures be scientific or artistic.

Roddenberry said he got the idea for PAX from James Hilton's LOST HORIZON. He explained, "It was a society of people who said, 'Let us preserve the books and knowledge until man is ready to come back.' When Rome fell, there was no one to preserve their society and culture and within a short while villages a hundred miles apart hardly spoke the same language."

Majel Barrett played a small supporting role in GENESIS II, while Mariette Hartley took a much larger part as the half human-half mutant Lyra-a. An erotic character, there were broad hints she sexually stimulated Dylan Hunt in order to sustain him after he awoke.

The suspended animation process required that the center of the brain controlling sex be stimulated when the subject is awakened. Since the drug for this was lost 150 years in the past, Lyra-a provided an effective substitute; one that Dylan gratefully accepted.

Lyra-a seemed a startling example of womanhood compared to the women of Pax, who practiced the Unisex manner of dressing. Whenever Dylan made sexual inuendo to Harper Smythe, she acted shocked. Clearly the sexually liberated Dylan Hunt had more in common with the passionate Tyranian Lyra-a than with the demure women of Pax. As a 20th century man, writer Roddenberry clearly identified with Dylan Hunt.

Lyra-a had two navels, a facet Gene later admitted he gave her for two reasons. He explained, "Back in the early days of STAR TREK, I had one episode where an actress' navel was exposed. This was before LAUGH-IN had made navels acceptable things on television. The network and studio supervisors made us re-shoot a whole segment because of that. So, when this new program idea was developing in my mind, I decided to give the mutants two navels to make up for all the bellybuttons I couldn't have back in the old days.

"Working in reverse, we then supplied a rationale as to why the Tyranians have two navels—because they had developed twin circulatory systems, etc. It was worth it."

Describing GENESIS II at the time, Gene stated, "Well, actually I was looking for a format that would give the kind of story latitude we had in STAR TREK without doing another space-hopping show. It seemed to me that what is usual when a civilization collapses is that the survivors withdraw into their enclaves and they each hang onto some distant memory of the past. It began to appear to me that the earth in a situation like that would be as varied as one hundred different planets, so I could have that story variety and still stay on earth and be talking about men.

"It's about the adaptability of man," Roddenberry added, "Every time a civilization falls, it springs back stronger. It was similar to what happened after the fall of Rome. The civilization was fragmented and each group hung on to some memory of the past."

Gene even write a complete 45-page series format with possible stories for episodes. These included pockets of civilization which had developed in eccentric ways, such as one which had reverted to the the Old West, another in the good old days of 1932 and a third where blacks hold whites in enslavement. Not exactly subtle ideas.

"Our stories were about how different parts of the world, or even different parts of our country, evolved into their own societies," Gene explained. "Our 20th century scientist, Dylan Hunt, becomes a member of Pax and joins one of their exploration teams that assists the world in moving back where it was before or beyond."

While STAR TREK was based on an optimistic premise of mankind surviving and advancing into the 23rd century with all its glories to behold, GENESIS II seemed to postulate the fall of civilization. Yet Gene did not see any contradictions, believing the two concepts could co-exist in our own sphere of reality.

He said, "I think that if we have an earth of the STAR TREK century, it will not be an unbroken, steady rise to that kind of civilization. We're in for some very tough times.

"Our twentieth-century technological civilization has no guarantees that it is going to stay around for a long time. But I think man is really an incredible creature. We've had civilizations fall before and we build a somewhat better one on the ashes every time.

"And I'd never consider the society we depicted in STAR TREK necessarily a direct, uninterrupted outgrowth of our present civilization, with its heavy emphasis on materialism. I think we're probably in for another Dark Ages.

"But my optimism is not for our society. It's for the essential ingredient in humankind. And I think we humans will rebuild and, if necessary, we'll lose another civilization and rebuild again on top of that until slowly, bit by bit, we'll get there."

While collapse of civilization stories are usually predicated on nuclear holocaust, Gene didn't believe that was necessarily why society would have fractured in the world portrayed in GENESIS II. "Our society is so fragile," he said, "so dependent on the interworking of things to provide us with goods and services that you don't need nuclear warfare to fragment us any more than the Romans needed it to cause their eventual downfall. You take large cities like Los Angeles, New York, Chicago—their water supply comes from hundreds of miles away and any interruption of that, or food, or power, for any period of time and you're going to have riots in the streets."

The first of Gene's new series pilots to premiere, the concept apparently had a more stable future than originally reported. Although CBS didn't snap it up right after the pilot was produced, they were interested, possibly as a mid-season replacement. In fact, CBS asked Gene to write more scripts.

He generated four before the show got the axe. In 1974 Gene explained that CBS dropped GENESIS II in favor of the PLANET OF THE APES TV series. He elaborated when he gave a lecture at Florida State University on January 23, 1975, saying, "GENESIS II was pencilled into the CBS schedule last year, but although it was the highest rated Thursday Night Movie of the Week that they had, before we could get on the air they put on the motion picture PLANET OF THE APES and it played to such a high rating they erased us and put that (TV show) on.

"I suspect they're sorry now they did it. We tried to tell them that once this one-joke thing of apes acting like humans got tiresome, where were they going to go? I was sorry to see (GENESIS II) go. I thought GENESIS II had the area for stories and comment very similar to STAR TREK, but I'm afraid that it's dead."

The CBS executive who chose the short-lived, poorly executed PLANET OF THE APES series over GENESIS II was Fred Silverman. Gene minced no words criticizing the former head of programming for his short-sightedness. He said, "It's a tragedy that opportunities like this to do exciting things and to talk about exciting things are pulled out by the roots by business executives who have no desire at all to give writers, directors and actors a chance to explore and elevate the art of film and television. And it could have been more exciting than the monkeys which captured his attention, but he seemed to be incapable of looking beyond and seeing the potential of something new and different."

THE MAN WHO CREATED STAR TREK

The GENESIS II concept owes a bit to Philip Francis Nowlan's original 1928 Buck Rogers story, ARMAGEDDON 2419 A.D. Nowlan's Anthony Rogers is trapped in a cave-in for 500 years while Dylan Hunt is trapped for 150. Most science fiction stories contain elements of what has gone before.

The series concept reveals facets not portrayed in the pilot. The skeleton shows similarities to STAR TREK, employing the "hundred new worlds" concept. Each episode can reveal a totally new facet of the world of 2133 while introducing a totally new civilization just as STAR TREK did.

The sub-shuttle provides the mechanism. Much was made of this conveyance in the pilot.

The system criss-crosses the entire globe in 2133. It is the major means of transporting Dylan Hunt into new adventures.

"I am particularly proud of the subterranean shuttle system we designed for the show," Gene said. "In the year 1979, as we explain in the series, air and sea travel had become no longer safe. So, this underground super subway was designed to link the continents.

"The tunnels are bored through solid rock by a laser and the car moves at hundreds of miles per hour, powered by a nuclear engine. When we mapped the design, we wanted to know how scientifically accurate we were, so we went to Cal Tech to check out the plans with a few scientists we often consult on such matters.

"You can imagine our surprise when they told us that our wonderful 'invention' had already passed the prototype stage for real!"

The series concept demonstrated how unique the civilizations could have been. In the series premise, Gene wrote, "As always, a few pockets of civilization had held out. In America, there was Barstow. Looking little changed from the 1970s, on its streets one might occasionally see an ancient automobile, wood-fueled now and used in forays against the desert barbarians.

Some farmland societies were said to still exist in Iowa, the Ukraine and Asian rice areas, rich enough in food to buy off aggressors. The metropolis of New York had escaped the short nuclear conflict only to become a giant prison for its inhabitants under ruthless police-state rule.

The seacoast plains south of New Jersey had become the black empire of Hagana; the Phoenix basin of Arizona was a traditionalist oligarchy rigidly modeled on American customs and values of the early 1900s. There were ecological experiments which had decayed into herdsman and hunter tribes; the fearful 'Snake God' was being placated through human sacrifice by the savage whites of the Greta Plains.

The London area had managed to preserve some stability but only at the cost of returning to rule by aristocracy under a king who called himself Charles X. Paris was gone as Nostradamus had predicted; Cairo had become a center of culture which rivalled ancient Greece as a seat of philosophy. Israel had withdrawn inward into a matriarchal society; in Central Africa a hidden but incredibly advanced technological society was believed to exist; in Central America a New Mayan civilization was born.

Added to this kaleidoscope were the mutant human groups where nuclear radiation had evolved new human types. While most mutant strains were retarded and dying out, the Tyranian group seemed a new and superior Homo Sapiens."

The woman Dylan met in the pilot, Lyra-a, would have popped up frequently in the series. One of Gene's first scripts explained how she escaped the nuclear holocaust at the power station by being in the sub-shuttle leaving the area at the time.

The series was also planned to have been fleshed out with other characters and plot devices. Dylan would have become the head of a PAX agent task force designated Team 21. Other characters introduced in the pilot, such as Harper-Smythe and

Isaiah, would have been featured, as well as such new characters as Piedmont, the team's black technology expert.

Each series concept includes a number of story springboards for possible use in the accepted series. Usually only about half of these springboards are ever made into full-fledged episodes.

Some of the springboards sound mundane, such as "Poodle Shop" wherein Dylan Hunt would have been trapped by a society where women rule and men are treated like domesticated pets. A version of this became PLANET EARTH, the sequel to GENESIS II in which John Saxon was recast as Dylan Hunt.

There was also "Who Dreams of Ivy" (suggested by Will Worthington's story) in which Hunt accepts the post of leader of an isolated community in order to accomplish his PAX mission, only to discover too late that this is an "honor" accorded only to criminals and strangers and will end in his sacrifice by a people who bitterly remember corrupt rulers as the cause of the Great Conflict. With his fellow agents held hostage, Dylan's only hope is to make himself seem irreplaceable, even at the cost of intrigue, deception, and the tyrant's trick of creating scapegoats.

Other projected stories included "Robot's Return," about the return to Earth of a team of humanoid robots, descendants of an astronaut team's automated equipment from an expedition sent to a moon of Jupiter in the late Twentieth Century. They returned to Earth to worship at the holy home of their creators. When they discover the helpless creatures that now inhabit Earth they realize that this shattered, savage place will someday be reaching into the solar system again, and doubt they should permit this to happen.

These were some of the many possible story ideas put forth in the concept. As the series concept stated, "The result is Genesis II, a science fiction series with Star Trek's 'hundred worlds' story variety but without duplicating the spaceship and planet-hopping concept."

These story concepts were never used, except for "Robot's Return," which was to get a second chance at life some years later, in a most unexpected fashion. It became the story springboard for STAR TREK: THE MOTION PICTURE.

Gene believed GENESIS II deserved another chance. In 1981 he stated, "I think GENESIS II should come back; somewhere in there is a marvelous premise for a series. Lots of excitement. You'll never know what we'll encounter from one story to the next. There were as many exciting story ideas at the start of GENESIS II as there were for STAR TREK. And some I still intend to do, especially one called 'The Apartment.' "

Interestingly, a comic book publisher, Innovation, has been seeking to obtain the comic book licensing rights to GENESIS II. Dylan Hunt would finally have his adventures told.

The one hundred minute TV movie THE QUESTOR TAPES, which first aired on January 23, 1974, was another attempt to launch a series. It was the best received of the aired pilots Gene either wrote or co-wrote. Originally titled QUESTOR, there was speculation at the time whether the last minute title change was meant to capitalize on the then big news story of Richard Nixon's White House tapes.

Questor is an android built by a mysterious Dr. Vaslovik, who disappears before Questor can be completed. The information tapes used to complete Questor were incomplete, giving him vast knowledge but no true human feelings.

"He's really an ambulatory computer," Gene explained at the time. "Externally, he looks exactly like a human being. He's capable of simulating human functions like breathing and eating. Only he would just as soon eat the china plate as the chicken scaloppine on it. He can convert either to energy in his power unit."

Questor's similarity to Data on STAR TREK: THE NEXT GENERATION is striking. Universal Television produced the pilot directed by Richard A. Colla. Gene Roddenberry and Gene L. Coon co-wrote the script.

Robert Foxworth very effectively portrayed the android who must search for his creator to fill gaps in his programming tapes.

Mike Farrell is coerced into helping Questor but soon loses his mistrust of the android and becomes his friend. Majel Barrett and Walter Koenig had small supporting roles.

Questor escapes from the government research lab where he was assembled and begins his search with government agents in hot pursuit. Similarities to THE FUGITIVE abound but disappear at the climax when the man chasing Questor sacrifices his life to throw the government off the trail and make them think the android has been destroyed. He does this after he learns Questor is the last in a line of android guardians created by an alien race to keep mankind from destroying itself.

Questor's predecessor, his creator Dr. Vaslovik, malfunctioned due to pollution in the atmosphere of late 20th century Earth. Questor learns his purpose in the pilot, and Jerry Robinson (Mike Farrell, shortly before he joined the cast of M*A*S*H) agrees to stay with the android and be his human half.

At the time, Gene stated, "We showed the program people at NBC the rough cut of QUESTOR yesterday and they seemed to like it very much. They had dozens of questions naturally about how the characters would relate and if there would be more message than entertainment content in the series. Messages frighten networks because they're in the position of not wanting to offend anyone. Their main reason for existence is to sell toothpaste, and the more you deal with real ideas the greater your chance of scaring some of your audience off and fewer people buy the toothpaste."

It was a good story, but it lacked the possibilities of Gene's other pilots, GENESIS II and SPECTRE. D.C. Fontana wrote a novelization of the script.

Gene related some problems he had with the network. He discussed these problems on the 1978 record album "Inside Star Trek." He said, "In the original draft of the show, this android that we called Questor was searching for the man who had provided his blueprints, and his parts, essentially the man who had created him. The robot wanted to know why he had been placed on this planet, which immediately got me in trouble with some of the television executives. One of them said, and I quote exactly, 'Who ever heard of a character in drama being interested in the reason for his existence?' In his case, I could have said, 'What about Pinnochio?'

"But the only way that Questor could locate his creator was through a very lovely woman who refused to talk. Fortunately, the android had been programmed in literature, which included the works of Maupassant, from which he had learned that sometimes the human female will open her mind to a man to whom she has opened other channels of communications. In my original script, the android then made love to her (he was programmed for excellence in many areas) and he immediately secured the information.

"I was called to a meeting of the executives. And they minced no words. A robot 'doing it' to a woman was absolutely unacceptable. The first thought that popped into my mind was, 'Thank god I hadn't written a gay robot— I really would have been in trouble!' But I carefully explained to these executives that the woman didn't know he was a robot. We would certainly use good taste in what we showed on the screen, but still, a great argument ensued.

"After a bit, I thought my opponents were showing human jealousy, perhaps even a masculine resentment against a mechanical man who could no doubt do anything he wanted, whenever he wanted, probably for as long as he wanted.

"After several hours I realized that our disagreement was much more basic. What they were actually trying to say to me was a version that has been heard so many times on this planet of ours, something that is so old that I couldn't keep from laughing. What they were trying to say was 'After all, Gene, how would you like your sister to sleep with a robot?'

"I lost the argument; Questor did not get the girl. I remember driving home that night, I was kind of happy. I was saying, 'You know, in your whole writing career, how many times will you get an opportunity to create a whole new area of intolerance?'"

When THE QUESTOR TAPES aired, he lost a hundred dollar bet with his wife, Majel. "My wife went and saw the final cut," Gene said, "with the music and everything and she said, 'Gene you'll get absolutely perfect reviews on this from the critics. (I'll) bet you a hundred dollars!' I thought, oh boy. Perfect reviews from every critic? No way I could lose my money so I bet her. It got perfect reviews from every critic."

Explaining the fate of QUESTOR, Gene said, "NBC did order sixteen of them and then we had a huge argument. For my money they wanted it to be too much like Superman and so I pulled out."

Gene said that NBC's thinking was "If ABC has the SIX MILLION DOLLAR MAN, we'll out do them and have the hundred million dollar robot!"

The Network also wanted him to retain the FUGITIVE-like chases, which he had deliberately jettisoned at the end of the story. "We had an office and a production date," Gene said. "Then they came and said the first thing they wanted was to get rid of Robinson, played by Mike Farrell, who I thought was vital to Questor. You can't have just an android; you've got to have a partnership between an android and a human.

"They also decided that they wanted to make it a copy of THE IMMORTAL and have Questor constantly on the run from the scientific consortium. And that's not the way I wanted to go and maybe I was wrong. But I really didn't want to do a chase series.

"And so I just let it die. Looking back, maybe I should have found some talented writer/producer who wanted to do the series in that format and just step back and let him do it. NBC wanted changes that were not acceptable to me at that time."

PLANET EARTH, the sequel to GENESIS II, aired April 23, 1974 on ABC, but failed to capture a series slot. After CBS had passed on their plans for a series, ABC decided to give it a try.

ABC insisted on recasting the show. It was produced by Warner Brothers Television under the hand of Robert H. Justman, who had held the same position on STAR TREK a few years before. Marc Daniels, one of the best directors on the original STAR TREK series, undertook the directing chores. The story was by Gene Roddenberry with the final script by Roddenberry and Juanita Bartlett.

"When we did PLANET EARTH," Gene stated, "ABC insisted on doing a story I thought was wrong. It was kind of a women's lib story set in the future and wasn't very interesting. I think what they had in mind when they pushed us in that direction was that they would be 'science fiction women' with long legs, silver costumes, and well-endowed.

"After we shot it, they came in very upset and disappointed. They didn't realize that's not my kind of science fiction and I was surprised they thought I might do that kind. I was trying to design a believable society that might exist under those circumstances—nothing like they had in mind. It was a breakdown in communications that contributed to the outcome of PLANET EARTH."

PLANET EARTH was a sequel to GENESIS II. Different actors continued the same format just as STAR TREK changed after "The Cage".

Gene explained, "Networks and studios have the philosophy that if something doesn't sell, the actors didn't make it work. That's not necessarily valid but they don't want to take any chances and John Saxon was chosen to star as Dylan Hunt.

"They also decided that the underground city of Pax was too 'down' and built it above ground. The subshuttle system remains as well as Pax being a secret order and helping the world anonymously. This is because most of the civilizations are hostile and they can do their work without being attacked as a threatening force. There were stories written where they would let themselves be known to civilizations where it was not a risk and they could coexist."

Other changes were good ideas, such as giving them all colorful uniforms. This lent visual unity to the PAX group and gave them a futuristic look. The addition of an esper was also a good idea although the actor who played him was miscast. He didn't project the awe and mystery of special powers. Instead, he came across as dull and mundane.

Ted Cassidy recreated his role as Isaiah from GENESIS II, but rather than being given anything interesting to do, he was reduced to playing the ignorant grunting savage. It was one of many flaws in a poorly written script.

The supporting actors were good but it was difficult not to miss Lynne Marta, who played Harper-Smythe in GENESIS II. She had far more character and seemed much less proto-typical than Janet Margolin.

John Saxon was not as effective in the lead as Alex Cord had been in the role of Dylan Hunt. Saxon had greater physical stature than Cord, and struck a more imposing figure. Saxon's martial arts expertise made him much more effective in fight scenes (he had co-starred in the Bruce Lee film ENTER THE DRAGON). In fact, it helped keep PLANET EARTH from completely falling flat.

Alex Cord as Dylan Hunt projected far more intelligence and personality than did John Saxon. After all, Dylan Hunt was supposed to be a scientist. He was a handsome man, but he didn't look like a football player.

Harper-Smythe looked more like a regular person in GENESIS II rather than the idealized version of a woman Janet Margolin presented as the same character in PLANET EARTH. Television all too often casts its characters from a standard mold.

Dylan Hunt and Harper-Smythe found their personalities replaced with movie star good looks. GENESIS II is a well-written, swiftly paced science fiction story while PLANET EARTH is a parody.

The concept was good, but poor scripting hurt. The script outline originally entitled "Poodle Shop" was selected by the network from a number of story treatments submitted by Gene. That was their mistake. The network apparently liked the Women's Lib theme even though it had been run into the ground on television in the early Seventies.

Diana Muldaur, an actress Gene would later use for the second season of STAR TREK: THE NEXT GENERATION, plays the head of a matriarchal society that captures Dylan Hunt. "When they offered this part," Muldaur revealed at the time, "I thought it would be the ultimate of women's lib. Men are called Dinks, kept as slaves, house servants and field hands, used, when necessary, for breedings.

"But do you know how we keep them this way—submissive and docile? We drug them. The only way to control men is by sedating them. It's the ultimate put-down of women."

Gene explained his views by stating, "I think sexual superiority is laughable either way." He thought of it as a fun story and not serious exploration.

Janet Margolin stated, "You should see the jumpsuits we wear. Can't tell men from women." Her character joined the Amazons to rescue Dylan, and the actress admitted, "I hate to say this, but when I'm out with the Dinks, riding among them swinging my whip, ordering these men around like cattle, you know what? I like it!"

PLANET EARTH wasn't very interesting. It dragged until the last twenty minutes, making token use of warlike mutants in the only good sequence.

With no money coming in from Paramount syndication of STAR TREK, and a young son (as well as a home in Bel Air and a condominium in La Costa), Gene had a real money problem. He continued to pitch the studios and networks. Nothing fuels creativity like bills.

In January 1975, Gene revealed that he was working on a script for 20th Century Fox for a futuristic underwater series set in 2115 called MAGNA 1. At the time he said the story "is an underwater science fiction [movie] which projects what man will be like underneath the sea a hundred years from now, which I accepted because for a long time I wanted to do something in oceanography. I'm holding everything else back because the STAR TREK motion picture negotiations are so close."

Or so it seemed at the time. It would actually be another year before Paramount gave Gene an office on the lot and signed a contract.

Gene explained the fate of MAGNA 1 by saying, "I wrote that in the middle of a studio change. By the time I wrote it, the people who had ordered the script were gone and there was no one to produce it."

In 1976, while discussions about his writing a new STAR TREK movie continued to drag on, he took on other projects. Some of them never went any further than MAGNA 1.

"I have two other projects that I'm working on concurrently," he said in 1976. "I have signed a contract to do a motion picture investigating psi phenomena (i.e. telepathy, telekenesis, etc). It's not a propaganda film. I'm not an advocate of them. I can't honestly say that I believe in them or disbelieve in them, but I'm going to do a movie investigating the whole phenomenon.

"I'm really looking forward to that because there's a lot of interest now among serious scientists. Do our minds have powers that we really don't understand and haven't really learned how to use?"

Gene was talking about MIND REACH, a book about the experiments of Puthoff and Targ of the Stanford Research Institute on parapsychology. In 1978 this project still hadn't gone anywhere. He was still hoping to develop it as a motion picture.

He continued, "The other project is just in the planning stages, the story in outlining stages, which is a science fiction musical for Broadway. I'm leaving shortly to go to New York to talk with the people who want to produce it and see how seriously we want to be about it. It sounds like it would be a lot of fun if we did it."

Gene had yet another project he wanted to tackle, one which would call on his own personal experiences, much as he had in the Fifties when he wrote crime dramas. After several years of trying, in 1977 he realized that TRIBUNES, a futuristic cop show, would never go beyond the development stage.

He said, "The police series was intended to have been an effect on my part to show police work as it should be done. It would have shown policemen having to have six years of college minimum, instead of the present academy, and also using the proper scientific method in solving cases. I would have liked to have done it. I think it's too late to do it now because there's already like thirty police shows on and I just don't want to be one of the thirty."

TRIBUNES was announced in 1973 as a 90 minute pilot slated to be made for NBC. Gene came up with the idea with Sam Peeples, drawing from their mutual experiences in police work. While Gene had been with the Los Angeles Police Department from 1949 to 1954, Peeples had worked in upstate California as a police commissioner.

The series would have dealt with an experimental police division of 40 to 50 men and women armed with the latest scientific and technological developments. The police no longer carried guns but weapons which splashed high-intensity light temporarily blinding a suspect or spraying nonlethal chemicals.

They also are magistrates, can take testimony, settle cases on the spot, issue suppoenas and the like. It was an interesting idea which if not gutted by network enforced rewrites, could have been provocative TV fare.

In the early Seventies, Gene stated that he'd sold four pilot ideas to television. While TRIBUNES was one of the four, and never produced, SPECTRE finally came to the small screen in 1977. The pilot was never picked up for a series.

It was written by Gene Roddenberry and Sam Peeples. Gene once stated he envisioned the main characters, William Sebastian and Dr. Hamilton, M.D., as a sort of modern day Sherlock Holmes and Dr. Watson, fighting the supernatural. It could have worked if the telefilm hadn't been gutted by lackluster directing and a mediocre final draft teleplay which cut the story's most compelling character from the denouement.

William Sebastian, the lead character, was described by Gene in his original story treatment of SPECTRE as "tall, slim with strong, almost arrogant features. His age is indeterminate mid-thirties, the kind of man who never looks young or never really old. He has long, straight hair, a high, broad forehead, an aquiline nose. His most striking features are his eyes— of a hunting hawk, piercing and always seeing more than most. His voice is deep, his accent American, his tone at times deceptively laconic. . . deceptive because he rarely wastes words and those he does use often carry several meanings. His clothes are that of a man who enjoys dramatizing himself. . . in the style popular in the early 1900s. This too is deceptive, for despite William Sebastian's display and affection for things of yesterday, he is entirely a man of today."

Dr. Hamilton, Sebastian's oldest friend and assistant, is described as "A big, heavily framed man, somewhat truculent in manner. He is flushed from a hearty appetite for good whiskey. Known to intimates as 'ham,' he's very British, a bit pompous without being aware of it. There is also a sense of humor under his British stiffness, also an innate gentleness and feelings that are easily hurt."

In the pilot which aired in 1977, these roles were filled by Robert Culp and Gig Young. The aired story differed in key respects while remaining essentially the same as the original.

In the early draft of the SPECTRE script by Gene and Sam Peeples, the story opens with Ham arriving at Sebastian's mansion. The draft specifies "The wind whips heavy rain along old Beacon Street in Boston. Our year is today but the object of our interest is a mansion of yesterday, adorned with cupolas, Tiffany stained-glass windows in narrow, arched casements. Unlike the neighboring houses, this once-lovely relic of the past has been allowed to fall into disrepair, its lawn and garden overgrown and tangled. The lights from the house are mostly the dim, yellow flicker of gas jets— an anachronism from the previous century which the owner has preserved; electricity appears only where its efficiency is mandatory."

In the original concept, written prior to the script, Ham was going to Sebastian's home to attend his friend's funeral as Sebastian had been stabbed through the heart with a ski pole in a sporting accident. Also, Ham was doubly depressed as his wife and child had recently been killed in an airliner crash.

The original story treatment by Gene has Ham enter Sebastian's house and, to his shock, find William alive and struggling with a beautiful woman who crumbles into dust when he rips her necklace from her. This is changed quite a bit for the finished pilot script, dispensing entirely with Ham's loss and having him merely visiting Sebastian in response to an urgent plea, having not seen William in many years.

The skiing accident is retained as Sebastian now has an artificial heart of his own design. He later uses it to convince Ham to stay with him, to keep an eye on him.

Sebastian and Hamilton fly to England on the Cyon jet at the behest of Anitra Cyon. During the flight, Sebastian explains to Ham that the world of the supernatural is real and that in combatting its evil manifestations he has rediscovered a challenge in life. He explains how supernatural beings come from another place that has natural laws different from ours and that the struggle between good and evil has, from the beginning, always been the struggle between mankind and those from outside who seek domination of the Earth.

This, to Gene, is what SPECTRE was really about. He said, "We haven't had a supernatural series where reality was the base."

He explained that the supernatural was "only science fiction understood as superstition. I had one of the characters suggest that East had been visited long ago by beings who lived by other physical laws than ours and some of them had been trapped here when the others left. This accounts for the supernatural forces, which I don't believe but it makes an interesting explanation."

Gene used a similar idea in his TARZAN screenplay. He had suggested that the alien Ba'al had remained behind thousands of years ago when the others left to return to the stars.

Gene's statement that he didn't believe his own explanation for supernatural forces illustrates an interesting point. Many think people who write fantasy, horror and science fiction believe the ideas they base their stories on. Actually this is seldom true.

In the many months since a crypt deep under the ground of Cyon House was opened, Geoffrey Cyon has become openly decadent both in habits and in the type of people he has infested his home with. His servants are all women, very beautiful and openly seductive, as are all the women Geoffrey has wandering around Cyon Manor. Once again a sexual undertone is present in one of Gene's storylines.

Other things are hinted at, and more than just hinted at. When Ham is in his room, he finds a small control panel by his bed. It operates little compartments all over the room, compartments which contain devices of a sexual nature.

One of the buttons even summons women to Ham's room. He chooses not to partake of this particular form of hospitality.

Cyon, the head of the family, is described by Gene as "tall, long muscled, obviously lithe and powerful. His piercing eyes and graceful movements have a feeling of animal magnetism—a man well at home in his body and proud of all his capacities. The mocking cast of his expression is that of complete assurance."

It is revealed later that Asmodeus, the demon of lechery, is behind the doings at Cyon House. Geoffrey Cyan, as an unwilling disciple of Asmodeus, has acquired the power to change into a were-tiger. During the climactic confrontation in which Asmodeus is revealed in all his horror only to be defeated by Sebastian, Cyon is caught in the middle of his change from human to tiger when he's shot with the same bullet made from the substance which drove off Asmodeus.

The closing scene of the original script occurs many days later in Sebastian's home in Boston. Cyon, it turns out, has survived. He retains many traits of the tiger he once was, physically noticeable in his eyes and on hands more like an animal's claws. Passing mention is made of his heightened senses.

Cyon has decided he wants to join Ham and Sebastian. He has given up everything in order to do this, as his house in London was destroyed in the aftermath of the battle with Asmodeus. Since Cyon's body was never found he is listed as dead. . .

a situation he'll not try to correct as he can no longer think of himself as the same man he was before. All of this was dropped from the pilot film.

SPECTRE was filmed in the late Seventies and premiered on May 21, 1977. Produced by Norway Productions and 20th Century Fox, with Clive Donner as director. The screenplay was by Gene Roddenberry and Samuel A. Peeples but it had been revised slightly when filmed. The cast included Robert Culp as William Sebastian, Gig Young as Dr. "Ham" Hamilton and John Hurt as Mitri. Majel Barrett appeared as Sebastian's assistant, Lilith, in the opening and closing scenes of the story.

"My interest in doing this kind of story was partially brought about because my wife, Majel, is a passionate fan of horror films," Gene stated, "and she had always wanted to play a witch. She did such a marvelous job that I'm sorry I didn't take her all the way through the film. Her performance was right on and certainly one of the more interesting characters. I wanted a change of pace and this story offered it."

The story follows the earlier script Roddenberry and Peeples had done (with some changes here and there), but the pacing and editing are too leisurely. Director Clive Donner had until that time worked in British films, much slower paced than those of America.

While SPECTRE is meant to be a horror film, it's pretty tame as television in the Seventies was still unwilling to push the limits. Gene went as far as he was allowed.

"I think the audience wants to be frightened, not cheated, at the end," he remarked. But unfortunately, the appearance of Asmodeus and his cabal of half-human followers is all but undone by poor special effects and makeup which was pretty cheesy, even by television standards. Asmodeus looks like a lizard, and while the costume isn't that bad, it's poorly filmed and barely shown.

The biggest disappointment in the filmed version is that the weretiger is jettisoned. When he's briefly shown as a beastman, in bargain basement makeup, he wears a furry headpiece and two ridiculous looking fangs.

In this version Cyon is supposed to rape and kill his sister, Anitra, but agrees only to kill her. He then refuses to do that. In the final conflagration, when Asmodeus is driven off, Geoffrey is apparently killed, but that's a bit hazy.

The aspect of Cyon trapped in a half animal form joining Sebastian as an investigator of the unknown was a terrific touch in the original script. Cutting it guts the climax, reducing it to a predictable confrontation. Combined with sluggish directing and editing, everything has been watered down and ultimately washed away. It's little wonder no one wanted to take this to series.

Gene later observed, "After having the STAR TREK experience, I probably should not have gone back and tried to do science fiction. I did one after another after another, getting nowhere in terms of another series. I really thought there was an audience out there and I could demonstrate it. As a matter of fact, we did sort of demonstrate it because on all of those movies made for television we did have huge audiences; some of the biggest audiences of the year for each movie. The studios and networks still weren't ready to support science fiction."

The Trek Revival

STAR TREK is the only series that died and went to heaven"—anonymous TV critic

Although the casual observer might have thought Gene's brainchild dead and buried, this was certainly not the case. During the Seventies, national interest in STAR TREK built at an incredible rate.

STAR TREK drew more fans as the series repeated in syndication. In 1972, Gene stated, "If I were getting six or eight letters a week about STAR TREK, I'd feel proud and successful. But I get 100 letters a week addressed to me personally. I have no idea how many letters go to NBC. I just can't afford to have my staff handle the mail any more!"

In the same year, TV GUIDE magazine noted, "All over the country today, people are wearing 'STAR TREK Lives' T-shirts, pasting Mr. Spock bumper stickers on their cars and maybe, for all I know, falling on their knees before graven images of Mr. Spock. Why? Well, it's because, back at the end of January, STAR TREK's fanatic band of followers held their first national convention— nearly three years after the series was shot out of orbit by NBC.

"We ran into Shirley Gerstel of Paramount Television, which had provided 13 STAR TREK episodes to be screened at the convention. 'The calls and letters that come into my office are tremendous,' she told us. 'I keep passing them on to the West Coast. I never thought that STAR TREK would come back, but now there's a rumor that Paramount might start making it again.'

"That, indeed, was the convention's principal rumor; it passed from one Trekkie to another, electrifying them. We asked Gene Roddenberry, STAR TREK's executive producer and creator, and the convention's guest of honor, about the rumor of STAR TREK's return. 'I didn't think it was possible six months ago,' he said a little dazedly, 'but after seeing the enthusiasm here I'm beginning to change my mind. It is possible to do it from my standpoint. We had such a family group on the show that it's totally different for us. We still meet and drink together, and we're all still friends, so for this show it is possible.' (Someone else added darkly that the GREEN ACRES crew did not still meet and drink together.)"

By 1973, all of the networks had switched to a new system for calculating ratings and did not exclusively base their decisions on the 1200 revolving homes measured by the Nielsen ratings. "NBC tells me they definitely want STAR TREK back on the air," Gene said in an August 1, 1972 interview. "To put it another way, the president of the network himself has told me he wants the show back. He's admitted to me that canceling it was a mistake. I suppose networks are entitled to make errors. I've made a few myself. Who hasn't?"

Before NBC would commit to a new series, they wanted Gene to make a new pilot. He said, "Paramount replied that the rebuilding of the sets and replacement of the costumes and props would cost $750,000. At this price they would proceed only if NBC would order four shows. NBC nixed the whole thing, and I went on a vacation to dream up something new."

In 1973, STAR TREK finally returned to the airwaves. The idea for the animated series was pitched to Gene by Lou Scheimer and Norm Prescott of Filmation, one of the higher quality television animation studios. Although their productions were not fully animated, they had more movement than the average Saturday morning fodder. Gene was swayed by their intention to honor the show's dignity and ideals; no cute kids or anthropomorphic canines would be added to the Enterprise crew.

He had already turned down several animation houses before Filmation made their offer. They allowed him to produce the series and insure that it wouldn't become typical Saturday morning fare.

He said, "That was one of the reasons I wanted creative control. There are enough limitations just being on Saturday mornings. We have to eliminate some of the violence we might have had on in the evening shows. There will probably be no sex element to talk of, either, but it will be STAR TREK and not a stereotype kids cartoon show."

Two new alien characters were added. James Doohan and Majel Barrett did extra duty, providing the voices for the new characters as well as most of the supporting cast. William Shatner, Leonard Nimoy, DeForest Kelley, George Takei and Nichelle Nichols returned to do their character's voices. Dorothy Fontana, David Gerrold, Stephen Kandel and others wrote scripts. While Walter Koenig didn't return as a voice actor, he did pen one of the scripts.

At the time the animated STAR TREK was in production, DeForest Kelley noted that Gene's involvement with the animated series faded somewhat after a strong beginning. Kelley said, "Dorothy Fontana was really running that show. Because it is so dependent on artists, there was not much Gene could do except see to it that above-average scripts were sent in for it.

"And you'll notice that most of the scripts were not written for children. They are adult scripts and some of them are very good, and would have made good [live-action] Star Treks.

"I did two animated shows here in Lubbock [Texas, where Kelley was appearing in the play 'Beginner's Luck' at the time of the interview] a couple of weeks ago. To do those two scripts took me a little over an hour because I gave four or five readings of each line. In case they didn't like the way I read a line, I'd read it three or four more times, so they could pick the one they wanted. It was a little bit time-consuming."

At the time, some thought the animated series might serve as the first step to get a live action STAR TREK back on the air in prime time. Kelley noted, "That was Gene's thought, I think. I questioned it at the time he said he was going to do it as I thought it was the death blow. Gene said, 'No, I don't feel that way at all. I think it's important to keep some form of STAR TREK alive and in the minds of people.'"

It wasn't the network, Kelley pointed out, that was keeping the series from being revived. The network wanted the show again. Paramount didn't want to make a new STAR TREK series because of the syndication money for the reruns.

They felt they'd be competing with themselves. Kelley continued, "I believe the popularity of STAR TREK is stronger than it has ever been. It will, in my opinion, be very difficult to ever have another show that has created the kind of feeling that STAR TREK has created. I doubt very seriously if there will ever be another one. It was a one-of-a-kind thing."

Kelley pointed out that the cast for the animated series often recorded their parts at different locations around the country. They read their lines with no other actor present, diminishing the feeling of camaraderie so important to the original series. The actors often came across as merely reciting lines.

Despite noble intentions, the animated STAR TREK was stiff and lifeless. The animation was partly at fault; the new characters were merely visual additions with no real personalities.

Some of the writing, such as Walter Koenig's "The Infinite Vulcan," which involved giant Spock clones, left much to be desired. Rehashes of bizarre aging diseases and tribbles did little to make the project a fountainhead of originality. Dorothy Fontana's episode "Yesteryear" remains the one true bright spot in the 22 episode animated series.

Another indication of STAR TREK's undying popularity came to light on September 19, 1974, STAR TREK Day at the Movieland Wax Museum in Buena Park, California. Gene Roddenberry and Majel Barrett were in attendance.

In response to frequent requests found in the museum's suggestion box, they unveiled a replica of the U.S.S. Enterprise bridge, occupied by lifelike wax representations of Kirk, Spock, McCoy and Uhura. Scotty, Sulu and Chekov were later added to the display in 1978.

Sculpted by Lia de Lio and detailed by Logan Fleming, these uncannily realistic figures made quite an impression on their real life counterparts in attendance at the gala opening. William Shatner, Nichelle Nichols, DeForest Kelley and Leonard Nimoy were startled to see themselves on the bridge.

In 1975, the TOMORROW SHOW hosted by Tom Snyder featured DeForest Kelley, James Doohan, Walter Koenig and Harlan Ellison. They discussed the enduring popularity of STAR TREK and rumors of a revival as a feature film.

It was a very windy hour. Among the more interesting comments were those of Walter Koenig. At one point he said, "The only problem is, if [STAR TREK]'s a feature film as opposed to a made-for-television show, they'll decide that they have to change the thrust of it in some way, make it monsters and huge battle scenes; something that you can't get on television. You may distort the entire feeling of the show."

Time would prove Koenig absolutely correct.

Finally, in 1975, Paramount Pictures announced its intention to spend two to three million dollars for a STAR TREK film, if Gene could provide a script that suited them. Gene returned to the Paramount lot to the same offices he had occupied from 1966 until 1968.

He had been talking story ideas for a STAR TREK film for years. As early as 1968 he said, "There are some discussions in progress. We didn't want to do a show that you might be able to see on TV. Obviously it should be bigger, different and so on, and one of the thoughts was to look for a motion picture writer who could do the story of Mr. Spock before he joined the Enterprise. Whether we come through or not, I will be pushing it, and we will be looking for the property and the company."

In 1975, this was the story Gene wanted for a motion picture. He said, "I think what we're going to try to do in this particular motion picture is to go back at the beginning, maybe see the Enterprise being built in orbit, maybe get into why this strange half-breed Vulcan/Earthman Spock joined a paramilitary organization, why the Captain picked this acid-tongued doctor and answer a lot of questions that the fans have had over the years."

When it was decided they had to appeal to a broader audience than hardcore fans of the television series, Gene went a different route. Im his initial submission, the Enterprise met God (or an entity calling itself God, a fine semantic and theological distinction, as the late Philip K. Dick once observed). It seemed a bit too outre for the studio.

"It was felt by some higher ups that my script might offend religious people," Gene recounted. "Perhaps it had just offended *them*. I had had the script read by a couple of Jesuit priest friends, a rabbi and a number of others, and they were not offended.

"Apparently, the skin was a little thinner at the top of the studio heads. What happened when Paramount and I had our quarrel was that they put four writers to work on various scripts and I have been supervising these writers."

They began to look at scripts from other sources. John D. F. Black submitted an outline, as did Theodore Sturgeon, Robert Silverberg and even Ray Bradbury.

Gene said, "What Silverberg and others are doing is actually coming up with ideas. At the end of getting all the ideas we want, we will then choose one and put a writer to work on the script."

Harlan Ellison's encounter with a dimwitted producer who insisted his proposed story include ancient Mayans has by now become the stuff of legend. It appears the exec had been reading Von Daniken's CHARIOTS OF THE GODS.

In 1980, after the creative dust had settled, Gene said, "[Paramount] wanted something that was good, staple Americana—like GREASE or SATURDAY NIGHT FEVER. They wanted something they could understand and deal with. So after they read my script and turned it down, they called in—over the period of a year—maybe 15 writers. And none of them did any better because all of these writers were trying to give them science fiction and that's the last thing they really wanted."

In the midst of this hunt for a marketable script, DeForest Kelley commented, rather drily, that what Paramount was really looking for was "JAWS in space." What the studio was trying to do was change STAR TREK by bringing in big name stars instead of the TV actors.

"They started off wanting to blithely recast," Gene revealed. "And until six months before we actually began shooting, they were still trying to get Kirk killed off in the first act. 'At the very least, Gene, you can promote him to Admiral and bring in a new star,' they said. I refused to do this because I think he [William Shatner] is an extraordinarily fine actor."

Gene wasn't idle during this time. In collaboration with writer Jon Povill (who would eventually become the associate producer of STAR TREK—THE MOTION PICTURE), Gene wrote another infamous rejected STAR TREK script. This was the time travel story rumored to have Kirk go back in time to kill JFK after the President's life is saved in 1963 and other key historical events are altered. Gene later denied this event was in the story.

On January 21, 1976, he issued a press release stating that Paramount was serious about producing a movie and had given him a start date of July 15, 1976. He said, "In eight months it's gone from casual disinterest to pressing enthusiasm. We don't have a script yet but then there are a lot of people with scripts who don't have a start date."

Gene underwent mood swings facing the pressures of coming up with an acceptable screen story for Paramount. They were in evidence in a wire service interview which, among other places, ran in the April 8, 1976 MONTREAL STAR. He candidly revealed his own constant surprise at the widespread fervor surrounding his famous creation, noting, "Sometimes I wish I could walk out the door and leave STAR TREK behind. I'm not a guru and I don't want to be. It frightens me when I learn of people treating a STAR TREK script as if it were scripture.

"It is scary to be surrounded by a thousand people asking questions as if the events in the series actually happened. I'm just afraid that if it goes too far and it appears that I have created a philosophy to answer all human ill that someone will stand up and cry 'Fraud!' And with good reason."

This didn't mean he was down on STAR TREK. While his association with the show typecast him in Hollywood, it also provided a higher than normal profile and opened doors otherwise closed to him. While the TV show pilot episodes he'd sold up until that time had not gone to series, Gene continued to work and entertain various offers.

The rise of STAR TREK conventions, a high profile phenomenon all their own, helped convince Paramount that STAR TREK was becoming more popular after cancellation. Gene said, "I expect that if the feature turns out well, Paramount will try to bring STAR TREK back to television. I would hope that it would take the form of occasional films in the long form. I don't think I could face the insanity of another weekly STAR TREK."

By July 1976 no script ideas had been approved but Paramount was determined to keep the dream alive. What they first looked on as a small film in the $3 million range, they were now committing to do as an $8 million motion picture.

Names were tossed around as possible writers and directors, including two up-and-coming talents named George Lucas and Steven Spielberg. They were unavailable due to their own films then in production.

Phil Kaufman was hired as the director of what was then called STAR TREK II. Two British screenwriters, Allan Scott and Chris Bryant, were hired by Paramount to write the screenplay.

Interest in STAR TREK remained high, particularly when a write-in campaign got the name of the first space shuttle changed to "Enterprise." Although Gene attended the rolling out ceremony for the shuttle in Palmdale, California on September 17, 1976, he really wasn't happy about it.

"I didn't like the idea and I still don't," he said in a 1977 interview. "I would have much preferred the space shuttle be named for Goddard or the famous Russian scientist. I would have preferred to have a non-military name and be representative of all the earth rather than a military history of the United States."

It was too late for that. An atomic power aircraft carrier had been named Enterprise years before.

Allan Scott and Chris Bryant turned in their STAR TREK II screenplay March 1, 1977. Paramount promptly rejected it. The pair returned to England and the rumor mills announced that the movie had been cancelled.

This wasn't the case. Gene blamed the problems on the studio. He insisted, "Paramount went about the movie in exactly the wrong way to accomplish anything artistic. They decided to make it a committee effort, and have no one really in charge.

"They told me that I had creative control—then told Jerry Isenberg that he had it, and then without his knowing it, they also told the director that he had creative control. You can't make a worthwhile movie that way.

"Good movies are made almost invariably by one person carrying the enthusiasm and the vision of it into completion. This is the way George Lucas made STAR WARS over three years of struggle. He fought hard because he had the vision of what he wanted. I found myself being second-guessed by people at the studio who had never even seen STAR TREK. It was just a horror tale."

On June 17, 1977, just three weeks after STAR WARS had been released to long lines, Paramount issued a press release announcing STAR TREK—PHASE II, the new television series. STAR TREK was to be the foundation for a new fourth network, Paramount.

"STAR WARS came out and was an enormous success," Roddenberry stated. "Somebody at Paramount misjudged the effect of this success and said, 'Wow, it's happened and no one can do it again. Therefore we don't want to risk doing STAR TREK.' In actuality, I think that STAR WARS merely proved that there was a huge market there for a STAR TREK movie."

Paramount wanted STAR TREK II (the new name of the TV series, the word "phase" having been dropped) to begin filming by late fall for a spring 1978 premiere. Robert Goodwin and Harold Livingston were hired as coproducers and Gene found himself producing the show after two years of being relegated to a secondary production role.

He also suddenly found his opinion worth something in Paramount's eyes again. Gene was now resentful over the way the studio had treated him since 1977 and he had to deal with that to do the job now expected of him.

"A major concern of mine was that the two years of bad treatment by the studio would affect the enthusiasm with which I entered the television project," he said. "Knowing that the worst possible thing I could do was to try to do a television series dragging a corpse of anger, defeats and double-crosses behind me."

In order to deal with his bitterness, Gene went down to his condo in La Costa for two weeks, "sort of commuting with myself, analyzing everything that had happened; analyzing just how badly I wanted to do the television series; what would be the best way to do it, what would be the best attitude. And I succeeded in really putting the abortive two years of the movie behind me," he realled.

Gene continued, "I came back to the studio and announced to all of the executives that as far as I was concerned, it was 'Day One.' I was going into my office Monday morning with excitement and enthusiasm, doing the best STAR TREK television series that I could conceive of. I would not carry into it any of the angers or disappointments and other things which would, in my opinion, have destroyed freshness and enthusiasm.

"This is the way I approached it and I must say that as far as the television people here at Paramount are concerned, they all have responded beautifully so far. I have had the creative control they promised, and everyone has been helpful.

"I hope now that Paramount has learned a lesson during the abortive attempt to make a movie and realizes that they must go ahead with one person and give him the equipment and support he needs to make the show." Roddenberry would take this promise of creative control quite seriously.

On July 25, 1977, sets for the new Enterprise began on stage nine at Paramount Studios. Joe Jennings was hired as art director along with Matt Jeffries, who had worked with Gene designing the Enterprise in 1965.

Soundstages eight, nine, and ten became earmarked as the new soundstages for STAR TREK. While William Shatner and most of the regular cast of the TV show had been signed for STAR TREK II, Leonard Nimoy wasn't interested in the rigors of a weekly series.

Gene created a new Vulcan supporting character named Xon. In the new writer's guide, it stated, "Can a twenty-two-year-old Vulcan on his first space voyage fill the shoes of the legendary Mr. Spock? Xon (pronounced "Zahn") was selected by the Vulcan Science Academy to attempt exactly that. Kirk was stunned when his new science officer reported aboard and found him to be little more than a boy. (Xon looks something like a young Michael York with pointed ears.) Kirk had assumed the replacement was someone near Spock's age. The reports he had read on Xon listed him as a prominent scientist and teacher." Xon was a full Vulcan and a super-genius even by Vulcan standards.

In the STAR TREK II writers guide, Gene wrote, "We will still use science fiction to make comments on today, but today is now a dozen years later than the first STAR TREK. Humanity faces many new questions and puzzles which were not obvious back in the 1960s, all of them suggesting new stories and themes. Also, television censorship has relaxed enormously during those same years, opening up still more new story areas, or certainly more honesty in some old areas. Television has become much more sophisticated in other ways. Older, ponderous dialogue patterns have given way (thank you, M.A.S.H.) to more realism through the use of fragmented sentences, overlaps and interruptions. Better camera techniques, new film emulsions and exciting new optical and tape effects all make increased realism possible.

"STAR TREK will take more looks into the private and off-duty lives of our characters." Gene continued, "More realism here too in very human areas such as when and what they eat, 23rd century bathing, changing clothes, playing and relaxing. . . The essential format will not change. Action-Adventure entertainment, and some fun for us too as we speculate where we humans are, where we're going and what it's really all about."

Among the writers for STAR TREK II, Gene approached novelist Alan Dean Foster. Giving Foster an old GENESIS II story premise called "Robot's Return," he made suggestions as to how the writer could develop it into a story treatment for STAR TREK.

Foster developed it into a 32 page story outline called "In Thy Image." This story involved the return of an ancient satellite to Earth, a satellite which has gained sentience and seeks its creator, a being called NASA.

Foster wanted to do the teleplay himself, but after reading sample scripts, co-producer Harold Livingston decided not to have him continue. Livingston decided to write the script himself since "In Thy Image" would be turned into the two-hour premiere of STAR TREK II.

Livingston stated, "So I sat down and for five weeks I wrote this script of 'In Thy Image.' I finished the first draft, delivered it to Gene and Gene said, 'God, it's good. You've done your job. Now just relax and I'll write the second draft.'

"He writes it in a week. Then he brought it in, gave it to us proudly in a bright orange cover, and there it is, 'In Thy Image' by Gene Roddenberry and Harold Livingston. He took first position.

"We all read it and I was appalled, and so was everyone else. There was [story editor] Jon Povill, [producer] Bob Goodwin, myself and Bob Collins, who was the director." They discussed what they were going to do until finally Livingston said he'd tell Gene what they all thought. Livingston recalled, "I went in and I said, 'Gene, this doesn't work.' Well his face dropped to his ankles.

"Then I got myself wound up and I told him why it didn't work, and I said, 'Why'd you do it? When something works, you don't piss in it to make it better!'

"In any case, he was pretty stubborn about this. He thought it was good and said, 'We'll give it to the front office.'

"Well, about three days later, we have a big meeting in Michael Eisner's [the head of Paramount in 1977] gigantic office. We sat around this huge table. There was Roddenberry, myself, Eisner, Jeffrey Katzenberg, the head of television, Arthur Fellows; and a couple of other guys." Michael Eisner held one script in each hand and explained that while Gene's script was television, Livingston's script was a movie. He said it was much better than Gene's. Livingston continued, "Well, holy shit! Everybody was clearing their throats. The great man had had his feathers ruffled.

"Anyway, after some heated discussion, it was decided to let [Bob] Collins write a third version using the best elements of both. So Collins did this after two or three weeks, and his was a total disaster!"

Other scripts were also being written during this time for STAR TREK II, including "Kitumba," by John Meredyth Lucas; "Deadlock," by David Ambrose; "Tomorrow and the Stars" by Larry Alexander; "The Savage Syndrome," by Margaret Armen and Alf Harris; "The Child," by John Povill and Jaron Summers; "Home," by Worley Thorne; "Home," by Theodore Sturgeon; and "Devil's Due," by Bill Lansford. Casting for the new roles continued with David Gautreaux hired as the Vulcan, Xon, and Persis Khambatta placed in the role of Ilia, both set as regular characters in the new STAR TREK television series.

The fans still hadn't recovered from the news that Spock wouldn't be back. Then the October 22, 1977 issue of THE LOS ANGELES TIMES quoted Nimoy about his on-going negotiations with Paramount about his returning as Spock. "I had a good relationship with the STAR TREK people," Nimoy said. "I considered doing the project, but the discussions became very complicated. They went on for a year and a half—it got to the point where I just didn't want to continue with them."

Gene knew this would set the fans off all over again. He issued a press release the same day which said in part, "It seems to me that STAR TREK's content must indicate that I have no small respect for our audience. I must now call upon our audience to return that respect in the form of some confidence that I am trying to make the best STAR TREK II possible under all the conditions faced in returning the show to television."

Over the years, Gene had come to regret creating a TV series in which the characters dominated the material as that left him at the mercy of the actors he had made stars. He vowed that if he had it to do over again, he'd create an ensemble in which no one or two characters dominated.

While stars on a TV show were common in the Sixties and Seventies, Gene could see benefits in an ensemble of players where the show was the star and the people could come and go without causing havoc. Gene said, "None of us were absolutely essential. There are writers and producers around who can do what I do—just as there are good actors around who could do another kind of Mr. Spock or Captain Kirk. STAR TREK would still have been STAR TREK. I'm glad we didn't have to, but I would never hold up a production because any one of us was not able to do it. That wouldn't be fair to the others."

As preproduction for STAR TREK II proceeded, plans also developed to make the pilot film something special that could be marketed as a theatrical release in Europe. This is often done with American TV shows.

Gene and company proceeded getting everything ready to begin filming November 30, 1977. He even had his novelization of "In Thy Image" half finished and a contract signed with Bantam to publish it.

Meanwhile Paramount was finding their fourth network idea wasn't being embraced by the advertisers. Without advertiser support, there was no point in doing the TV show.

Noting that STAR WARS continued to rake in money and was passing the $100 million mark, Paramount reversed their decision once again. On November 11, 1977 they halted production on STAR TREK II and announced that STAR TREK would become a motion picture after all.

Harold Livingston rewrote his script of "In Thy Image" for the motion picture. Livingston said, "Along that time, Roddenberry and I really began to get at each other's throats. December came along and my contract was coming up. Before they could fire me, I quit.

"We had too many problems there. I just didn't think that Gene was a good writer. He, for his part I'm sure, considered me a total interloper. Who the hell am I to come in?

"I understand that. In fact I understood it, but I wanted to instill some literary value into these science fiction myths. He had his own formula which worked. He was obviously saturated with science fiction. I think he knew a lot about a lot of things, generally, and he had a great following. Here I was getting on his nerves."

So Livingston left Paramount and went to work for Aaron Spelling Productions. He firmly believed he was leaving STAR TREK and Gene Roddenberry far behind.

While Paramount retooled STAR TREK for the motion picture screen, Gene issued a press release on January 6, 1978 detailing the trials and tribulations of returning STAR TREK to active duty. In the release, he revealed that they were closer to success than ever before. [See APPENDIX THREE]

The movie was given the green light. The director of STAR TREK: THE MOTION PICTURE was to be Robert Wise, director of the classic THE DAY THE EARTH STOOD STILL.

At that time STAR TREK's planned budget was $12 million, $3 million more than Star Wars cost to make. No one would have predicted this would swell to $40 million by December 7, 1979.

VIII Trek On the Big Screen

"Gene has a brilliant story mind for this kind of thing, but he's a bad writer." —Harold Livingston

Crucial to bringing STAR TREK—THE MOTION PICTURE to the screen was the casting of Leonard Nimoy. He was signed only a week before the huge March 28, 1978 press conference held at Paramount Studios, the largest such publicity event since Cecil B. DeMille announced THE TEN COMMANDMENTS.

Although not revealed until STAR TREK—THE MOTION PICTURE opened in December 1979, Nimoy had agreed to make the picture in return for a lump sum settlement of his long standing grievance with Paramount. They had endured a running feud because the studio insisted on standing by their contract, saying no royalties for the use of his likeness on STAR TREK products were due him.

The fee paid, including his salary for acting in the film, was reportedly $2.5 million. Paramount caved into Nimoy because they believed STAR TREK without him would be bad box office. Director Robert Wise believed this as well. He insisted Paramount cut a deal with the actor. The budget of the film was now up to a planned $15 million.

Once Paramount decided to go for a big budget motion picture, they went all the way. The entire original cast was assembled on stage for the first time since 1969. When Gene Roddenberry was introduced from the dais, the entire cast came to their feet and cheered. Gene remarked later that "I was never so touched and moved in my entire life."

He had issued a press release that same day to all fan clubs and others on his mailing list. It simply stated: "Well, we've made it. STAR TREK—THE MOTION PICTURE is now a certainty, as you can see from the enclosed official announcement released by Paramount today. It has been a long and sometimes frustrating road for all of us, but I'm sure you now will agree with me that that the delay was worth it. To obtain a director like Robert Wise, to be able to get Bill, Leonard, De-Forest and all the other members of the original cast together again, is a tremendously exciting achievement.

"I do wish to express my personal gratitude to you and all those others who have supported this project with so much enthusiasm and played such an important part in making it become a reality. We'll continue to be in touch as further news develops and as we finally get in front of the cameras."

Behind the scenes, things were still contentious even after Harold Livingston quit the project in December 1977. The script was still being worked over, but Gene had the basic idea. As associate producer Jon Povill explained, "We knew we had to have a big special effects ending. The problem of what was going to happen at the end and why it was going to happen was one that plagued the script from the very start. Then Gene came up with the idea of the machine dumping its data into Decker with a light show of all the information it had accumulated.

"We were going to get all this amazing, incomprehensible stuff that V'Ger had accumulated in its travels across the universe, and of course nobody could come up with these images, so that didn't work. It was pretty much my contribution to say that the reason for what was happening was that this thing needed to go on to the next plane of existence; that it was transcending this dimension and going on to the next."

Dennis Lynton Clark replaced Harold Livingston, but he and Gene got off to a bad start. Gene loved playing practical jokes, but such jokes should be played on friends, not someone you barely know.

This led to real problems. "Gene's a good guy," Clark explained. "I try never to bum-rap people. The problem with Gene is that his heart was never in the right place at the right time. It's a good heart, but he puts it aside at the wrong times.

"I was the subject of a practical joke from him. An awful one, and it was right at the beginning of the relationship and it set things off badly. Gene's a nice man, unless you give him some power."

Throughout his writing career, Clark always used the same assistant. He eventually married her.

Clark came in to work one morning and was told Gene had replaced her with a different secretary, actually actress Grace Lee Whitney. She pretended to be an obnoxious, gum-chewing secretary who played loud rock music in the office.

In Susan Sackett's book THE MAKING OF STAR TREK THE MOTION PICTURE, she explained that, "Gene's practical jokes had done much to loosen up taut nerves during the original STAR TREK television series, and it seemed past time to lighten up STAR TREK's return, too."

Sackett went on to say, "Finally he was let in on the joke and he took it quite well, considering he had almost been driven to a nervous breakdown."

Sackett's book shows Clark didn't take the joke well at all. His is the only name carefully not mentioned of all the people the book describes.

"It wasn't fun for me," Clark stated very matter-of-factly. "I almost killed her. It was bad taste, but that was Gene.

"I do have to say that he is the only person who made STAR TREK work over the years, because he makes very bad mistakes with the people that work with him. He alienates them.

"I was always a Trekkie. I would have been very proud to have my name on the first STAR TREK movie. That practical joke was the beginning of the end."

Clark spent three months on the film. He says he spent most of his time hiding from Shatner and Nimoy because Gene didn't want the actors having any input on the script. Clark explained, "He didn't even like Bob Wise's input."

When Clark left the film, Paramount's Jeffrey Katzenberg, Robert Wise and Gene all asked Harold Livingston to return. The writer reluctantly agreed, so long as Gene agreed to keep his hands off the script.

Livingston had a certain style he wanted to use and directions he wanted the characters to explore. The first time Livingston rewrote pages and sent them to the studio to be sent by pouch to Eisner and Katzenberg in Paris, Gene intercepted them.

Livingston recalled, "Eisner called up from Paris and said, 'What kind of shit is this?' Then Wise and I had to explain what happened.

"This kind of thing continued and Gene would be very remorseful and contrite: 'I was just trying to help.' I said, 'Listen, Gene, I'm not going to do this if you're going to keep this up.' "

Although Livingston was being paid $10,000 a week by Paramount, he quit three times over Gene's constant interference. Each time Livingston would be talked into returning by either Robert Wise or Jeffrey Katzenberg.

"As we began shooting," Livingston continued, "we would get to a point where I would send in pages and then Gene would send in different pages and Wise would get two different versions. Sometimes I would write it and put my initial on them, and Gene would put 'G.R., 4PM' under mine, as though that's what should count and my pages should be ignored.

"This was the way the picture was made. For the third time I quit. I said, 'Screw it, nothing is worth this.' Now we weren't talking to each other. Gene has a brilliant story mind for this kind of thing, but he's a bad writer. He's clumsy."

Finally studio president Michael Eisner coaxed Livingston to return and rewrite the script. Livingston agreed only if Gene wouldn't do anymore writing. Gene agreed but quickly went back on his promise.

In Susan Sackett's book, she describes the multiple rewrites in a different context: "Robert Wise was involved in all the important script meetings also, and on many occasions he brought in Bill Shatner and Leonard Nimoy to offer their contributions. The input from so many people saw the script being constantly rewritten, right up until the actual day many pages were to be shot.

"At one point, each day's scenes were being rewritten *several times a day*, and it became necessary to note on script pages the *hour* of the day when these pages had been rushed to the stage so that the actors could learn their most recent lines and Bob Wise would know what he was shooting."

The emphasis on specific words appears this way in Sackett's book. She never says that Gene contributed to the problem of multiple rewrites.

Problems continued when the Writer's Guild proposed that the credits read: "Screenplay by Harold Livingston and story by Alan Dean Foster". Roddenberry protested. He wanted the credits to read: "Screenplay by Gene Roddenberry and Harold Livingston and Story by Gene Roddenberry."

When the Guild decided otherwise, he threatened to protest. "I knew he couldn't win an arbitration because it wasn't his script," Livingston stated. "Anything he'd done was tossed out, or most of it."

Livingston convinced Alan Dean Foster to give Gene a shared story credit, which Foster reluctantly agreed to. When Gene wouldn't accept shared credit, a livid Livingston threatened arbitration. Livingston recalled, "When I said that, he withdrew, and he withdrew in a funk; he was mad."

Gene said he didn't want to take it to arbitration because he didn't want to lower himself. "At that point, I guess," Livingston said, "he decided to withdraw and assume this injured pose. He would have lost this arbitration because he didn't write any script. All he did was rewrite, patch up, fool around and screw up everything."

Gene publicly commented during production of STAR TREK—THE MOTION PICTURE, stating, "I'm not taking screen credit because we had a writer who worked very hard on it. He felt he deserved the credit and my policy is never to get into a credit dispute. That was my policy all through STAR TREK. If a writer felt he wanted it and wanted it badly enough to have a Guild action on it, I'd withdraw."

Alan Dean Foster wanted the credit to read the way it did on the script: story by Alan Dean Foster and Gene Roddenberry, since it was based on Gene's one-page idea. "I then get this very strange letter back saying that Gene Roddenberry is off in La Costa some place recuperating, he's very busy and he really doesn't have time for this. I just laughed. Is this real life or kindergarten? I just threw up my hands and said, 'Fine, whatever,' and that's why I have sole credit on the movie."

Foster described what happened to him on STAR TREK—THE MOTION PICTURE as his worst experience in the movie business. He recalled Gene hugging his shoulder once and saying, "You remind me of me when I was getting started—I'm going to teach you everything I know about the business."

"He did teach me quite a lot about the business," Foster admitted, "although I don't think that's what he originally had in mind."

These contentious behind-the-scenes conflicts recall something Gene said on March 30, 1988 when he was honored in Los Angeles at the Museum of Broadcasting. Although it could be argued this is taken out of context, Gene said, "Writing for the television audience does the same thing as the great sculptors and painters and composers also do. What you do is you bring alive that day and you say to the world, 'Hey! These are things as I see it! These are my comments. This is how I see the world!' And you do this with utter selfishness, which is what an artist should always do.

"All writers should be selfish and say, 'This is the way that I see it,' and under the voice should say, 'Screw you! If you want yours, you can do it, too!'"

Clearly, Roddenberry was a person of great passions. He needed to see his work accepted and recognized.

Whatever else one might say, Gene appreciated his fans. In October 1978, he said, "Since when has a producer ever invited two hundred fans to come in and be extras?! My affection must be obvious."

While the fan phenomenon surrounding STAR TREK sometimes gave Gene pause, he ultimately accepted it. He once said, "I think the reason for the popularity of STAR TREK is a really old-fashioned sort of reason. STAR TREK came along at a time in which most television leads were anti-heroes. On STAR TREK we decided to go for real heroes in an old-fashioned sense, people whose word was their bond, who believed that there were things more important in life than personal security or comfort. That, indeed, there are some things worth risking your life for—even dying for if necessary.

"As a result, our principal characters were ones about whom a person could say, 'Hey, I'd like to be like that!' or 'I'd like my children to be like that.' And it seems to me that possibly the greatest hunger there is in the world today is for heroes to admire and to emulate.

"When I grew up it was much simpler—it was the president of the United States. But we don't even have that left.

"One reason I don't object to the STAR TREK fan phenomenon is the fact that if there's got to be some show that people want to model their lives after or point to for their children, I'd much rather they do it out of this show than some limited show that is saying that all doctors are Jesus Christ, or if we just let our police have more guns we could solve the crime problem."

On August 2, 1979, STAR TREK—THE MOTION PICTURE completed principle photography. All of the scenes involving actors were finally finished.

Gene was interviewed on August 3rd, 1979, over the phone for a convention in Baltimore, Maryland. He explained, "It all seems to be going well. The pressure and the amount of time we have between now and the beginning of December is not as much as we would like to have.

"On the other hand, Paramount has given us all the backing and money and help they can give us to try to see that we get a first class picture done by that time, and it's going to be a race. I think that we will have a fine picture. Whether we might have needed another two weeks to make it even greater or whether we can push it through and get everything we want in is up in the air.

"Now, we certainly will get enough to make it a good picture. We are pushing right now, trying to get everything in.

"The date [for release] is still December 7th. Bob Wise, the director and friend, keeps muttering in executive committees over there that he would rather have it be the 18th or the 19th or something like that; I don't know if anything will come of that.

"We're fairly pleased. I keep popping out to optical viewings and to cutting rooms. Oh, yes, we're into music now with Jerry Goldsmith. He's been in several times and it sounds terribly exciting. I'm working extraordinarily closely with him. In this, I feel we're very fortunate to have a Bob Wise, who has won Oscars in musical production.

"And during the same time I've been novelizing the script into a STAR TREK novel, which will go on the market at the same time. So I've had sort of the unusual experience of watching us cut scenes and finding myself, later on, sitting at a typewriter and writing the scene, and having the opportunity to see and study what is there that you get with a camera that you've got to do with words in a novel and what are the differences. How do the two compare? It's almost been, for me, like a college course in cinematography and writing. It's been a delightful experience."

Gene went on to reveal that by August of 1979, Paramount was already thinking about sequels. He said, "Paramount has asked me a couple of times did I have any sequel ideas? Basically I said to them, 'Christ, can I have a week off in between so I can think about it?'

"I think everything depends on the way that this movie is accepted and how it comes out. I think very likely there will be a sequel movie or STAR TREK into television, but I think everything depends now on the movie and how it runs for the first three or six months."

Gene added interesting observations about the merchandizing as he remembered the old '60s model kit showing Spock holding a phaser on a monster. Gene noted, "Merchandizing has been a very big part of our concern. It's become big business since those early days, God, ten years ago when we used to send out a 5 x 7 black and white of the stars in the days when Lincoln (Enterprises) slowly got into it. I don't have a great deal of control over it, except the control of the fact that they kind of feel that they have to listen to me because I might get mad and say nasty things to people.

"I've tried to use that without being an ass about it as best I can, and I have found people here who seem to understand and seem receptive. I've said to them a number of times that whatever we do must see that fans get a square deal, that they get a dollar's worth for their money. I said I would not stand this time for putting out toys with box labels of Mr. Spock killing some monster with a zap gun because it happened to look ugly. I told them that all future models of phasers I wanted a little sign on it for kids that said 'set for stun only,' and a few things like that, and so far I've gotten cooperation.

"It is hard for one man like myself, who is at the creative end of it, to have great effect on a multi-million dollar corporation, which Paramount and Gulf & Western are. There has been some effort to be cooperative, and there has been in some places some understanding that 'Hey, maybe there's something special about this and the people that are attracted to it, and maybe we ought to listen a little bit to Roddenberry, as long as it doesn't really cost us an awful lot of money, or doesn't get too annoying.'"

Gene was very conscious of the many fan-produced STAR TREK items which had helped sustain interest in the series during the Seventies. He believed such items had their place in the scheme of things, and said, "I think we've got them fairly well convinced that this really is bad business to create trouble, and that fanzines, etc., are the life blood of the movement and they always have been. And I said, the day we start sending cops to arrest a junior high school student because he's using STAR TREK on a mimeographed thing he circulates to fifty friends, why, that's the day I walk out of the studio. They said, yeah, but come on, there's a limit, too, isn't there? And I said, yeah, there's a limit.

"I don't like to pick up a magazine and see our blooper reels on sale, and I don't like to see rip-offs on honest merchandizing contracts that other people have paid good money for and my hope is that as long as I stay here and as long as we keep talking to them, their attitude will be roughly what we've had over the past years when we shut our eyes to some things and complained about others."

STAR TREK—THE MOTION PICTURE appeared on December 7, 1979. That this was Pearl Harbor Day escaped no one's attention. Paramount was determined they would not be sunk.

Due to a commitment made theater chains involving millions of dollars in advance payments, Paramount had to deliver STAR TREK—THE MOTION PICTURE on schedule. For this reason, special effects units working on the film were forced into 24 hour shifts as late as October 1979.

Paramount footed the bill. Such costs help explain the final $40 million production budget.

Anticipation was great. Rumors that Kirk and crew met God persisted from years earlier, only to be disproven. The adventure developed from the old "Robot's Return" story treatment had reached its final stage.

When all was said and done, what fans saw was a slow movie which exhibits awe-struck reverence for special effects. It gives short shrift to character relationships. Like Spock in his initial appearance, the film is too clinical and dispassionate to engage the emotions.

Scenes cut from the theatrical release but restored on video lessen the problem; each character has his moments. Spock weeps after his mind meld with Vejur. Why these scenes were cut remains a mystery. Another restored scene, showing Kirk in a space suit emerging from a cargo bay, is notable in that no special effects were cued in. The viewer can briefly see the soundstage structure behind him.

Leonard Nimoy said, "I think we should say, in deference to the people who made the first STAR TREK motion picture, that they had a very special set of problems. For example, there had not been a STAR TREK project for eleven years. We finished making the series in 1968 and here we were in 1979, coming together to do a different STAR TREK project. That meant that a lot of very special circumstances had to be addressed.

"Ground had to be broken in a special kind of way. Do you make comment in the film that eleven years has passed and therefore things have changed? The ship has changed, the uniform has changed, the sets have changed, rank has changed, relationships have changed. We were faced with the concern that we should not be perceived as a blown-up television episode, but should be looked upon as a motion picture. therefore there were certain changes that were expected by the audience, and they must be addressed."

Looking back on the film now after the five which followed, it is clear ST: TMP has a completely different style. It is arguably the only one produced expressly for the big screen without thinking of its appearance on home video six months later. It is a wide screen extravaganza. However thin the story may be, it is visually an epic on a grand scale.

One Paramount executive dubbed the production a "thirty-five million dollar turkey," but cost estimates actually make that figure ten million higher. The film grossed one hundred and five million dollars in the United States.

The scuttled ending featured the Enterprise being ejected from Vejur, followed by the three Klingon ships from the start of the movie. A battle royal ensues, in which the triumphant but damaged Enterprise undergoes a saucer separation— an idea that would eventually turn up elsewhere.

Director Robert Wise was supposedly unhappy with the final cut of the film and Paramount vetoed re-editing in order to make the all-important release date. People who attended the Washington, D.C. premiere reported observing Wise burying his face in his hands at various points in the film, obviously embarrassed.

Gene's novelization of the script contains the background information and human interest the film sorely needed. For instance, Kirk, it seems, was semi-retired, involved with a woman managing him as a public relations figurehead for Starfleet. Based in San Francisco, Kirk spent his off years lecturing extensively about his space adventures. The person who dies in the transporter accident with Sonak was actually the woman in Kirk's life, a detail left out of the film.

Also in the novel, Ilia's potent sexual chemistry effects Sulu. He becomes physically aroused in her presence. The scene reveals a lot about both characters, but never made it to the screen, not even in the video restoration.

Gene's novel is good and it's surprising he didn't try his hand at more. He wasn't that busy. In fact, he said he was going to write a novelization of the script Paramount rejected for the sequel to ST—TMP. A couple years later, he said he only wanted to write novels based on original ideas, not STAR TREK.

Although ST: TMP enjoyed huge boxoffice grosses, this was offset by huge cost overruns. The film received mixed reviews. Paramount blamed Gene for the poor reviews and determined to make a sequel without giving him control.

In Walter Koenig's book about the making of ST: TMP called CHEKOV'S ENTERPRISE, he relates times when Gene worked over scenes in the script with director Robert Wise on a daily basis. While his name does not appear on the screenplay credits, Gene's hand is evident. Harold Livingston implied as much in his criticism of the movie.

"I was upset with the film," Livingston stated. "It just wasn't what I wanted. I can't honestly say this wasn't my fault, because in the end I took the rap for it anyway. But if I do a poor job, I'll tell you it's bad. I know it's bad and I'll welcome help. I'm certainly not infallible.

"Gene would never admit that he wrote a bad line or couldn't write. He's made an industry of STAR TREK and he's really done nothing else. Gene's values lay in his knowledge, his experience. If he had imparted that and let the professionals do their job, you'd have had a picture."

Gene had his own view. He said, "I discovered on the first movie that the director is everything. The writer-producer type, really, no one listens to him. . . It's just the way movies have always been made."

He felt that the picture would have been better if they'd had more time to develop the script from the two-hour TV version into into a real motion picture story. He tried to hold out for that and said that the film couldn't be done correctly if released in December 1979.

"I felt we wouldn't have time to finish the film in the image I'd visualized," he explained, "but I went along with my director and my optical expert. If we'd waited, STAR TREK—THE MOTION PICTURE certainly would've been more complete. The question is, as an economic venture it would've been a much finer picture with an Easter release, but would we have done much better? Nobody can answer that."

He acknowledged the film's short-comings but he doesn't view it as a creative failure. Gene admitted, "They used optical effects too much, but they thought, well STAR WARS had optical effects so we'll give them three times as much. These were studio decisions.

"I think that it appeared to resemble [earlier episodes] more at the end because many of the things that made the script different were, bit by bit, sliced out of the movie. They were the 'talky things. The personal stories were excised from the script or the shooting schedule. Then it became more and more like things we had done in the past.

"The film has some failures, it also has some remarkable successes. Considering the way it all happened, we came out with a remarkably good film and I'm very pleased to have been a part of it.

"It could have been better—yes! I don't ever expect to make a film where I don't look back and say to myself, 'Ah, I'd like to change this and this. . . "

He was optimistic about the sequel. Gene explained, "We know a little bit more about how to use TREK in motion pictures. The second run in anything is easier. If you've ever played golf, the second try you can always sink the putt. It's that first shot at the hole. . . "

Gene kept his office on the Paramount lot in the early months of 1980 and wrote a script for the sequel to the STAR TREK movie. In this script the Klingons go back in time and change Earth's future and thus destroy Earth. The Enterprise, traveling in a space/time warp, remains unchanged and tries to intercept the Klingons.

They stop the Klingons but are badly damaged and must make repairs without being discovered by Earth, thereby changing history. It was apparently "that first shot at the hole" (recalling Gene's golf metaphor) that the studio was mindful of when Paramount rejected the script and Gene and his assistant, Susan Sackett, were asked to pack up their office and move off the studio lot.

It would be a year before Paramount decided how to approach a sequel.

STAR TREK—THE MOTION PICTURE grossed over $100 million in the United States alone. Only its huge cost prevented it from making a lot of money. Subsequent STAR TREK films grossed less but returned higher profit to the studio.

Gene was relegated to an advisory position on subsequent films while Harve Bennett, who had worked on the TV series THE SIX MILLION DOLLAR MAN, was brought in as producer. "It just about killed me on the first movie when the studio and the director made all the decisions," Gene stated. "So I invented the term 'executive story consultant' and set the rules that they have to show me everything they do. . . from the first lines [through] all rewrites and the dailies."

The way he described how all this came about made it clear this was the best deal he could cut. Paramount didn't want him involved.

Gene said, "I think Paramount realizes the way I work is intensely personal and perhaps the market isn't there for that kind of work today. And the show would be better off with someone who doesn't get so personally, deeply and emotionally involved. Which is fine with me because I made it clear to Harve Bennett in our first meeting that I feel I'm kind of 'Star Trekked out.'

"It's not the same market that I knew and I feel it's time to go out and do something new."

Harve Bennett had an interesting view of his role on the four STAR TREK films he produced. He explained, "Credit for the success of the show, of course, goes to Gene Roddenberry. There's no disputing his genius. But it also goes to Gene Coon, the hard-headed rewriter who made a lot of things work.

"I think of myself, sometimes, as the Gene Coon of the feature movies. Fandom never understood the contribution Coon made, not withstanding Roddenberry's genius.

"It's my gut feeling, knowing all the players and the material, that whenever the name Gene Coon is on an episode as a producer, they are generally the best shows."

Bennett read Gene's script for STAR TREK II regarding the Klingons going back in time and altering Earth history with the Kennedy assassination, but he didn't think it worked. "It had the same problem that Shatner's story did on [STAR TREK] V," Bennett said, "which is that you know you're not actually going to meet God, and you know you aren't going to stop Oswald's bullets, so why bother?"

Bennett viewed a number of episodes and was particularly interested by "Space Seed" and the sequel possibilities of Khan. The film built from there. Nicholas Meyer was hired to direct and a screenplay was written.

While Gene made suggestions, they weren't always followed. He said, "The movies can be good and I think they'll be getting better. Before, the producers didn't listen to me enough.

"In STAR TREK II Chekov says, 'I remember you.' I told them, look, the fans will *know* that Chekov wasn't in that show ["Space Seed"]. And the producers said, 'Oh, the audience doesn't care about those things!' You should've seen the mail they got on that!

"So I hope there'll be more cooperation on the next one. I wish sometimes that I had been Edgar Rice Burroughs on the thing so then I could've written the novels myself or licensed them myself, and so on. Without NBC censors. But Paramount is basically the owner of STAR TREK and I'm supposed to get one-third of the profits."

Regarding STAR TREK II: THE WRATH OF KHAN, Gene went on to say, "A number of things about that film bothered me and since then Paramount and I have come to, I hope, an agreement so that they will listen more carefully.

"Something that few fans have ever picked up on is when the little creature crawled out of Chekov's ear and Kirk, with a look of disgust, grabs his zap gun and zaps the thing out of existence. That should not have been. If Kirk is indeed a space traveller, this unusual unique thing that was there to be exterminated and studied should not have been squashed. That's the way Twentieth Century people act. Our people should not.

"That's what makes it hard to do and makes similar shows hard to do. You really have to think in those terms. There's a thousand small things like that which make a difference. If you land on a planet and they start zapping things because they're ugly, then that's the day I call a press conference and announce my way out."

He also didn't much care for the new uniforms, saying, "I understand why they've got them. They're handsome." He thought that the uniforms looked like costumes from a production of "The Student Prince."

Gene didn't seem comfortable comparing STAR TREK II to the first motion picture in the series. He said, "They are two different things. What we've been doing with the movies is what we'd been doing the first five or six episodes [of the sixties TV series] which no one is aware of because you didn't see them shown in that order. But we've been trying to find the movie format. Television and movies are not the same.

"The first one was, I thought, a very brave effort to talk about a very deep subject—of whether machines can become life forms. The second one was more exciting, but in some ways, that I mentioned earlier, it kind of got away from it.

I think three will be more on the nose than any of them. We're really searching for a format is what we're doing."

In 1982, the second STAR TREK feature, STAR TREK II: THE WRATH OF KHAN redressed the failing of its predecessor. It contains a strong, engaging plot, plenty of action, a powerful nemesis, dramatic relationships, and a famous controversy— the death of Mr. Spock.

Paramount kept tight reigns on STAR TREK II's budget. It only cost thirteen million to make, less than a third of the first film's cost. It grossed eighty million in its initial domestic release alone. Paramount made a big profit on THE WRATH OF KHAN.

Hedging their bets over Spock, the studio introduced a new Vulcan, Lieutenant Saavik, portrayed by Kirstie Alley. Saavik, was the first character to appear in STAR TREK that Gene didn't have some hand in creating. When asked whether the part Romulan, part Vulcan character had any human in her background, he observed, "I'm afraid not. I thought it might be nice if there was but that's not their plan.

"As a matter of fact, my recommendation to them is that they make her even a bit more alien in her dialogue as we did with Mr. Spock. I thought a few times too often she sounded like an American girl who had just laid down her tennis racket, and I think you have to build in those mysteries and those mysterious ways, especially when you have aliens."

Nicholas Meyer, a successful novelist (THE SEVEN PER CENT SOLUTION) turned movie director (TIME AFTER TIME and the TV-movie THE DAY AFTER), brought a deft hand and a humanizing touch to directing the film. Production began on November 9, 1981 and wrapped on January 2, 1982. After post production work was completed, the film was released on June 4, 1982.

Although Majel Barrett had appeared in STAR TREK—THE MOTION PICTURE, she was not invited back for the second film. Since the first one, she has only appeared in STAR TREK IV: THE VOYAGE HOME. Majel never disguised her bitterness, especially after her return in THE VOYAGE HOME was marred by having most of her scenes left on the cutting room floor.

She characterized the attitude that keeps her out of the films by saying, "It might not be a good idea for Majel Barrett to go running around the set. Not for Mrs. Gene Roddenberry. The movie series hasn't gotten past the point where they can handle the fact that Gene Roddenberry is the creator. It's just unfortunate."

Originally, Spock's death in THE WRATH OF KHAN occurred midway through the movie, a placement altered by director Meyer. Meyer recalled, "I said he has to die at the end because there is no way you're going to top it. The movie is going to be anticlimactic if he dies in the middle."

With such an overwhelming climax, interest was immediately focused on the next picture. Was Spock really dead— and what part, if any, would Leonard Nimoy play in the future?

Nimoy was approached by the studio. The information was kept under wraps until Paramount devised a means of linking Nimoy with STAR TREK III— without revealing anything about Spock.

During negotiations for STAR TREK III, Nimoy offhandedly suggested he could direct as well as either of his predecessors, and that he knew the basic material more intimately. To his surprise, producer Harve Bennett liked the idea.

A directorial career was launched almost by accident as Nimoy took the helm. From a marketing standpoint, it was brilliant. With Spock dead, The SEARCH FOR SPOCK could be advertised using Leonard Nimoy's name— while preserving the mystery of the beloved Vulcan's ultimate fate.

Nimoy's return was further brightened by a new enthusiasm for STAR TREK brought about by a more positive experience on the previous film. The unpleasantness of the first feature was a matter of the past; the cast had a great time under Nicholas Meyer's direction. They had finally regained the old camaraderie sadly missing from the first big-screen voyage.

Gene had much to say about the death and resurrection of his favorite Vulcan. "I'll tell you what the true story of this was," he revealed. "Leonard Nimoy wanted to get away from the Spock character; he wanted the Spock character to die, and I understand why he did.

"This character had fastened himself on him like the Old Man of the sea. He sang Tevya in the road company of 'Fiddler On The Roof,' and the first night he did it he had five curtain calls, and on his way to the dressing room a stagehand said, 'Nice going, Mr. Spock.' And so he decided that the character had to die because he's a serious actor and has a right to be that.

"So his price for doing another movie was to have Spock die, as he did. However, during the making of it, Leonard, quite naturally, began to look at the Spock character and the fun he'd had with it, and the acting challenges there were in that, too. And when the time came to do the next movie he said, 'Is there some way he couldn't die?'

"To prove to you (we are) willing to listen to everybody, my secretary figured out a way that he could come back logically and believably. And that was the way we did it; the way she suggested it."

Asked about the destruction of the Enterprise in THE SEARCH FOR SPOCK, Gene replied, "Yeah, I approved it, but I hated it! But it somehow worked out."

Production on STAR TREK III began on August 15, 1983; principal photography wrapped on October 21, 1983. STAR TREK III's cost and profits were similar to those of the third feature.

While Gene had expressed reservations about THE WRATH OF KHAN, he had no qualms about STAR TREK III. He said, "THE SEARCH FOR SPOCK is by far the best STAR TREK movie they've made. I think they've finally captured the right format with this one. Leonard Nimoy has done a better job of directing than anyone preceding him—it's really outstanding work. I think he's made a new career for himself if he wants to be a director. He knows STAR TREK better, too— he's been so many years on the inside!"

Gene seemed more comfortable in his consultant role by this time. Reportedly his contract with Paramount paid him a flat fee each year, which meant that some years he was busier than others.

"I've been an executive consultant on it, which is all I really want to be. I've produced STAR TREK seventy-eight times already," Gene explained, "and I figure what's to win by doing it any further?"

Gene often forgot exactly how many episodes the series ran, and technically, including the first pilot, he produced eighty episodes. One could argue, though, that since he wasn't really involved much with the third season of the series that this number should be reduced by a third.

Gene continued, "Basically my contract gives me about the same no matter what I do now. I guess after sixteen or eighteen years you get certain privileges. I'd say that the main difference is that they're listening to me a little more carefully than on the last movie. I think Paramount's come around to decide that, well, maybe it [ST—TMP] wasn't just a big mistake—maybe there *was* some thought behind it all."

There was no doubt there would be a fourth picture. Leonard Nimoy was signed to direct once more, the first person to direct more than one film in the series. An initial script draft was completed in August 1985 by the writing team of Steve Meerson and Peter Krikes.

The script was later rewritten by Harve Bennett and Nicholas Meyer— the serious parts apparently by Bennett, the humorous ones by Meyer. All four writers received screen credit after the Writer's Guild of America determined that all parties had contributed significantly to the project.

Director Nimoy had some input as well, particularly in the choice of whales as the focus of the plot. The movie also promised to feature the largest number of STAR

TREK alumni of any of the motion pictures. Not only did Dr. Chapel, now a Commander (Majel Barrett), and Commander Janice Rand (Grace Lee Whitney) make their first appearances since STAR TREK—THE MOTION PICTURE, but Sarek (Mark Lenard) and Amanda (Jane Wyatt) were also on hand to check up on their son's well being.

While Gene served as a paid creative consultant on the STAR TREK motion pictures, and was listened to if not strictly obeyed, pointing out the mistakes other people were making was not creatively satisfying for him. He wanted to do more.

Between the time of his removal from the Paramount lot in July 1980 and when he returned on a full time basis in 1986 to create THE NEXT GENERATION, Gene explored other creative avenues. The primary one was being a novelist.

He had already written a novelization in 1977 of the story which would become STAR TREK—THE MOTION PICTURE. He stated at the time, "I guess that if I had my absolute choice, I'd like to end up writing only novels. It's the one type of writing which you have about the greatest freedom. You can live anywhere. You don't have to live near Hollywood. You can work on your own time and schedule."

In 1981, with one published novel under his belt and the conflicts over creative control of STAR TREK—THE MOTION PICTURE behind him, he reiterated his interest in becoming a full time novelist. Gene said, "This is the reason why I'm turning toward novels where I have more latitude and freedom that commercial television no longer offers and that cable and satellite television may offer, at which time I'll come back. I may continue to work in today's television for economic reasons depending on how other projects develop."

He didn't work in television again until he returned to create and develop STAR TREK: THE NEXT GENERATION in 1986.

On a Seattle radio show in January 1983, Roddenberry stated, "I'm writing a book, REPORT FROM EARTH that—if you like TREK—I think you'll like. It'll be out in about a year."

The book was never published. That didn't stop him from talking about it, but talking about writing is always more fun than doing it.

In the November 1985 STARLOG, Gene was still talking about REPORT FROM EARTH, but now he was willing to share more information about it. He said, "I'm in a period of growth and expansion. I'm taking long, hard looks at the world and what's happening in it, analyzing and thinking. I'm trying to become acquainted with the universe—with the part of it I occupy—and trying to settle, for myself, what my relationship with it is.

"I'm writing and making notes, but I haven't quite decided whether they're going into the novel on which I've been working. It's called REPORT FROM EARTH, and the main character is an alien. This began for me with Spock, but this new alien character, Gaan, is from a far-off planet and has a different body style and even different chemistry. Spock was connected with Earth by being half-human, but Gaan is totally unconnected. And while I've been trying to see the world through Gaan's eyes, it has changed the way I view us—the human animal.

"All of us carry a considerable amount of prejudice about ourselves around with us. You and I naturally think in terms of the white man's viewpoint—Western society's viewpoint—no matter how hard we try not to. That's how we live; how we relate.

"I began analyzing the world as this character would probably see it and judge it. Gaan finds us to be remarkable creatures, although he believes us to still be in childhood—or just barely getting into adolescence. But considering all we've achieved, we're remarkable!"

Gaan was obviously a viewpoint character for Gene's own philosophizing. While fictional characters don't always share their author's point of view, he often commented on humanity as being in its childhood. Through Gaan he'd be able to further expound on this and other personal points of view.

"And what I've discovered," Gene continued, "is that to practice seeing the world through an invented alien's eyes is not only an exhilarating and fun way to examine yourself and the whole planet, but it creates an unusual kind of logic system.

"The secret is identifying with the alien so completely that prejudice about myself and Earth begins melting away—and somehow shedding of personal prejudice seems to open up a person's mental processes. You think in new dimensions and at new speeds. The more I polish Gaan and practice putting myself in his place, the more discoveries I make."

Gene delivered a speech at Worldview '84, the World Future Society's Fifth General Assembly, in June 1984. Among other subjects, he discussed Gaan in this lecture and offered insights into both the character and the book. "Gaan was originally a marine life form, it's home being a far distant methane sea planet," Gene revealed, "its profession scholar, its specialty the study of life on ocean planets similar to its own, which all members of Gaan's life form had believed to be the only environment capable of evolving intelligence.

"Their way of studying other intelligences is to stay unobserved while learning the languages and customs of a new world, after which they fabricate a perfect duplicate of that world's intelligent life form, into which a scholar like Gaan then places its own consciousness. It is a study method we ourselves may learn to use in centuries to come. What better way to study another intelligence than from the perspective of living with them as one of them?"

Describing his book, he stated, "My novel has so far gotten Gaan to our planet, let him recover from his shock of finding an intelligent form on the dry crust of this strange poisonous world, and watched him grow accustomed to these ugly human things stumbling about on stalk-like appendages, burdened with the full weight of gravity.

"While this is happening, Gaan's technicians in orbit discover a dead, frozen, perfectly preserved human body whose bulky outer covering bears the initials CCCP. Having now a pattern from which a human replica can be fashioned, there is no way a scholar like Gaan can resist this opportunity to study a remarkable new world. In the novel, the time is today and Gaan has begun to live among us, studying us."

Gene was excited by the idea of using an alien to turn a mirror on humanity. He explained, "How enjoyable and informative it is to look at this world through the eyes of an extraterrestrial scholar and stranger!

"Try to imagine how wildly funny each evening's TV news report becomes—and what it is like to go out onto the streets, into shopping malls, and to other places and see the incredible and colorful things that are happening. I have difficulty seeing a better way to gain new perspectives and test old perspectives on the happenings of today.

"The more one becomes a Gaan, the less encumbered one is by earthly racial backgrounds, politics, beliefs, passions, superstitions, preferences, intolerances, hopes, and fears. All that one sees through Gaan's eyes is what exists, what is happening, at what rate, affected by what other factors. Observe, compute, analyze, and voila!—perhaps not all of tomorrow appears, but some very useful approximations of it will almost certainly come into view. Those capable of using an extraterrestrial's eyes as an exercise, as a challenge, as an exciting game, improve on their ability to estimate where today may be taking us."

As egocentric as Roddenberry was about the centrality of the humanity species, he didn't wholeheartedly accept the Eurocentric view of our world. "Once you begin looking in Gaan-like fashion at much of what is being published in the futurism field," Gene said, "you will begin encountering predictions that read like propaganda pamphlets endorsing our Western world, our political and economic systems, our religious beliefs—or if not actually recommending such things, still leaving no doubt but that our way represents the world's only possible future."

Gene went further, describing how the extraterrestrial entity Gaan views our small blue world and the beings who scurry across it. He explained, "When Gaan looks at the topics we are studying today, he confesses some puzzlement over why we are not paying more attention to the following questions:

"If automation puts half our work force on the street (and we dare not call that impossible), what of the police? If they are overworked and outnumbered, how do we increase their numbers, their legal powers? What kinds of better tools should we provide? Better weapons, too? What limitations? Shouldn't we be considering possible scenarios, recommending options and limits?

"Prison experiments have demonstrated that implants can trigger alarms if the wrong prisoner enters the wrong area. Or even trigger chemical releases incapacitating the person. Is this a valid parole device? Is this a legitimate possibility for the protection of law-abiding citizenry from 'trouble makers'?"

Clearly Gene's earlier life as a policeman influences his approach to subjects. He is far more the peace officer than the alien viewing human territorial psychology.

"If disorder threatens our cities," Gene continued, "should we consider travel passes that limit which vehicles can travel through which areas? What about cordoning off trouble areas or designing special television networks to produce 'patriotic' TV, motivating changes in people's attitudes and desires and values?

"We are perilously close to being able to manufacture non-narcotic drugs offering a broad selection of mood alterations at a cost of pennies. Do we distribute these legally? Do we prefer that these become criminal substances? Do we continue to maintain the criminal status of all drugs?"

This has been a recurring issue with him over the years, although he had never been able to address it in the public venue of the marketplace of ideas. While political pundits have debated the prospect of legalized drugs, the entertainment arena of television has steered a wide course around this subject. Only legalized abortion is more explosive than legalized drugs. Both go to the very core of the way our society views itself.

Gene has a very libertarian view of the subject of drug use. While not an abuser himself, what he had seen convinced him the problem will never be solved by punishment. In fact he believed punishment failed to address the situation.

He said, "The truth is that drugs actually represent something that's very wrong in our society. I submit it is frightening that when a person reaches adulthood or adolescence they need some sort of help to make life happy. What emotional things are we doing to those people who need a substance to get by?

"We should be examining that, not the criminal aspect of drugs. It may be that unless our world becomes more perfect, some people are always going to need mood changers."

Returning to Gaan's view of our globe, and his questions of Western civilization, Gene wondered, "Can our political system survive television's Hollywood method of casting candidates and presenting issues? Is there a self-ordained messiah in our future? Are there indications of a public hunger for this? Is there a very obvious trend toward more and more simplistic answers to life's problems?"

He went on to quote Gaan in regard to the alien's long-term prospects for the human species. Gene, quoting Gaan, continued, "Despite what sometimes seems insurmountable evidence to the contrary, I am now inclined to believe that they will ultimately survive. I look forward to the day when these humans, who are so much more than they yet believe they are, will at last understand that the Cosmos outside and the Cosmos inside themselves are one and the same."

Gene continued working on the book in the Eighties. In 1985 he still believed he would complete it in the near future, stating he was only a couple years away from finishing REPORT FROM EARTH.

"I think about these things and I make notes," he said. "Being a computer nut, I put them in my computer and file them away and data-base them, so I'm accumulating a great deal of information."

The book remained unpublished at the time of his death.

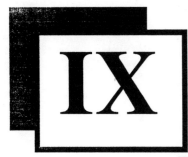

Gene Gets His Star

"As a Los Angeles policeman, I walked on this boulevard on foot patrol, and to have a star here is a double pleasure."—G.R.

When Susan Sackett (Gene's longtime assistant) nominated him for a star on the Hollywood Walk of Fame in 1984, she didn't realize it would ignite a controversy. This controversy came to light in the DAILY VARIETY dated November 2, 1984, in a story by Will Tusher headlined: "Roddenberry First Writer Nominated For H'Wood Star."

Tusher wrote, "Gene Roddenberry, creator of STAR TREK, the tv series that found a second life as a trilogy of theatrical features, is the first writer nominated for a sidewalk star in the 24-year history of the Hollywood Walk of Fame. His name, the Hollywood Chamber of Commerce has confirmed, was submitted last January but will not be considered by the selection committee until late January 1985.

"Chamber president Bill Welsh said the year's delay between submission and consideration is because of the vast number of applications for stars and the fact that the selection committee meets only a 'couple of times' a year. Meanwhile, the number of sidewalk stars has risen to 1790 — the last conferred on Eva Gabor — without recognition for a writer.

"When the WGA made an issue of the oversight (DAILY VARIETY, Sept. 19), Welsh contended that no writer's name had ever been submitted. He said yesterday that he 'couldn't recall' that Roddenberry's name had been offered. Roddenberry is a hyphenate writer-producer. The Writer's Guild has yet to make its own recommendations for sidewalk stars, but it is working on the matter."

Once the Writer's Guild complained, the finger was pointed right back at them. The guild had ignored the issue for two decades, apparently not caring whether the names of well known Hollywood writers appeared on the sidewalk. This is understandable since most people in Hollywood consider the Walk of Fame a tourist gimmick, not on the level of the Oscars or the Emmys.

In November 1984, Susan Sackett sent out a form letter to her mailing list. It included, "At last — the dream is coming true! When I submitted Gene's name in nomination for a star on the Hollywood Walk of Fame almost a year ago, I was told that there would be a long wait. Therefore, I vowed that I would personally put up the $3000 needed if his Star were approved before I had a chance to collect from his fans. Now it seems a virtual certainty that Gene *will* be receiving his well-deserved Star some time in 1985. We're all aware that without Gene Roddenberry there would have been *No* STAR TREK, *No* Mr. Spock, *No* Captain Kirk, *No* U.S.S. Enterprise. His mind created the spark that ignited life in our beloved program and its characters."

She then asked for donations, for if only 3000 fans sent $1.00 each, that would cover the costs. And if you think that $3,000 to put a brass star on a sidewalk seems excessive, by 1991 the Walk of Fame committee had increased that fee to $4700.

On September 4th, 1985, Gene was honored with a ceremony unveiling his star. Nearly all of the cast from the original STAR TREK series were there, including Leonard Nimoy, Deforest Kelley, James Doohan, Walter Koenig, Nichelle Nichols, George Takei and Majel Barrett. Also on hand were actors Roger C. Carmel, Susan Oliver, Grace Lee Whitney and the original STAR TREK makeup artist, Fred Phillips.

Due to work commitments, William Shatner was unable to attend. He was ten minutes away at the Burbank Studios lot filming T.J. HOOKER. Most of the STAR TREK actors have received stars on the Walk of Fame, but to date the only ceremony Shatner appeared at was his own.

The unveiling of Gene's star on the Hollywood Walk of Fame was the culmination of over a year of lobbying efforts by fans, spearheaded by Susan Sackett. Donations paid the fee covering the cost of the star and the ceremony. It was a touch and go for a while because a great number of names are nominated each year but only a few are chosen.

It was overcast before the ceremony began at 12:30 PM. As the Los Angeles Police Pipe Band broke into a rousing bagpipe melody prior to the festivities, the clouds parted and spirits brightened.

As usual, Johnny Grant, the "Honorary Mayor of Hollywood" and Chairman of the Walk of Fame Committee, served as Master of Ceremonies for the event. With a recording of "Hooray for Hollywood" playing over the loud speakers, the festivities began.

Grant kicked off by saying, "Hello, everybody, and welcome to another Walk of Fame ceremony. Today we honor the creator and producer of the original Star Trek television series, Gene Roddenberry!" Cheers greeted the honored guest's name.

Grant introduced Bill Welsh, President of the Hollywood Chamber of Commerce, the sponsoring organization of the Walk of Fame. Welsh stated, "I am particularly thrilled that today we honor a man who has had a long association with our community of Hollywood, and indicative of the fact that the whole world loves him are the people who have come from so many far away places to be a part of this ceremony today. Johnny's going to tell you more about Gene Roddenberry and the things he has done here in Hollywood, as well as what you know about the STAR TREK activities. But this is our chance as a part of the Hollywood community to say to Gene, 'We want the world to know that we love you and that we respect you!' and Gene, we have a slogan in the Hollywood Chamber of Commerce—we say that we're building the Hollywood for the 21st century. That means, Gene, that when the next century rolls around and people walk up and down Hollywood Boulevard as you used to, they'll see this star and they'll know that this community had this great affection for you, and was proud that you were one of us who went on to great heights of success."

Grant then read telegrams received from friends and supporters of Roddenberry who had been unable to attend, but wanted to convey their feelings publicly, "Congratulations Big Bird—to the creator and prime spirit, it will be a pleasure to walk on you. The Vulcans send their love—Mark Lenard."

Then he read, "Dear Gene, everywhere I go, I hear your name on the lips of people saying how incredible is the talent of Roddenberry for having written THE MARTIAN CHRONICLES. At the same time, everywhere you go, do you not hear the magic name Ray Bradbury, who created STAR TREK? No matter how you play it, isn't it wonderful? Love to you on this special, fine day—Ray Bradbury!"

Grant then introduced Gene by giving a brief rundown of his accomplishments, ending the introduction by stating, "He has served as a member of the Writer's Guild Executive Council, is a former governor of the Television Academy of Arts and Sciences, and is a member of the board of directors of the National Space Institute. The father of three, Gene lives in Los Angeles with his lovely wife Majel. Ladies and Gentlemen, family, friends, and Trekkies from around the world, please help me and the Hollywood Chamber of Commerce give a warm welcome to Mr. Gene Roddenberry as we dedicate to him this star on the Hollywood Walk of Fame. Scotty, beam him aboard!"

Bill Welsh gave Gene a special Walk of Fame jacket emblazoned with Gene's name. Maria Hernendez, from City Councilman Michael Woo's office, then stated, "The Mayor has proclaimed today Gene Roddenberry Day and the council has said: 'Now therefore be it resolved that the City Council of the city of Los Angeles congratulates Mr. Roddenberry on his many accomplishments and wishes him continued success.'"

Then guests were introduced to the assembled multitude.

Leonard Nimoy said, "This is a wonderful day for Gene, obviously, and for all of us connected with STAR TREK. I'll tell you just one brief story.

"When we were preparing the series, I wasn't sure that the ears were going to work out right, and I thought if these ears don't work, I'm going to be Dumbo of the year. So I went to Gene and said, 'I'm really nervous about it Gene.' Before we started shooting I said maybe we should just drop the ears because they don't look right, and he said, 'I'll tell you what. You wear them for thirteen weeks and if it doesn't work out, we'll get you an ear job.'

"Gene, I'm glad you talked me into it. Congratulations today. I think it's wonderful for you, wonderful for STAR TREK, and we're really happy to be here with you to celebrate."

When Walter Koenig was introduced, he noted, "Not only is Mr. Roddenberry an extraordinary man and a gentleman we all admire, but he is also the very first writer to be honored on the Hollywood Walk of Fame."

Johnny Grant quickly jumped in, interrupting Walter, to add, "Just to keep the record straight, he has several colleagues who are already here. There has been much controversy over this. He is being honored today for everything he did in television." That Roddenberry was also a producer helped blur the distinction of his being honored as solely a writer.

When her turn came, Nichelle Nichols said, "Gene Roddenberry, I'm so proud of you, as I've always been. I'm so grateful to you for thinking of Uhura, and my hailing frequencies are always open for you!"

Harve Bennett, the producer of STAR TREK II, III and the then-upcoming IV added, "I have only one word for a man who makes what has followed his genius so easy, and that is mazel tov!"

When Gene finally spoke, after all glowing praise from his friends and colleagues, he voiced his thoughts about this very special moment in his life. He said, "As a Los Angeles policeman, I walked on this boulevard on foot patrol, and to have a star here is a double pleasure. Actually, when I walked the boulevard as a Los Angeles policeman, my scripts were beginning to sell and my producers didn't know I was a policeman. I was afraid if they found out they might not buy them, so I really spent my time here on Hollywood Boulevard jumping from one dark doorway to another." Gene acknowledged how great it was to have the Scots section of the

Los Angeles Police Band on hand for the event. He then introduced his mother, Carolyn Roddenberry, his son, Gene Jr. and his two daughters, Darleen and Dawn, as well as his brother Robert and his sister, Doris, whom he described as, "a much better writer than I am."

Clearly nervous, surrounded by people present to pay him tribute, Gene said, "I want to thank some other people, too. When I go places, people often ask me, what are Trekkies? What are STAR TREK fans? Some of them got an idea that they are people who dress in funny clothes and go around making signs and so on. Some of them do that and have fun doing that, but STAR TREK's Trekkies range the entire audience and include astronauts, physicians, physicists and yes, they also include twelve and fourteen year old kids. We have also been associated with STAR TREK for almost twenty years now, and in twenty years I have never had a bad experience with a STAR TREK fan. They're incredible people and I want you to applaud them! They are people who believe in humanity and believe they are going to make it."

Gene also made observations about the city in which he had lived and worked for so many years. He said, "I also concur with you folks on this Hollywood Boulevard—this city, Los Angeles, is the Twenty-first Century city in the making. It is becoming a Third World city. I think that's marvelous. The mixture of races and colors and religions here says that democracy, damn it, does work and it's a great thing and you haven't seen anything yet. The Los Angeles that's ahead of us, if we can keep peace and order on our streets, we can become anything we want and do anything we want to do in Los Angeles. And I think we will."

When asked to do the "Space, the final frontier," introduction from the STAR TREK TV series, Gene drew a blank. Even with coaxing, he was unable to recall it. Finally, he laughed and said, "I just write these things. I'm not a performer. But I believe them all and I believe in humanity, and I'm not done writing about humanity. We are an incredible species. You've seen Los Angeles, you've just seen humanity.

"We're still just a child-creature; we're still being nasty to each other around the world and all the children go through those phases, but we are growing up and moving into adolescence, now. When we grow up, man, we are going to be something and we're going to do it , too! Thank you all so very much. Thank all of you that came out and bless you all."

When Roddenberry finally saw the star unveiled, he was surrounded by his friends as Johnny Grant said, "Ladies and gentlemen, we welcome to the Walk of Fame, Gene Roddenberry!" The crowd cheered and applauded. The moment had arrived. STAR TREK had really made a star out of its creator.

Following the ceremony, a special reception was held for Gene on the Paramount Studios lot. Gene's star was once again on the rise in Hollywood. New people were coming into power at Paramount and decisions were being made which would once again put him in a position of creative power at the studio. A new era for STAR TREK was just around the corner, but no one knew it yet, not even Gene.

The 1,810th star on the Hollywood Walk of Fame, located at 6683 Hollywood Boulevard, stands forever as a lasting tribute to the imagination behind the spirit that endures — the spirit of Gene Roddenberry and his creation, Star Trek.

X The Next Generation

"I do not perceive this as a universe that's divided between good and evil."—G.R.

Even as STAR TREK IV: THE VOYAGE HOME was being prepared for a launch which would set a new boxoffice record for the movie series, Gene was hatching plans for a new Enterprise all his own. . . with a baldheaded Frenchman as Captain, a woman doctor, an android science officer, and, horror of horrors, a Klingon on board! Many thought it couldn't, or perhaps even shouldn't, happen, but Gene Roddenberry was going to give it one heck of a shot.

Gene recounted, "When Paramount originally approached me to do a new series, I turned them down. I did not want to devote the tremendous amount of time necessary to producing another show. In order to keep the original series going, I practically had to disown my daughters. I had no time for them when they were school age. I did not want to do that to my life again.

"There is only one way to know to write and produce and that is to throw my energy at the project all the time. So when they began to think about a second series, I said I would not do it.

"Then they said, 'Well, suppose we figure a way that it could be done so you would be in charge?' I thought they were kidding. The studio said that I could be in full control of the creative standard. I asked a few questions, and they said, 'Yeah, sure, you must know these things because you've been doing them anyway under network guidance.'

"I told the studio that if they went the syndication route I would go for it. Not only would I go for it, I would go for it full blast. I told them I would find ways of doing STAR TREK that would give them extra elements. I think we have done that."

The STAR TREK series would be launched with an all new cast, set (somewhat vaguely) seventy-five or so years after the original series, and feature the Enterprise of that farther future, the fifth of its line, NCC 1701-D. Paramount was banking that a syndicated show would generate revenues.

It seemed impossible. But. . . it happened. Gene worked hard to produce a new STAR TREK that would be true to the ideals of the original but still have its own flavor.

THE MAN WHO CREATED STAR TREK

Asked what was the most difficult aspect of creating STAR TREK: THE NEXT GENERATION, Gene replied, "The most difficult aspect? Leonard Nimoy said it. You can't catch lightning in a bottle twice, and I was thinking, yes, he's probably right.

"The thing that attracted me to doing it was, number one, they said I wouldn't have to deal with networks. And then they said, maybe you shouldn't because it's impossible, and my ears perked up over that.

"Nothing's impossible, goddammit! Nothing's impossible really, is it? But the most difficult aspect was to go against all of that and put a show together and believe you could do it, and collect people that could do it, and collect a cast that in its own way has the qualities of the old cast. It was the impossibility of it that was the most difficult."

Roddenberry continued, "What we want to do is to grapple now with the problems of the '80s and '90s and the turn of the century. I think we are going to surprise you on technology.

"You can only go so far in making things smaller and faster and more powerful. What other things should technology be worrying about? We're going to be getting into those areas.

"There's a reason to do another STAR TREK now. We did the original STAR TREK about the problems of the '60s. Many people forget that, in the mid-'60s, when we put on a multi-racial crew, that was considered awful. People were shocked."

That's one argument he didn't have to fight any more. He also didn't have to deal with network, or studio, interference. Early in the new show's production, a group of junior executives walked into Gene's office and began going over a script demanding changes. He pointed out they had no right to do this under the terms of his contract, and threw them out!

Asked what he kept from the old STAR TREK to please audience expectations, Gene explained, "While I listen to the audience, one of the secrets of whatever success I've amounted to was that I never make shows for the audience. I listen to good advice, but the only person I make shows for is myself.

"I love any help you can give me, but I'll be damned if I'll make a show for you! I make it for myself and if you happen to like it, I'm delighted; we've got the best of both possible worlds.

"Writers and producers and directors and so on that create a show for specific audiences do schlock work. They should do selfish work; proudly selfish work, and that happens to be true about painters, and sculptors, too."

Resistance from old fans proved not to be a problem. Still, creating a new series when the original has grown to mythic proportions is difficult. The new characters take time to settle in. Once they did, they were believable.

First there was Captain Jean-Luc Picard. For this demanding role, Gene cast British actor Patrick Stewart, a noted Shakespearean with roles in films such films as EXCALIBUR, LIFEFORCE and DUNE in addition to extensive stage work.

Stewart had become highly regarded in Great Britain due to his roles in such BBC productions as I, CLAUDIUS, SMILEY'S PEOPLE, and TINKER, TAILOR, SOLDIER, SPY. All had aired in the United States, making his work familiar to American audiences as well.

His face is also known to American film-goers. For David Lynch's adaptation of DUNE, he played Gurney Halek, one of the more prominent roles. In EXCALIBUR, he assayed Leon Degrance. More recently, in 1985, he was seen in the strange science fiction film LIFEFORCE in the character of Dr. Armstrong.

Stewart also starred on London stage in a production of "Who's Afraid of Virginia Woolf?," garnering the prestigious London Fringe Best Actor Award. As an associate artist of the Royal Shakespeare Company, Stewart was considered one of the leading talents of the British stage.

Gene said, "Patrick Stewart was my first choice because I'm faced with a bald-headed man for a captain and I'm used to him being jolly with hair. Bill was rather athletic. The longer I looked at Patrick Stewart and saw the power that was there that was a different kind than Bill's, the more I became sure that he was the man. I'm so delighted to have him I cannot tell you!

"When you look at dailies, you always watch Picard even when he's not doing anything! Because he is doing something here [points to his head] constantly! England produces great actors and he's an example of that."

Stewart has been difficult to work with during the five years of THE NEXT GENERATION. The cliffhanger in which Capt. Picard was turned into a Borg in the third season was concocted when Stewart threatened to quit.

A former staffer reported that Stewart walks off the set in a snit at least once a week. His co-workers have unflatteringly nicknamed him "Baldilocks".

When Stewart appeared on a TV talk show with William Shatner, the notoriously egotistical Shatner came across as the picture of charm while Stewart appeared overimpressed with himself. He seemingly enjoyed making fun of the older cast members of the original STAR TREK. Some felt this public display finally pulled the cover from Stewart's supposedly genial exterior.

Gene wisely anticipated problems like this. The second STAR TREK series is fashioned so no one character could emerge as the star—not even the captain. An ensemble of players was created for the new Enterprise.

Since Capt. Picard would never beam down to an uncharted, possibly hostile planet in this modern version of STAR TREK, Gene split the command function in two. Picard has an executive officer, William Riker. There has been speculation Picard and Riker are two aspects of Captain Kirk.

In a nod to the old show's first pilot, as well as to nautical history, Riker is often referred to as "Number One." A canny poker player, he doesn't fear risk, but weighs them carefully. Riker assures the safety of his superior officer.

The notion of using "Away Teams" instead of sending the ship's executive officers on dangerous missions was suggested by David Gerrold. Jonathan Frakes, the seasoned television actor who stepped into the role of William Riker, credits Gene with giving him insight into the character.

"Gene is so very non-Hollywood and really quite paternal," Frakes noted at the time. "One of the things he said to me was, 'You have a Machiavellian glint in your eye. Life is a bowl of cherries.' I think Gene feels that way, which is why he writes the way he does. He's very positive and Commander Riker will reflect that."

Gene also created a new crew position for THE NEXT GENERATION, that of Ship's Counsellor, and a new alien race—the Betazoids. Although this position can be occupied by a member of any race, Picard is fortunate his counsellor is a Betazoid. They are extremely empathic, if not telepathic, and can read minds to varying degrees. Picard's counsellor, Deanna Troi, is a gorgeous half-human woman, who can sense emotions with great acuity.

This ability, combined with extensive psychological training, makes her a vital part of the Captain's decision-making process. "Captain, I sense. . ." has become as familiar a line to NEXT GENERATION fans as "I'm a doctor, not a. . ." is for those of the original series.

Deanna once had a relationship with Riker, but it seems to have mellowed into an abiding friendship. When asked, the actress dismissed it as an idea that the show would no longer explore.

Marina Sirtis enjoys the irony of being a British actress playing an alien on American television. Sirtis initially auditioned for the role of Security Chief Tasha Yar, rather than that of Deanna Troi.

Most controversial at the show's inception was the android science officer Data. Many saw him as a transparent Spock substitute. Indeed, there are many similarities between the two, but the differences have been developed most.

A much closer predecessor of Data is the android in THE QUESTOR TAPES. Gene cast Texas-born Brent Spiner as Data.

Spiner was well prepared for his role by a strong belief in extraterrestrials. "Obviously I'm from another planet," Spiner laughed, but added that he seriously does believe in beings from other planets and would continue to do so until such things are disproven.

An Enterprise without a ship's doctor would be unthinkable. Gene provided Chief Medical Officer Beverly Crusher. Dr. Crusher is the first regular role in a television series for actress Gates McFadden. A compassionate, dedicated doctor, Crusher is also the mother of a precocious youngster, Wesley, played by Wil Wheaton. (Not coincidentally, Gene's middle name was Wesley.)

McFadden was the director of choreography and puppet movement for the late Jim Henson's LABYRINTH and assisted Gavin Milar in the staging of the fantasy sequences for Dreamchild. "Those films were my baptism by fire into the world of special effects and computerized props," McFadden revealed.

The actress was replaced by Diana Muldaur for the second season of THE NEXT GENERATION. Gene issued a press release telling fans not to write him about the decision because his mind was made up—until he changed it again and brought Gates McFadden back to the role in the third season.

Another new character, eventually to be promoted to the post of Chief Engineer, is Geordi LaForge. The role was named as tribute to the late STAR TREK fan George LaForge, a cerebral palsy sufferer whose long survival was attributed to his strong identification with the show.

A black man, Geordi maintains the tradition of a multi-ethnic cast in STAR TREK. He is blind, but, due to the advanced technology of the 24th Century, can see by means of an electronic visor linked with his nervous system. He can even see visual ranges inaccessible to most human beings.

Geordi is a sincere, likeable, confident man with slight insecurities. He always perseveres, communicating freely with others. The opposite of Picard, he affects an informal approach to life, and is not hung up on protocol.

Actor LeVar Burton, best known as the young Kunta Kinte in the classic miniseries ROOTS, plays the role. The character was reportedly created by David Gerrold.

The biggest shock in THE NEXT GENERATION's crew roster was Worf. . . a Klingon. Since Kirk's heyday, peace has finally been negotiated between the Federation and the Klingon Empire.

Negotiations were underway at the time of the events of STAR TREK III: THE SEARCH FOR SPOCK. This further developed in STAR TREK VI: THE UNDISCOVERED COUNTRY. The two spheres of influence now strive to get along, and have established some mutual trust.

Worf is unique. There are no other Klingons in Star Fleet. He was raised by humans after his family was killed in the massacre of their outpost during a surprise Klingon attack—an event that haunts him.

Worf is like Spock in that he is the product of two cultures, a warrior Klingon dedicated to his own culture but tempered by exposure to human ideals. Worf was added after the pilot for THE NEXT GENERATION and does not appear in "Encounter At Farpoint."

For a time, he would be little more than a grouchy guy with lots of hair standing in the background, recommending aggressive action. He would be featured in more and more episodes, eventually opening up a window on the fascinating world of the Klingons.

The 6' 5" Michael Dorn was cast as Worf. Dorn was born in Liling, Texas, but raised in Pasadena, California, just minutes away from Hollywood.

With the cast set, THE NEXT GENERATION got under way. Creator Gene Roddenberry handed the executive producer's reins over to Paramount's Rick Berman.

D.C. Fontana signed on as story editor, but soon left, unhappy with the treatment received by her script "Encounter At Farpoint." Sadly, the episode kicked off the new series with less than a bang.

Fontana's initial story received a forced graft of Gene's "Q" subplot. The two concepts didn't merge. Instead of a genuine, two-hour movie, audiences received a poorly-shuffled sandwich of two separate stories.

Like STAR TREK—THE MOTION PICTURE, "Encounter At Farpoint" moved slowly, too enamored of its own special effects. These featured a saucer/hull separation at a climactic moment.

It was no surprise that Gene Roddenberry's name was on the screenplay. Clearly whatever lessons he had learned from the STAR TREK: THE MOTION PICTURE debacle were forgotten.

"In the first STAR TREK, I rewrote or heavily polished the first thirteen episodes so that Mr. Spock would be the Mr. Spock that I had in mind," Gene said during the first season of the new series. "This was enormous labor, and then it began to catch on and we got some good writers.

"In STAR TREK: THE NEXT GENERATION I rewrote thirteen episodes. I don't want to act out a big 'I did this, I did that,' but as far as the basic original writing, I had to do that again, with few exceptions. It is the way episodic television is.

He continued, "Now as the year's gone on, I've found some good people and I hope to find more. We got some good writing in the old series, and we've had some good writing in the new series. But most of the writing comes from a very few, very good people who labor hard and very often they are staff people."

Special effects for the first season were provided by Industrial Light And Magic, but they soon proved too expensive. Other effects teams were sought out. With a per-episode budget of over a million dollars, THE NEXT GENERATION was a major gamble for Paramount. They had to use the budget to the best of their ability.

The first season of THE NEXT GENERATION was erratic. The actors had yet to settle into their roles, and the scripts, often rewritten by Gene, were uneven.

Controversy ensued when both D.C. Fontana and David Gerrold felt they had contributed to the development of the series concept and neither received credit. Gene never acknowledged them. In fact, in regard to Gerrold, he went so far as to comment that ". . . Gerrold [had] been condemning the show, constantly. I had him on staff for many, many months, [and] he never wrote an episode we could shoot."

Fontana is harder to dismiss. She worked on a total of four scripts for the first season of THE NEXT GENERATION.

The dispute between Gene, Fontana, and Gerrold was settled behind-the-scenes for an unspecified sum. No on-screen credit was given.

The second season of THE NEXT GENERATION showed marked improvement. Changes were evident.

Jonathan Frakes now sported a beard. Some viewers, unimpressed by the first season, now use sight of a clean-shaven Riker as their cue not to watch an episode.

Claiming Gates McFadden's character didn't click, Gene summarily dropped Beverly Crusher from the roster with an offhand mention of her going off to head Starfleet Medical. Her replacement was another woman, Doctor Pulaski, ably played by Diana Muldaur, a veteran guest star of the original STAR TREK.

Despite Muldaur's fine acting, this character didn't work. Perhaps the problem was that the crusty, no-nonsense Pulaski seemed to be a female "Bones" McCoy. The character provided much-needed friction on the bridge, but never really came to bear on the plots much, leaving her an unengaging character.

Another new character also came on board in the second season, although she may have been aboard all along. Guinan is a mysterious alien woman of great age who functions as bartender and freelance counsellor in the Enterprise's open lounge, Ten Forward. She serves synthahol, a marvelous brew whose mildly intoxicating effects can be shaken off at will.

Guinan's background is intentionally shrouded in mystery. Although not featured on a weekly basis, she is a recurring presence.

Whoopi Goldberg described her character Guinan as "a cross between Yoda and William F. Buckley," but freely admits she's put a lot of herself into the role. Growing up in New York, young Whoopi was inspired by the harmonious message of the original STAR TREK, and especially by Nichelle Nichols. "He explained that I had a place in the future," Whoopi said of the original STAR TREK.

When Goldberg learned her friend LeVar Burton would be on a new STAR TREK series, she asked him to tell Gene she wanted to come aboard. Everyone thought Burton was joking.

A year later, Goldberg took matters into her own hands. She contacted Gene and the two worked together to create the mysterious alien bartender.

By this time, Gene had developed a stable of writers he could trust. His production team learned to work his way. Gene said, "We have a lot in store, and a lot of things we want to talk about. We can no longer claim we're brave because we have mixed races which, twenty-three years ago, was very exciting. When we did that we had women in jobs other than secretaries and so on, and people were saying, 'My God, how far can they go!'

"Now we want to talk about hostage situations. I am amazed to see the hostage (takers) treated as bad guys always. Many of these people have legitimate complaints. The world is not as simple as we lay it out—good guys here, bad guys there.

"I am very concerned and want to find a way to get into the fact that most of the warfare and killing going on in the world is going on in the name of religion; organized religion. Not that I'm saying that there are not great plans and that we are not part of some great thing, but it is not the type of thing you see preached on television.

"I don't hold anyone up to ridicule. My mother is a good Baptist and she believes in many great things. But I cannot sit still in a series of this type and not point out who's killing who in the world."

Gene did an episode questioning religion, "Who Watches The Watchers?" in season three. On a primitive planet, an off world survey team is accidentally discovered by the inhabitants, who come to regard the Enterprise crewmen and their miraculous feats (appearing and disappearing) as the actions of gods.

"I've always thought that, if we did not have supernatural explanations for all the things we might not understand right away, this is the way we would be, like the people on that planet," Gene explained. "I was born into a supernatural world in which all my people—my family—usually said, 'That is because God willed it,' or gave other supernatural explanations for whatever happened. When you confront those statements on their own, they just don't make sense. They are clearly wrong.

You need a certain amount of proof to accept anything, and that proof was not forthcoming to support those statements."

Gene was disappointed at the little recognition it received. "It is a source of considerable amusement to me that we can do shows like this," he said, "and on various other subjects large and small, and get little or no public reaction. If these things were to be done on Broadway or in motion pictures, they would have stunned audiences.

"The audiences would have said, 'How wild, how forward, how advanced.' But because these subjects are done on a syndicated television show, in our time slot, no one really notices them.

"I thought several times that the world of drama would have stood up and cheered us, but no, only silence. But there is one advantage, one thing happening: all of these episodes are brought back and rerun every year. What will happen with STAR TREK: THE NEXT GENERATION is almost identical to what happened to the original STAR TREK as larger and larger audiences become acquainted with the program.

"The original STAR TREK audience now says, 'Hurrah, what fine shows!' This has brought us considerable pleasure that they would notice it. STAR TREK: THE NEXT GENERATION is on that same path now and more so.

"The time will come when the second series will attain its true stature. I just hope some of it happens while I am still alive. I'm not jealous that I don't have praise. This happens very broadly in contacts with humans. The world is not necessarily poorer because a painter or playwright is not recognized in his or her lifetime."

While STAR TREK: THE NEXT GENERATION continued to pick up steam and gain recognition, things didn't work so well for the next outing of the classic STAR TREK characters. STAR TREK V: THE FINAL FRONTIER, directed by William Shatner, was a disappointment to film-goers— and to Paramount Pictures.

Nimoy, meanwhile, enjoyed great success as director of the smash hit THREE MEN AND A BABY. When Shatner's negotiations with Paramount proved slow, Nimoy took another job, directing THE GOOD MOTHER for Touchstone Pictures. The film, starring Diane Keaton, was not a great success but received wonderful critical notices.

This led to another delay in starting STAR TREK V's production, prompting the petulant Shatner to threaten a Spockless feature. When Nimoy called his bluff, Shatner admitted he couldn't do it without him. Production was also stymied by 1988's Screen Writer's Guild strike, which continued into the Fall.

While all this was going on, everybody had forgotten something—no one had ever shown line one of the story to Gene. Harve Bennett and Paramount had already approved the storyline and David Loughery was writing the screenplay before Gene even knew it was this far along. When he found out about it he made a stink.

Work on the screenplay stopped until he could read the outline and comment on it. He said, "I created STAR TREK. I don't take anything away from Leonard or Bill or anyone, but I'm the guy who did it. How dare they start something without listening to my comments, whether they follow them or not?

"And I've never insisted they follow them. If I had strong objections to the story, I would have stated them."

His comments definitely caused a rethinking of Shatner's Captain Kirk meets God storyline, though. "I thought it was very unwise to do a story which seemed to be talking about God because there are so many versions about what God is or isn't," Gene said. "And living in a time in which you have Tammy Bakker and the young lady who got screwed—not that that's an unusual happening in any religion—I think the public was beginning to see that many religions are nothing but flim flammery, dedicated to getting as many bucks as possible. And I didn't want STAR TREK to be associated with any one of them.

"The original story I saw was, 'The Enterprise Meets God.' And my point was that it had to be even more obvious [that 'God' is an actual alien]. I didn't object to it being an alien claiming to be God, but there was too much in it that an audience could have thought was really God or really the devil, and I very strongly resist believing in either.

"I do not perceive this as a universe that's divided between good and evil. I see it as a universe that is divided between many ideas of what is."

Gene also felt certain incidents violated the integrity of the characters he'd created so long ago. Gene said, "I had some objection to McCoy and the others believing it was God. McCoy was saying, 'Hallelujah, I'm with ya, I'm with ya!' and only Kirk and Spock understood the difference.

"I said, Hey, these are people that have been with you for twenty years, through thick and thin, through a variety of things, and I don't really think you serve them well by having them fall on their face and say, 'I believe, I believe.' I suggested that he [Sybok] better have some power over them if you were going to have someone like McCoy say, 'I believe.' You'd better have some reason to do it."

They heeded Gene's criticism, even to giving Sybok the mindmeld power. Gene also pointed out that the script's journey to the center of the universe premise was impossible because the universe has no center, plus Starfleet had still not explored beyond eleven percent of our own galaxy by the 23rd century.

Other problems occurred during the making of STAR TREK V, one of which drew Gene's attention. Shatner had been one of the earliest critics of a new STAR TREK television series. He feared it would pull interest away from the motion pictures just when his would be hitting the theatres.

Wil Wheaton, who played Wesley Crusher on THE NEXT GENERATION, walked across the Paramount lot to visit the soundstage where Shatner was directing STAR TREK V one day. When Shatner found out he was part of the cast of THE NEXT GENERATION, the elder actor began mocking the notion of a child on the bridge of the Enterprise, causing the sixteen year old boy to leave the set in tears.

Gene was furious when he heard, and went right to Harve Bennett, insisting he speak to Shatner. "He's your problem now, not mine," he reportedly told the producer.

Shatner apologized to Wheaton shortly thereafter. The incident is still so sensitive they no longer discuss it.

Not all the fault for the film lay with Shatner, even though he was the director and the story concept for the film was his. Paramount, convinced humor was the key to the success based on response to THE VOYAGE HOME, insisted on comedic moments even when they didn't belong.

From a boxoffice standpoint, this feature was a washout. It cost thirty-two million dollars to make and grossed only fifty million, less than half the take of THE VOYAGE HOME.

Nimoy was asked to direct STAR TREK VI but turned it down. He had already experienced the rigors of starring and directing the same film.

Gene's role in the STAR TREK features beyond the first remained advisory. He argued against producer Harve Bennett's idea for STAR TREK VI, though. It involved recasting the crew and going back to tell of their days at Starfleet Academy and how they all met.

Interestingly, Gene had thought along similar lines fifteen years before. At that time the original crew of actors would have been young enough to pull it off.

Gene stated quite simply, "I didn't like it. Who was going to cast the new Kirk and Spock? No one has ever cast a TREK character besides me that's worked."

This is an obvious reference to of Saavik, who went through two actresses before being quietly dropped from the movies.

Gene continued, "Braggadocio or whatever, that is the history of TREK. I could have done so had I thought it was a good idea, but it didn't fit in with the rest of TREK.

"It wasn't good. Some of it was like POLICE ACADEMY. You could hardly do this without the magic of a group of characters tailored for STAR TREK, which this was not."

When Paramount officially turned the idea down, Bennett terminated his association with STAR TREK.

XI Honors For Roddenberry and Trek

"I sometimes get a feeling I seem to be saying STAR TREK is an inspired vision of the human future, which it is not."—G.R.

During the first year of STAR TREK: THE NEXT GENERATION, Gene was honored with a special program by The Museum of Broadcasting. Every Spring the Museum in Los Angeles spotlights individuals and television programs which excel.

On March 30, 1988, Gene was the focus of such a tribute, not just for STAR TREK, but for his entire career in television as both writer and producer. When Gene came on stage that night in 1988, he was greeted with thunderous applause. After the auditorium finally quieted, the writer-producer smiled in appreciation and began reading the speech he had prepared.

He began, "I think, very briefly, I should've started this tonight with a confession. Sometimes appearing like this, I sometimes get a feeling I seem to be saying STAR TREK is an inspired vision of the human future, which it is not.

"I really don't believe that, honestly. I made STAR TREK for a Twentieth Century audience using Twentieth Century people and morals and situations. And were I to present the 23rd or 24th Century as I really believe it will be, the audiences would hate me. I'd probably be arrested.

"My view is that there is no way that you're going to have an Enterprise flying up there and going from star to star in the next fifty years, or the next hundred years, or the next three hundred years. The next big move humans are going to make is to fly out there and visit this new world that's coming closer and closer."

Gene continued, with great feeling. "We can now get to the shores of some of these worlds out there with no more trouble than our ancestors had bringing ships over to these shores. In my opinion, we will no doubt spend the next thousand years, probably, conquering our solar system about the same way we conquered this new world. It's well worthwhile conquering this solar system because at the center of this solar system of ours is a nuclear-powered furnace which has all the energy we'll need for a thousand years to to take the incredible raw materials that are out there on these nine worlds and bend it into things we need.

"Just as standing on the shores of New England when the whites first landed there, they would have found it impossible to believe that we would fling highways across this great nation. They were freezing and starving to death just standing on those shores. And that we would gird the entire world with airlines and all sorts of transportation, and that we would scratch this earth for raw materials; oil and minerals.

"Out there, there is so much more. We are only a child race now. We may get into our adolescence up there in the enormous challenges of what lies ahead in civilizing and taming the solar system and making it into our solar system. Which is kind of nice, because it really makes you believe that there is a God, or at least Isaac Asimov would've written it this way—that while we're in our adolescence, we're not allowed to travel to the stars.

"Most people don't realize how incredibly far away the stars are. We've got all we can do to travel around this solar system, which is fine with me because I don't want these people out here going to stars where there are other life forms and screwing them up! After we've conquered our solar system, and presumably grown into an adult species, then we can be trusted to go to the stars and to contact other life forms. It's a system I like very much.

"The fact that I am here commenting," Roddenberry continued, "is a tribute to Arthur C. Clarke. It happened in the summer of 1969, ten weeks after the first STAR TREK [TV series] had finished shooting and had been cancelled for consistently low ratings.

"So being unemployed, I was able to attend a conference in Arizona where Arthur was the principle speaker. As I'm sure all of you know, he is the author of things from CHILDHOOD'S END to SPACE ODYSSEY and is an equally brilliant scientist and futurist. And it became clear to me that he knew a lot about American television and I could hardly believe my ears when I heard him congratulating me on what we had managed to accomplish in three years of this utter failure—particularly since it had been labeled by the American television industry as a childish and expensive flop.

"I told Arthur that no advertising company had the slightest interest in even our first rerun of this monstrosity. I remember Arthur smiling and saying and pointing out to me that during the end of the television series, man had landed on the Moon. Man—human—had actually walked on another world, and he said that in his opinion I should relax and that in time it would no longer be considered a foolish fantasy.

"Well, it's a pleasure to be here," Gene said with great warmth and pride.

Moving on to his other work in television, Gene discussed the first series he was head writer for—HAVE GUN, WILL TRAVEL. He remarked that, "It's been twenty-five years since I wrote that series, but I realize now that I was writing science fiction then, too."

Gene had kind words for the star of that show, the late Richard Boone. "Richard Boone, unlike many in our business, really treasured writers and directors and was a very nice man to work with, and I wish he was still here."

The program that night involved showing clips from shows Gene had worked on, from HAVE GUN, WILL TRAVEL to THE LIEUTENANT, which he produced and wrote right before he did STAR TREK. Upon viewing these segments from shows he hadn't seen in 25 years or more, Gene stated, "It's fascinating to me to watch these things because I realize that I've been writing and studying the same type of thing, and gravitated toward the same type of writing, all my life."

Clips were then shown from other shows, including the STAR TREK first season episode "The Devil In The Dark," which Gene commented on afterwards. "You'll notice how crude the first STAR TREK appeared," he said. "Like in the cavern, the floors were all level. Believe it or not, we didn't have the money to ramp them. We made those STAR TREK's for $184,000. It was the first time in a science fiction show that anyone had a monster and decided to make it a mother. This had never been done, and when I suggested it, everyone was looking around saying, 'Are you sure we can do that?'

"That was one of the first shows we did, and we were still learning to do STAR TREK. For me it was a very heartwarming thing to watch that one and see where we were at and where we've come today."

Gene talked about what it was and is like to be a writer in Hollywood. Speaking from his then-current position as producer of STAR TREK—THE NEXT GEN-ERATION, he stated in no uncertain terms that, "I promise you, any producer, like myself, would stand in the driving rain for two days to get a show that is somewhat shootable. You don't have to know anyone. You have to be good. You have to practice your trade. You have to do as I did and as all the writers I knew in those days did—watch television with the sound turned off so you can see how picture goes to picture. Then listen to just the sound without the picture. Learn your art and you'll sell. And write, write, write. You may get by easier, but you'll never really be good unless you do these things."

Then someone in the audience, who was apparently ignorant of much which was already well-known about the behind-the-scenes problems on the first season of STAR TREK: THE NEXT GENERATION, asked Gene if he was going to get writers like Harlan Ellison or David Gerrold to work on the series.

"Most of those I wouldn't want in the same room with me," Gene promptly re-plied. Inexplicably, many in the audience thought this was funny, and some even applauded.

"I've given all of them a chance," he continued. "David Gerrold has been con-demning the show (THE NEXT GENERATION) constantly. I had him on staff for many, many months; he never wrote an episode we could shoot! So beware these people that are loud voiced. Give your attention to people who quietly do good work."

Of course Gerrold, Fontana, and Ellison have related very different recountings of these conflicts. Now, with Gene's death, it is too late to repair these rifts and per-haps they are best left forgotten. Many conflicts of ego arise in a creative and high-ly paid industry such as television.

On a lighter note, Gene was asked how he would explain the difference in appear-ance between the Klingons in the old series and the Klingons in the new series. "Easiest thing in the world," he replied. "In the old series we had no money! And the cheapest thing we could do was to stick moustaches on them. In the new series we had some money and we said, 'Hey, c'mon, not everybody looks like central casting.'"

When someone inquired whether it was a conscious effort that THE NEXT GEN-ERATION did not employ as much violence as the old STAR TREK, Gene ex-plained that "I think we tried to stay away from violence in the old, but don't for-get, we started the old series in the time of cowboys, and all of us became more and more civilized as the years went by. The third year of STAR TREK, and the second, were more civilized than the first. In STAR TREK: THE NEXT GEN-ERATION we're very much changed people. We grow and our characters grow with us. Those of you who really want to be in the creative elements of television or film or whatever, you're on to a great thing."

Gene felt he learned much from his career. He said, "I have had, on STAR TREK, in the reading and studying and so on that I've done, the equivalent of several doc-torates. You grow. You learn. You study astronomy and science. You study pol-itics. All of the things that are worthwhile.

"I wake up, and have for thirty-five years now, at five o'clock in the morning. I get at least two hours of good reading in before my family is up at seven, and I've been doing that for thirty-five years. I invite you to the wonder of that, and you can realize, too, on whatever shows you write, science fiction or otherwise."

He felt very strongly about the importance of drama and what it could accomplish in reaching people. He believed his speech a perfect forum to explain just why television drama was important. "You learn," he insisted. "You test humans. Drama is an incredible school in life, and many scientists today are beginning to say that science and art are sort of the twin faces of the same kind of thing facing different ways.

"I've found, over these years, that the great profit I've made on STAR TREK is the circle of acquaintances I have. I can go to M.I.T and lecture there. NASA invites me there every year or two. The Smithsonian Institute; I participated in helping design some of the Air & Space Museum."

A common question regards crossover possibilities between the two STAR TREK series since "Encounter At Farpoint" featured a guest appearance from Dr. McCoy. In 1988, Gene downplayed the overlap. He explained, "We've got a new show which has to be different. I don't have the enthusiasm of the writers and the technicians unless they have their show that they can do. And so, I've kept the old characters out.

"I hate to! Those are my children, too. And I love them. But I have a new family and I must be true to the new family.

"The easiest way to fall on your ass is to be nice to everybody and never take a firm stand one way or the other. Those of you who produce, or are going to, have the courage of your convictions. You may make a lot of mistakes, and I have, but at least if I go down to defeat, it'll be on the basis of my mistakes; not on others."

Although Gene was sixty-six in 1988 while producing a major television show, he remarked that the directors of the original STAR TREK were too old to work for the new series. "We did that show twenty-three years ago," he said. "Many directors that we used then were people in their maturity at that time. Styles of directing change and so on!

"I love our old directors. Some of them got very busy and very rich.

"I choose what I think is best for the show, and I know sometimes people think that I'm a little hard-hearted. Thank God I'm behind the camera because I find my actors getting a bit old on that [earlier] show. I don't (get old)."

Unfortunately Gene perpetuated the Hollywood system which deems most talent over 40 as "too old," even though he himself escaped the consequences. He was 66 when THE NEXT GENERATION first aired in the fall of 1987.

Gene seemed more open to the idea of using writers from the original series, but he revealed his concerns quite openly. He said, "I like those writers. I like Bloch. I haven't seen anything he's done recently, but certainly I would listen very carefully to anything he had to say if he wanted to come by and suggest some ideas. But I'm also looking for young new writers.

"Some of them [the old writers] I feel might be set kind of in the mold of science fiction of those [earlier] days, and I'd be glad to find out I'm wrong. We have not had much luck calling in the old writers. A lot of time has gone by. They have become set in their ways. And they have become successes in their own ways. I'd love to use them. . . " Gene almost revealed behind-the-scenes disputes he was having with the Writer's Guild of America West when someone asked how he felt about the Hollywood writer's strike which was then in progress. "I'm a charter member of the Guild," he said. "I've supported them in strike after strike and I wish them good luck this time. I have some quarrels with the Guild now because there's some things that have come up where the Guild hasn't been representing me.

"When you're a success, you're no longer represented because they want to represent the freelance writers. I feel that I should be represented as well as any writer who's sold two or three scripts.

"The hyphenate [Writer-Producer] quarrel has always been out there and I don't think it's been resolved by the Guild. But I'm passionately a Guild member and I think there's good things they've done."

Gene insists he's suffered no interference with THE NEXT GENERATION as he had with the original series. He stated, "It's been so successful that everything I've asked for on the show I've gotten. I'm not asking for unreasonable things and they certainly have been supportive.

"I have gone, on a couple of the shows, a hundred eighty, a hundred ninety thousand dollars over budget, and that's serious money, but I explained why it was necessary. They listened and nodded and said, 'Okay, watch what you're doing, but we're not going to fire a guy who created this thing a second time.'

"I'm going to try not to take advantage of them. The new Paramount has a new level of executive that I haven't seen before in television where they honestly care about what you do and care about the writing and the tools you need. And I think we writers should encourage studios like that."

The highlight of the evening arrived when Gene announced that "The Big Goodbye" episode of STAR TREK: THE NEXT GENERATION had won the coveted Peabody Award for television excellence. Clearly Gene felt his efforts to bring back STAR TREK had been recognized.

He had rewritten the first dozen episodes, including "The Big Goodbye." Even though the series has since offered stories superior to what was accomplished in this episode, it has not been so honored again.

The evening proved a fitting tribute to three decades in the industry. None then imagined Gene would die just three and one-half years later.

On June 9th, 1988, Universal Studios launched its own addition to the growing tributes to the mythos of STAR TREK. Just so people arriving at Universal Studios knew that something unusual was going on that day, a gigantic balloon in the shape of the Enterprise seemed to hover over the top floor of the huge parking garage. While the balloon was by no means full scale, it was about forty feet long and well crafted so that there was no mistaking it for anything except The Enterprise.

The unveiling of this latest addition to the Universal Studios Tour was set for 10 AM with the press and a few hundred selected fans in attendance. As with most anything like this, it ran late, not starting until about 10:30. In the meantime, press were allowed access to the stage.

The bridge set was crowded with people. Camera tried to keep out of each others way while Gene was off to one side being interviewed. Deforest Kelley answered questions while William Shatner arrived and walked up to his co-star, giving Kelley a good natured hug.

Also on hand were George Takei, Nichelle Nichols, James Doohan and Walter Koenig. Fans in the audience wouldn't learn who was there for the show until later.

In the auditorium in front of the stage, fans became restless. "STAR TREK, STAR TREK, STAR TREK," they chanted.

Finally, it began. On an overhead screen, a film featured the history of STAR TREK as though Captain Kirk had called up the information on the ship's computer.

The film began revealing the history of the Enterprise, starting with its first Captain, Christopher Pike. It then gave mini-profiles of each character, beginning with Spock, showing snippits from "This Side of Paradise" and "Amok Time."

Leonard McCoy came next with a series of lines of classic dialogue, including several versions of the immortal: "He's dead, Jim." This was followed by brief descriptions of the movies, with reference to the new Enterprise.

Kirk then asked the computer to extrapolate into the future to see what the next generation of the Enterprise might be like. this led into descriptions of Jean-Luc Picard and company.

The film ended with Captain Kirk saying, "Happy birthday, Enterprise. Let's see what's out there," whereupon, one after the other, all three versions of the Enterprise sped off into warp speed.

Unfortunately, the film short was later dropped from the STAR TREK Experience.

After the film, a generic host stepped from behind the curtain and announced: "Universal Studios Tour welcomes you to the premiere of Paramount Pictures STAR TREK Adventure. And a special welcome to the fifteen hundred fans who, as contest winners, are here to celebrate this premiere with us.

"Just prior to you coming into the theatre this morning, we went out and selected twenty-nine members from your group and they're going to participate as stars in our very first episode. My name is Jerry Green and I'm going to be director for our show today and I have to be real honest with you here, I'm a little nervous.

"Usually before openings of shows you get nervous butterflies, but when you're doing a show based on STAR TREK for fifteen hundred people who know almost everything there is to know about STAR TREK, you want somebody here who is. . ."

Gene Roddenberry stepped out from behind the curtain to thunderous acclaim.

"Ladies and Gentlemen," Green continued, "the creator of STAR TREK, Mr. Gene Roddenberry!"

"Thank you so much," Gene said, beaming proudly. "You're very kind. I love you all; I really do."

"Mr. Roddenberry," Green stated, "I'm glad you showed up, believe me. I can see me making a mistake on some of this STAR TREK knowledge and these guys would nail me to the cross!"

"Well why not, they do me!" quipped Gene.

"They wouldn't dare. Listen, as long as you're here and because you know more than anybody; you've worked with cast, you've worked with crew. You've been around the fans for many, many years, what can you tell me that might help me get through this alive?"

"Well," Gene added, "I think that the important thing is for us not to depend on our own cleverness so much, but depend on what is basically with the fans. They are the ones who make STAR TREK possible because they believe in the things we talked about, and the networks and others have never really believed the fans were of the quality group that they are, but they are wonderful and they make all this possible."

The moderator then announced they were going to proceed making a movie "based on the STAR TREK Adventure!" A recorded voice welcomed the audience to this behind-the-scenes experience.

One of the fans sitting on stage apparently pulled a lever, a turbo-lift door opened—and out stepped William Shatner! The fans exploded into applause.

Then DeForest Kelley, Nichelle Nichols and James Doohan came out on stage. The moderator put the chosen fans through their scenes, which consisted of looking busy and dealing with smoke drifting over the scene.

One was made up with smudge marks so he looked as if he staggered out of an explosion.

When the next set rolled out, Jerry announced, "Ladies and gentlemen, we are proud to announce, an actual working transporter room. You've heard Captain Kirk say it a million times, Beam me up, Scotty! Ladies and gentlemen, through special authorization and permission by Mr. Roddenberry, this is a working transporter room. Let's step over here, Mr. Roddenberry."

"Amazing, I've never seen this before," said Gene in seemingly mock amazement, but actually he was surprised because he hadn't seen what this mock-up of the transporter would really do.

Jerry Green, the moderator, instructed the fans to get into position. He cautioned, "Be very still. Last time we did this in rehearsal, somebody moved and they wound up with their hand stuck in their ear. So be real careful. Be still, and stand by and energize to those predetermined coordinates."

The transporter effect, seemingly created live on stage, looked very real.

"I've never seen this before, really," Gene insisted, and he did seem genuinely impressed.

"I think we've uncovered a lot of talent here today," he later remarked.

"Well, we'll cover it back up. Don't worry," Green quipped. "We are now going to watch all of this put together in one composite package. We'd like to thank Paramount Pictures for making this all possible, and now ladies and gentlemen, Universal Studios, Paramount Pictures and our guest actors, and Mr. Roddenberry, proudly present—The STAR TREK Adventure!"

The lights dimmed. Screens overlooking the audience displayed a scene in space and then the Enterprise emerging from a dazzling display of special effects complete with the powerful Jerry Goldsmith score backing it up.

William Shatner's voice was heard saying, "Captain's Log. Stardate 4121.7. We are in route to Akimov VII, an obscure planet in the Klingon Neutral Zone. Our mission is to answer the distress call of a marooned space freighter which is carrying an invaluable cargo. I am confident in the capabilities of my new crew who are seasoned professionals, the best assembled crew in the entire Starfleet Command. I am proud to serve with them."

Scenes from STAR TREK II intercut with video of the fans in costume. The "movie" was marred by jarring transitions. The difference between film and video was painfully obvious, but the final effect was entertaining.

At the end of the film presentation, Gene Roddenberry, Nichelle Nichols, James Doohan, DeForest Kelley, George Takei, and Walter Koenig all came back on stage to wave to the audience. Green explained that William Shatner was beamed away to another appointment.

It was surprising Shatner had showed up at all. He never participates in public displays. In 1976 he was the only cast member who didn't show up for the dedication of the space shuttle Enterprise; the only Walk of Fame star ceremony Shatner showed up for was his own.

"STAR TREK Lives!" proclaimed Nichelle to the cheering multitude.

Then they all went back stage. When the curtain opened again, everyone who had appeared in the premiere performance of "The STAR TREK Adventure" appeared together on the bridge set— even the Klingon dragon-hound. Thus ended the coming out party for the latest addition to the Universal Studios Tour, and yet another marker of the enduring power of the STAR TREK legend created by Gene Roddenberry.

The STAR TREK Adventure continues as a popular attraction at Universal Studios. The storyline has been revised several times. Leonard Nimoy, who had been unable to make the opening of the Universal Attraction, made a special appearance for four hours four months later.

In November 1990, when THE NEXT GENERATION surpassed the marker set by the 79 episode run of the original STAR TREK, Gene observed, "We grew beyond the original show. We love the original and those actors, but we see the world differently now and our show reflects that.

"The revival of THE NEXT GENERATION had no emotional import for me. I don't live from despair to vindication. I never say it's just a TV show because it was once my center of concentration."

From 1989 until 1991, Roddenberry turned more and more of the daily control of THE NEXT GENERATION to Producer Rick Berman. "Oh, I look at every script," he said, "but I don't necessarily study every rewrite. I see the original when it comes in and so trust Rick Berman and Michael Pillar that probably the next version I see is the semi-final or final."

Gene's age was finally catching up with him. A series of strokes, one left him confined to a wheelchair until he fought his way back to mobility through physical therapy.

Gene began to serve as a consultant on THE NEXT GENERATION, much as he had on the STAR TREK motion pictures. By 1991, he had virtually no daily involvement. His creative team was in place and they proved they could helm the series successfully.

Gene said he expected STAR TREK would continue on and people would remark, "What they're doing now is much better than what that Roddenberry guy did with it!"

In July 1991, Paramount, who eleven years earlier had closed his office and ordered him off the lot after rejecting his script for STAR TREK II, honored Gene by naming a new building after him. William Shatner and Patrick Stewart represented the two generations of STAR TREK.

This miffed Leonard Nimoy who, due to a slip-up, hadn't received an invitation to the ceremony. He contacted Paramount to correct the oversight.

Gene was the only other speaker from among the STAR TREK people at the ceremony. He looked remarkably well, having largely recovered from his stroke. His speech wasn't noticeably slurred and he seemed strong.

Possibly offended at being left off the speakers roster and at almost not being invited, Nimoy chose to exercise a contractual right with Paramount. He refused to approve any photos featuring him which were slated to be used in the $45.00 coffee table book about the 25th anniversary then on the verge of publication by Pocket Books. The book had been written by Gene Roddenberry and Susan Sackett. This would have left the STAR TREK book with no pictures of Mr. Spock.

Nimoy also reportedly objected to some textual references. As a result, the book has been placed on "indefinite hold," according to a source with the publisher. It had been slated to appear in September 1991.

In August Gene suffered another debilitating stroke. It prevented him from participating in public events.

A 20th anniversary party for STAR TREK had been held on the Paramount lot in 1986. A similar event had been planned for September 1991, but when Roddenberry fell ill, it was scaled down from the huge event previously planned. Perhaps when Gene improved a party could be held.

OPPOSITE PAGE: Gene Roddenberry with his wife, Majel, and his longtime friends Walter Koenig, DeForest Kelley, Leonard Nimoy, Nichelle Nichols, James Doohan, George Takei and Roger C. Carmel, taken on Sept. 4, 1985 on the Hollywood Walk of Fame.
THIS PAGE: Gene Roddenberry proudly displays the plaque he was awarded.

Gene Roddenberry with cast and crew of STAR TREK IV: THE VOYAGE HOME.

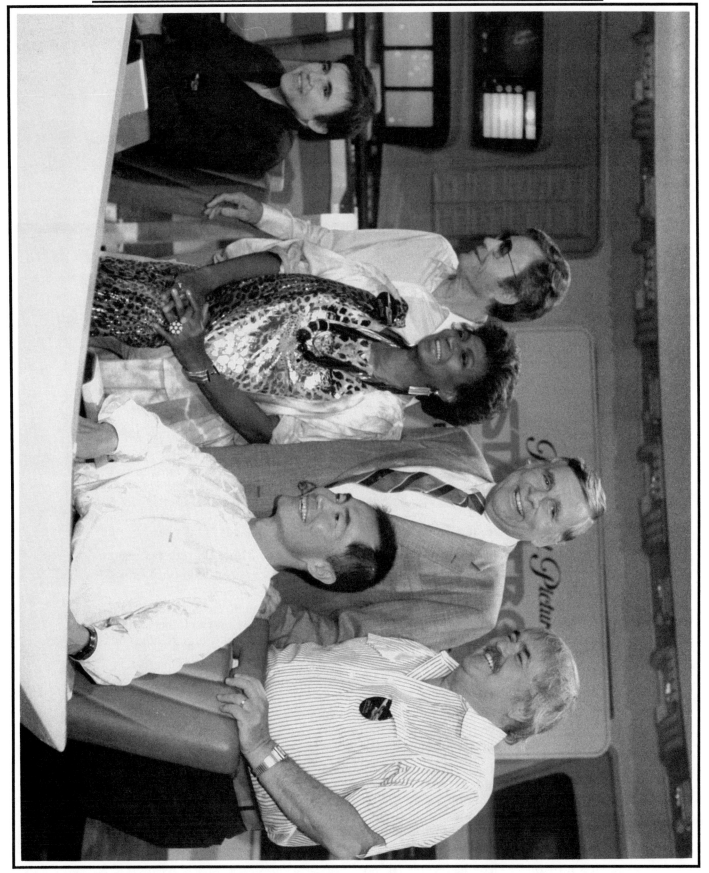

Gene Roddenberry with Walter Koenig, DeForest Kelley, Nichelle Nichols, George Takei and James Doohan, June 9, 1988.

XII Final Bow

"If it deserves recognition, I may get it sometime after my death. . . " —G.R.

(Based on unpublished interviews conducted during a press junket in November of 1991, approximately one month after Roddenberry's death)

On Thursday, October 24, 1991, Gene Roddenberry tragically succumbed to the illness which had plagued him all that year. He suffered a heart attack in his West Los Angeles home. Rushed to the Santa Monica Hospital-Medical Center, he died at 2:46 PM. Ironically, after years of struggle, it was his powerful heart that failed him. Official cause of death was ruled to be a major blood clot in his heart.

Gene was seventy years old. He is survived by his wife Majel Barrett, two daughters from a previous marriage (Darlene Incopero and Dawn Compton), a son, and his mother, Carolyn Glen Roddenberry.

Not all his friends fared well after his death. Susan Sackett, his personal assistant for fifteen years, was reportedly fired by Majel Barrett the day Gene died. Richard Arnold, a close associate who had supervised book licensing and related areas, found his job non-existent in the wake of Roddenberry's death.

Some months before Gene's death he had been asked what he would do if Roddenberry died. Arnold reportedly replied, "Oh, Gene's taken care of me in his will—I'll have a job at Paramount for life."

This, of course, begged the question of how Gene, an employee of Paramount, could guarantee another employee their job from beyond the grave. He couldn't.

Gene was interred at Forest Lawn Memorial Park in the Hollywood Hills. Unfortunately, some fans who attended the memorial service saw nothing disrespectful in showing up wearing STAR TREK uniforms and regalia. To make a bad situation worse, some showed up uninvited at the private graveside ceremony, making their presence known when the coffin was being lowered into the grave by saying: "Beam him up, Scotty!"

It's no wonder Gene had said in 1986, "I don't want STAR TREK on my tombstone."

When news spread of the death of The Great Bird of the Galaxy, response from the STAR TREK faithful was overwhelming. Many, who had never met him, felt as if they had lost a close friend or family member. Those who had known him, had much to say about their old friend and mentor.

Leonard Nimoy observed that the man who created Mr. Spock changed his life forever. He said, "Not only did he have a great vision but he had a great stubbornness; a great sense of self-assured stubbornness even when it must have been scary! When people were saying, 'That's no good, you can't do that, it won't work,' and so forth. But he was stubborn about what it should be.

"When the network wanted to know, 'Who's the monster this week? Who's the heavy this week?' There wasn't necessarily one, and I tried to perpetuate that vision in STAR TREK IV.

"There was no heavy in STAR TREK IV. Nobody got shot. Nobody was the person you point a finger at.

"At the end of STAR TREK III, I said to Harve Bennett, 'If we make another one, I want to make one where nobody gets killed. Where there's no black hat heavy that we can point to and say—if that person dies, we'll be okay. Where circumstances come at us in such a way that we have created our own problem. That our ancestors have created the problem for us, even unknowingly, unconsciously—not intentionally.'

"It turned out to be the most successful of the films and was very rewarding. I'm a Roddenberry disciple. I grew up with him, sort of."

Nimoy revealed that although Gene's health had been declining the past couple years, he was still very much involved with STAR TREK VI. "I went to him for regular meetings on this script," he revealed. "Every time we had a draft of the script I went to Gene for a meeting.

"He was very intrigued with the idea that we would be exploring this relationship with the Klingons. He was very much involved."

Nimoy strongly dismissed the notion that Gene's executive consulting position essentially froze him out from participation in the movies. He said, "Who said that? That he was frozen out?! Not true and very unfair. Gene was concerned, in this particular story, about the prejudice question because it's an interesting issue.

"Sometimes when you show people showing a prejudice, even though your intention is to show that they're wrong, there are going to be people who identify with it and say the people who are finding them wrong are wrong. And here you've got a couple of guys saying, 'What do you think of the smell?' and 'Only the top of the line models can even talk.'

"Gene was concerned about this. He said, 'I don't feel good about Enterprise crew talking that way.' And we pointed out that these are bad people! These are bad people who are racist and who turn out to be assassins.

"But he was just uncomfortable knowing that there were a couple of guys walking around in Federation uniforms who will talk that way about another race. And I understood it—it's a danger. But by and large he was quite taken with the idea that this would be a Klingon detente film. It was his idea to put Klingons into the Federation in THE NEXT GENERATION. This was the beginning of that link."

DeForest Kelley had been a friend of Gene's for a long time and knew him well. "Gene had a down home, earthy quality about him," Kelley recalled. "He was a big man. If you encountered him you would never dream that this man has this mind that he has. In a one on one conversation with him, he could be just as down to earth as possible until you start to engage him in some sort of philosophical conversation and suddenly this thing turns around!

"He was an intriguing human being but he never sprung that brilliance until it was called upon. He just was a guy who loved life, loved to have fun, and loved everything. He loved to drink, he loved to eat, he loved women—he loved everything.

"He was great fun to be with. But he changed the course of my life and he changed the course of every life in this cast, whether they know it or not. Bill would not be who he is today and Leonard would not be who he is today. Not only that, but I know, from certain mail—whether you agree with it or not, what the fans write—but he's also changed the lives of God knows how many thousands of other people who view what he's done and I think will continue to do so for some time. I think that he's a terrible loss and went out much too early. He will be missed, deeply."

George Takei observed that STAR TREK is "Gene's vision—we are his creation. He left us a great legacy and his absence is definitely going to be felt. But another part of the legacy that he left us is that he was aware of his mortality.

"As a matter of fact, his passing was not unexpected. It was a jolt, but it was very painful to see this vigorous, dynamic man being reduced by small hits. His speech getting slurred—he was at one time confined to a wheelchair, but he was determined *not* to be confined to a wheelchair and with therapy he got to the point where he could get up, and with a cane and his male nurse assisting him, he could walk.

"It wasn't that strong policeman's stride—it was this old man's shuffle. It was painful to see that. But Gene made sure that what he had given birth to would continue on. With THE NEXT GENERATION he had people who shared that vision and had talent and the kind of integrity and strength that kept that vision intact.

"Certainly with the STAR TREK movies, his participation was as an executive consultant, and the real active creators were people that he had charged with carrying on the plane, so to speak. I think this vision is intact.

"Two days before he passed on he saw the final cut of STAR TREK VI and he was very, very happy. So that was another pat on the back that he gave us before he passed on. So his vision and his legacy will continue because he's left *us* as part of that legacy—people who share his talent and philosophy and what STAR TREK is all about."

Walter Koenig said, "My association with Gene was generally very nice. He's certainly responsible for what's happened to me for the last twenty-five years.

"No matter what isolated instances there were in which I felt frustrated by his behavior and angry at him, my very basic and overall feelings are one of gratitude toward him for involving me in this and what has happened all these years. He was a man who was always very warm and very friendly. Always had time to say hello. Intransigent when it came to his own ideas, which is really a virtue because he could not be compromised. And although he suffered for it early on, I think ultimately it was one of the reasons why NEXT GENERATION is so much his vision because the studio knew that he could not be swayed—could not be made to change his mind.

"He lost projects in the earlier days because of that obdurate posture, but THE NEXT GENERATION was really his vision undiluted. The good and the bad, it was his vision undiluted, and that must have been enormously satisfying for him because this is a business where there's a dozen cooks for every project. I admire that. I admire his integrity to his own beliefs."

James Doohan had become good friends with Gene and recalled, "Gene and I would go sailing a lot and he was one hell of a navigator. We were fogged in on Santa Rosa island, which is about fifteen miles away from Santa Barbara harbor. I said, 'You set the course and I'll handle the boat.' So he said, 'Okay, take this heading here.' We arrived within about fifty yards of the harbor—just unbelievable.

"But engineering-wise he wasn't so hot. There was a day that looked as if it was going to be a very calm day. We headed out from the marina. I said, 'Let's stop and get some gas.' And he said, 'No, let's not take that time; we'll be okay.' So anyway we got out there about a mile out and we were crawling along at a quarter of a knot an hour. It was terrible, and it would have taken us forever to get to Catalina over to Avalon. So we started up the motor, but about ten or fifteen minutes later the motor stopped.

"At nine o'clock at night we limped in to Avalon harbor doing a knot an hour, I suppose. Gene called over to San Pedro and flew a mechanic over and he checked the motor and said, 'You're out of gas.' I said, 'Gene, let me handle all the engineering!'

"We got along well together. Gene and I knew each other quite well. I hadn't met him before STAR TREK, but we became good buddies. I was a little older than he was so I was able to tell him off every now and then. I think that Gene has left STAR TREK in good hands with the people that are in charge now."

Nichelle Nichols has some of the most emotional memories of Gene, and knew him perhaps longer than any of the other STAR TREK actors. "He was a wonderful, beautiful man," she recalled. "I loved this man—very much, very deeply. I knew Gene for over thirty years.

"Before STAR TREK, he gave me my first episodic TV job and with an introductory guest-star billing. It was in THE LIEUTENANT. It shows you how the man is. If he likes your work he never forgets his friends.

"Three years later when he was doing STAR TREK, he insisted that they bring me back from Europe to the show, and I'm real glad he did."

Nichelle Nichols had composed and recorded the song, "Gene," some time before his passing. She said the song, "Was my tribute to Gene to let him know, in all of those thirty years, how much I loved him and what I thought of him."

Strangely, William Shatner's own comments about Gene seemed somewhat distant. He said, "I met Gene twenty-five years ago. He had made the first pilot of STAR TREK, which NBC didn't buy but they wanted to recast it and try again."

Shatner explained how Gene had called him about starring in the second pilot and how he then came to California to perform in the role. He described their working relationship at the time as being wonderful.

Shatner continued, "Then he moved upstairs and there were other people slogging around in the trenches and so we didn't see as much of him as we had. When the series was over, I saw him not at all, and then the first film ten years later we saw him around.

"He was executive producing it but Bob Wise was the man in charge. And then he wasn't there for any of the subsequent films, so I didn't see him very much.

"I really had no contact with him for many years. I'd heard that he was ill in the past few years and occasionally I'd see him at the studio and say hello. But I had nothing but the most profound respect for him as the man who started all of this, and certainly has started STAR TREK: THE NEXT GENERATION. So when he died it came as a shock and I'm deeply saddened by it. But I really didn't know him at all."

On the E! channel at the time, Shatner sounded more enthusiastic in his recollections. He said, "Gene Roddenberry was the force that created STAR TREK. His creative abilities and his desire for perfection all made STAR TREK so much of what it is and we're going to miss him very, very much."

Ray Bradbury fondly recalled how fans would sometimes mistake him for his friend. Bradbury's response was never to deny he was Gene; instead, he'd play along, telling fans he'd created the show especially for them.

THE MAN WHO CREATED STAR TREK

"I don't know how much longer I can go on pretending that I'm Gene Roddenberry, now that he's gone," lamented Bradbury, "but I will carry the sweet burden to the end of my life."

For some, Gene's passing left the future of STAR TREK uncertain. Would his vision be altered, even betrayed, now that he was gone?

Rick Berman, the executive producer of STAR TREK: THE NEXT GENERATION, was quick to point out that the torch had already been passed. Berman has filled Gene's shoes for some time, with his mentor's blessings.

"What [he] created during his lifetime is certainly going to continue. His death is not going to in any way stop the flow of his vision," said Berman. "The thrust of our series has always been to continue Gene Roddenberry's vision of the future. It will be easy to keep doing that because we've never stopped doing it."

Gene himself expressed similar views in a 1990 interview, when he said, "I've trained so many executive producers now, they pretty much think as I think. When I'm gone, others will come along and do STAR TREK so well, people will say, 'Oh, that Roddenberry stuff, it was no good compared to this.'

"I would be pleased by that statement."

Indeed STAR TREK: THE NEXT GENERATION's fifth season was already underway at the time of Gene's passing. Although he didn't live to see it broadcast, the season was highlighted by the two-part crossover, "Unification," which bore a dedication to Gene at the beginning. It offered the long hoped-for linkage of the old and new series using Spock as the meeting point.

Although Gene did not live to see the release, and subsequent success, of STAR TREK VI: THE UNDISCOVERED COUNTRY, he did see the finished film. After his passing, of course, a dedication to him was added.

When VARIETY published a special issue (December 2, 1991) honoring twenty-five years of STAR TREK, many of the cast bought ads and used the occasion to lament the passing of the creator of the series which had given them so much over the years. For instance, George Takei's ad read: "A zest for the adventure of exploration; A shining affirmation of the human potential; A stellar voyage of the glorious vision of Gene Roddenberry."

Jonathan Frakes took the opportunity in a full page ad to say: "I'm proud to be a part of the family. We all miss our leader, Gene Roddenberry."

Nichelle Nichols printed the lyrics to the song she'd once written honoring Gene, and which ended with the phrase: "Gene, you showed us galaxies afar. You tied our hopes to every star. We're lucky you are who you are... Our loving... Gene."

DeForest Kelley's ad said: "25 Years of Wonderful Memories—Congratulations to all who have shared in the success of STAR TREK. All that is missing is... Gene."

William Shatner and his wife, in their full page ad, stated: "Our love and admiration to the cast of STAR TREK and our deepest sorrow that Gene Roddenberry will not share another 25 years with us."

Leonard Nimoy had no ad. When VARIETY had contacted him about buying one, he asked if William Shatner had one. When told that he did indeed, Nimoy said he wasn't interested in buying one then.

STAR TREK VI opened December 6, 1991 to an $18 million weekend, the best opening weekend of any STAR TREK film.

At the end of the film, Kirk's final voice-over muses on the adventures that will be had by the next crew of the Enterprise. He is certain they will continue to "Boldly go where no man— or no one— has gone before."

STAR TREK was a framework on which Gene hung his philosophical ideas. He once said, "Our show did not reach and affect all these people because it was deep, and great, literature. STAR TREK was not Ibsen or Shakespeare.

"To get a prime-time network show on the air, and to keep it there, you you must attract and hold a minimum of eighteen million people every week. You have to do that in order to woo people away from Gomer Pyle, Bonanza, Beverly Hillbillies. . . we tried to do this with entertainment, action, adventure, conflict and so on. But once we got on the air, and within the limits of those action-adventure limits, we did not accept the myth that the television audience has an infantile mind.

"The whole show was an attempt to say that humanity will reach maturity and wisdom on the day that it begins, not just to tolerate, but to take a special delight, in differences in ideas and differences in life forms," he continued. "We tried to say that the worst possible thing that can happen to all of us is for the future to somehow press us into a common mold where we begin to act and talk and look and think alike.

"If we cannot learn to actually enjoy those small differences, take a positive delight in those small differences between our own kind here on this planet, then we do not deserve to go out into space and meet the diversity that is almost certainly out there."

Rick Berman, the executive producer of STAR TREK: THE NEXT GENERATION, was quoted in the December 2 VARIETY, saying, "Gene felt strongly about the goodness of mankind. He knew there were rotten things also, but he liked to think of the future where wonderful things would continue and man could enhance the quality of his life."

Gene was very happy to learn, late in his life, that Tibetan Buddhist monks enjoyed STAR TREK. He said, "If the Dalai Lama likes us, I suppose the message is getting out."

Every day brings Gene's message to more and more people. Perhaps, now that he no longer walks among us, and he would certainly have hoped that this was so, his visions of the future might be the inspiration that creates a better future for all of humanity.

Gene thought a great deal about God and the nature of the human existence throughout his life. Some misinterpreted the things he had to say as an atheist's dismissal of God when it was actually an agnostic's dismissal of the superstitious trappings of all organized religions.

He admitted he believed the characters on STAR TREK believed in something higher. "Oh, yes. They have their own beliefs," he once said. "Which are private to them, and they don't evangelize or go around discussing them with other people. I've always assumed that by this time [the 24th century] there is a belief that is common to people in STAR TREK that, yes, there is something out there. There is, perhaps, something that guides our lives but we don't know what it is and we don't know if it is."

Gene also once said, "Whatever God is, it's got to be so much more than we can imagine. But I know that I am a piece of it. I don't fear death—you can't kill God, and I am a part of him."

APPENDIX

APPENDIX ONE

Television Writing And Producing Credits Of Gene Roddenberry

(ROBERT WESLEY was a pseudonym used by Roddenberry primarily while he was still working as a Los Angeles police officer.)

This list was complied from information obtained through the Academy of Motion Picture Arts & Sciences and the Television Academy. We know it is incomplete as certain shows Roddenberry said he worked on, like DRAGNET, were not in their files. It is possible he used a second pseudonym as the Robert Wesley shows, for example, are not cross-indexed with Gene Roddenberry and were only obtained because we were aware of the existence of this pseudonym. On the other hand, most of the pilots Roddenberry worked on were obtained from the Lee Goldberg book UNSOLD PILOTS (McFarland, 1989) as the Television Academy did not have most of them listed in their files.

1954
MR. DISTRICT ATTORNEY
"Court Escape" (by Robert Wesley)
"Police Academy" (by Robert Wesley)
"Wife Killer" (by Robert Wesley)
"Gambling" (by Robert Wesley)

1955
HIGHWAY PATROL
(Episode #1381 - by Robert Wesley)
(Episode #1429 - by Robert Wesley)
(Episode #1445 - by Robert Wesley)
(Episode #1468 - by Robert Wesley)

MR. DISTRICT ATTORNEY
"Police Brutality" (by Robert Wesley)
"Patrol Boat" (by Robert Wesley)

1956
I LED THREE LIVES
"Discredit The Police" (by Robert Wesley)
"Radioactive" (by Robert Wesley)

CHEVRON HALL OF STARS
"Secret Defense of 117" (by Robert Wesley)

WEST POINT STORY
[half hour anthology series dramatizing actual events from the files of the U.S. military academy at West Point.]
Producer: Maurice Unger
ZIV Production
Host: Donald May (also played Cadet Thompson in 1956 season.)
[Life in the West Point military Academy]
(Episode #1623 - title unknown)
(Episode #1624 - title unknown)
"Highway Patrol"
(Episode #1651 - title unknown)

(Episode #1752 - title unknown)
(Episode #1755 - title unknown)
(Episode #1818 - title unknown)
(Episode #1830 - title unknown)
"One Command"

DR. CHRISTIAN
[Medical series based on a film and radio series]
"Bullet Wound"

1957
KAISER ALUMINIUM HOUR
"So Short A Season"

WEST POINT STORY
(epsode #1854 - title unknown)
"Guest of Honor"
"Drowning of the Gun"
"His Brother's Fist" (Airdate: 12/3/57)
(with Leonard Nimoy in his first major TV role)

HAVE GUN WILL TRAVEL
"Helen of Abajinian"
"The Yuma Treasure"
"Ellow West"
"The Great Mojave Chase"

JANE WYMAN'S FIRESIDE
"The Perfect Alibi"

BOOTS & SADDLES
A California National Prod.
[Story of the Fifth Cavalry]
Series star Jack Picard
"The Prussian Farmer"
"Rescue of the Stranger"
"The Golden Gun"

HAVE GUN WILL TRAVEL
"The Hanging Cross"

BOOTS & SADDLES
"The Marquis of Donnybrook"

1958
HARBOR COMMAND
"The Psychiatrist"

JEFFERSON DRUM
[A story about a lawless gold-mining town called Jubilee in the 1850's. Jefferson Drum was a newspaper editor or was also a fast gun.]
Cast - Jefferson Drum: Jeff Richards
Lucius Coin: Cyril Delavanti
Joey Drum: Eugene Martin
Big Ed: Robert Stevenson
"Law And Order" (Episode #2 of series, airdate: 5/2/58)

"Madam Faro" (Ep. 7 - airdate: 6/6/58)
"The Poet" (Ep. 11 - airdate: 7/4/58)

SAM HUSTON
"The Man From Texas"

HAVE GUN WILL TRAVEL
"Maggie O'Bannion"

1959

THE NIGHT STICK (unsold pilot - never aired)
also known as THE BIG WALK
"Jim Ireland Meets the Giants"
[A show about a typical street cop.]
Producer/Writer: Gene Roddenberry
Cast - Jim Ireland: Richard Shannon
Gail: Ann Robinson
Mr. Komansky: Barry Nelson

HAVE GUN WILL TRAVEL
"The Tiger"
"Posse"
"Episode in Laredo"
"Charlie Red Dog"
"Golden Toad"
"Les Girls"

1960

THE DETECTIVES
Capt. Matt Holbrook: Robert Taylor
"Karate" (airdate: 1/8/60) (Guest star: John Anderson)
"Blue Fire" (airdate: 1/15/60)

JUNE ALLYSON SHOW
"Escape"

HAVE GUN WILL TRAVEL
"The El Paso Stage"

333 MONTGOMERY (unsold pilot - 30 min.)
(Airdate 6/13/60 as episode of ALCOA GOODYEAR THEATRE)
[Kelley as a criminal lawyer in San Francisco.]
Producer/Writer: Gene Roddenberry
Director: Paul Wendkos
Executive Producer: Robert Sparks
Based on the book NEVER PLEAD GUILTY by Jake Ehrlich
Cast - Jake Brittin: DeForest Kelley
Eva Fremont: Joanna Barnes
Secretary: Joanna Davis

1961

TWO FACES WEST
"The Lesson"

SHANNON
"The Pickup"
"The Embezalor's Daughter"

TARGET: THE CORRUPTORS
"To Wear A Badge" (with Harry Essex)

HAVE GUN WILL TRAVEL
"Alice"

1962

APO-923 (Unsold pilot - one hour)
"Operation Shangri-La"
[World War Two action show set in the Pacific.]
Producer: William Sackheim
Writer: Gene Roddenberry
Director: George Sherman
Cast - Pat Harrington, Jr., James Stacy and Ralph Taeger

DEFIANCE COUNTY (unsold pilot - one hour)
Also known as TY COOPER
[Show about a District Attorney in San Francisco.]
Producers: Clarence Green and Russell Rouse
Writer: Gene Roddenberry
Cast - Ty Cooper: David Gardner

DR. KILDARE
"The General"

HAVE GUN WILL TRAVEL
"Taylor's Woman"

NAKED CITY
"Rydecker Case"

G.E. TRUE
"V-Victor Five"

HAVE GUN WILL TRAVEL
"Trial At Table Rock"
"Marshall Of Sweetwater"
"Cage At McNaab"
"The Savages"

1963

THE LIEUTENANT (pilot - "A Million Miles From Clary")
(Airdate: 9/14/63)
[one hour drama about Camp Pendleton, based in Oceanside, Ca.
Story revolved around three officer's lives.]
Exec. Producer: Norman Felton
Producer: Gene Roddenberry
Writer: Gene Roddenberry
Capt. Raymond Rainbridge: Robert Vaughn
2nd Lt. William Rice: Gary Lockwood
Lt. Samwell Panosian: Steve Franken

THE LIEUTENANT
"The Alien" (by Robert Wesley - Why he used pseudonym in unknown)

THE VIRGINIAN
"Runaway Home"
THE LIEUTENANT
"A Very Private Affair"
"To Kill A Man"

1964

POLICE STORY (unsold pilot - 30 minutes)
(Airdate: 9/8/67)
[Ihnat, Johnson and Clark are three policemen on special assignment.]
Producer/Writer: Gene Roddenberry
Director: Vincent McEveety
Cast - Capt. James Paige: Steve Ihnat
Lt. Roy Haggerty: Rafer Johnson
Questor: Gary Clark
Garrison: Malachi Throne
Lab Chief: DeForest Kelley
Sgt. Lilly Monroe: Grace Lee Whitney

THE LONG HUNT OF APRIL SAVAGE (Unsold pilot - 30 minutes)
[Western show about a vigilante searching for the bandits who
murdered his family.]
Producer: Gene Roddenberry
Creator/Writer: Sam Rolfe
Cast - Robert Lansing

1971

ALIAS SMITH AND JONES
"The Girl In Boxcar Number 3"

1973
GENESIS II (Unsold pilot - 90 minutes)
(Airdate: 3/23/73)
[Science fiction about a NASA scientist who awakens from suspended animation
after 154 years.]
Producer/Writer: Gene Roddenberry
Director: John Llewellyn Moxey
Music: Harry Sukman
Cast - Dylan Hunt: Alex Cord
Lyra-a: Mariette Hartley
Harper-Smythe: Lynne Marta
Primus Isaac Kimbridge: Percy Rodrigues
Isiah: Ted Cassidy
Primus Dominic: Majel Barrett

1974

THE QUESTOR TAPES (Unsold pilot - 100 minutes)
(Airdate: 1/23/74)
[Science fiction about an android created to be a guardian
of humanity.]
Executive Producer: Gene Roddenberry
Producer: Howie Hurwitz

Writers: Gene L. Coon and Gene Roddenberry
Director: Richard A. Colla
Music: Gil Melle
Cast - Questor: Robert Foxworth
Jerry Robinson: Mike Farrell
Geoffrey Darro: John Vernon
Vaslovik: Lew Ayres
Dr. Chen: James Shigeta
Dr. Bradley: Majel Barrett
Administrative Assistant: Walter Koenig

PLANET EARTH (Unsold pilot - 90 minutes)
(Airdate: 4/23/74)
[Sequel/reworking of GENESIS II]
Executive Producer: Gene Roddenberry
Producer: Robert H. Justman
Writers: Gene Roddenberry and Juanita Bartlett
Director: Marc Daniels
Music: Harry Sukman
Cast - Dylan Hunt: John Saxon
Marg: Diana Muldaur
Harper-Smythe: Janet Margolin
Isiah: Ted Cassidy
Baylock: Christopher Cary
Yuloff: Majel Barrett

1977

SPECTRE (Unsold pilot - 2 hours)
(Airdate: 5/21/77)
[Supernatural detectives Culp and Young investigate mysterious
doings at a lavish English manor.]
Executive Producer: Gene Roddenberry
Producer: Gordon Scott
Director: Clive Donner
Writers: Gene Roddenberry and Samuel A. Peeples
(From a story by Gene Roddenberry)
Music: John Cameron
Cast - William Sebastian: Robert Culp
Dr. "Hamm" Hamilton: Gig Young
Mitri Cyon: John Hurt
Sir. Geoffrey Cyon: James Villiers
Anitra Cyon: Ann Bell
Lilith: Majel Barrett
Synda: Jenny Runacre
Inspector Cabell: Gordon Jackson

APPENDIX TWO

ORIGINAL STAR TREK PROPOSAL
DATED MARCH 11, 1964

STAR TREK is. . . A one-hour dramatic television series. Action-adventure-Science Fiction. The first such concept with strong central lead characters plus other continuing regulars.

And while maintaining a familiar central location and regular cast, explores an anthology-like range of exciting human experience. For example, as varied as. . .

THE NEXT CAGE. The desperation of our series lead, caged and in exhibition like an animal, then offered a mate.

THE DAY CHARLIE BECAME GOD. The accidental occurrence of infinite power to do all things, in the hands of a very finite man.

PRESIDENT CAPONE. A parallel world, Chicago ten years after Al Capone won and imposed gangland statutes upon the nation.

TO SKIN A TYRANNOSAURUS. A modern man reduced to a sling and a club in a world 1,000,000 B.C.

THE WOMEN. Duplicating a page from the "Old West"; hanky-panky aboard with a cargo of women destined for a far-off colony.

THE COMING. Alien people in an alien society, but something disturbingly familiar about the quiet dignity of one who is being condemned to crucifixion.

STAR TREK offers an almost infinite number of exciting Science Fiction stories, thoroughly practical for television. HOW? Astronomer(s) express it this way: by multiplying 400,000,000,000 galaxies (star clusters) in the heavens by an estimation of average stars per galaxy (7,700,000,000,000,000,000,000,000,000,000), we have the approximate number of stars in the universe, as we understand it now. And so. . . if only one in a billion of these stars is a "sun" with a planet. . . and only one in a billion of these is of earth size and composition. . . there would still be something near 2,800,000,000,000,000,000,000,000,000 worlds with a potential of oxygen-carbon life. . . or by the most conservative estimates of chemical and organic probability), something like <u>three million</u> worlds with a chance of intelligent life and social evolution similar to our own.

[Roddenberry admitted years later that he'd made this all up and was surprised when an astronomer told him that his calculations weren't as wild as he'd imagined they must be.]

Or to put it in the language of television . . . STAR TREK is a "Wagon Train" concept—built around characters who travel to worlds "similar" to our own, and meet the action-adventure-drama which becomes our stories. Their transportation is the cruiser "S.S. Yorktown," performing a well-defined and long-range Exploration-Science-Security mission which helps create our format.

The time is "Somewhere in the future". It could be 1995 or maybe 2995. In other words, close enough to our own time for our continuing characters to be fully identifiable as people like us, but far enough into the future for galaxy travel to be thoroughly established (happily eliminating the need to encumber our stories with tiresome scientific explanation).

The "Parallel Worlds" concept is the key to the STAR TREK format. It means simply that our stories deal with plant and animal life, plus people, quite similar to that on earth. Social evolution will also have interesting points of similarity with ours. There will be differences, of course, ranging from the subtle to the boldly dramatic out of which comes much of our color and excitement. (And, of course, none of this prevent an occasional "far out" tale thrown in for surprise and change of pace.)

The "Parallel Worlds" concept makes production practical by permitting action-adventure science fiction at a practical budget figure via the use of available "earth" casting, sets, locations, costuming and so on.

As important (and perhaps even more so in many ways) the "Parallel Worlds" concept tends to keep even the most imaginative stories within the general audience's frame of reference through such recognizable and identifiable casting, sets and costuming.

PRINCIPAL CHARACTER

Robert M. April—The "skipper", about thirty-four, Academy graduate, rank of captain. Clearly the leading man and central character. This role is designated for an actor of top repute and ability. A shorthand sketch of Robert April might be "A space-age Captain Horatio Hornblower", lean and capable both mentally and physically.

Captain April will be the focus of many stories—in still others he may lead us into the introduction of the guest star around who that story centers.

A colorfully complex personality, he is capable of action and decision which can verge on the heroic—and at the same time lives a continual battle with self-doubt and the loneliness of command.

As with similar men in the past (Drake, Cook, Bougainville and Scott), his primary weakness is a predilection to action over administration, a temptation to take the greatest risks onto himself. But unlike most early explorers, he has an almost compulsive compassion for the plight of others, Alien as well as human, must continually fight the temptation to risk many to save one.

OTHER REGULAR CHARACTERS

The Executive Officer — Never referred to as anything but "Number One", this officer is female. Almost mysteriously female, in fact — slim and dark in a Nile Valley way, age uncertain, one of those women who will always look the same between years twenty to fifty. An extraordinarily efficient officer. "Number One" enjoys playing it expressionless, cool—is probably Robert April's superior in detailed knowledge of the multiple equipment systems, departments and crew members aboard the vessel. When Captain April leaves the craft, "Number One" moves up to Acting Commander.

The Navigator — Jose Ortegas, born in South America, is tall, handsome, about twenty-five and brilliant, but still in the process of maturing. He is full of both humor and Latin temperament. He fights a perpetual and highly-personal battle with his instruments and calculators, suspecting that space, and probably God too, are engaged in a giant conspiracy to make his professional and personal life as difficult and uncomfortable as possible. Jose is painfully aware of the historical repute of Latins as lovers — and is in danger of failing this ambition on cosmic scale.

Ship's Doctor — Phillip Boyce, an unlikely space traveler. At the age of fifty-one, he's worldly, humorously cynical, makes it a point to thoroughly enjoy his own weaknesses. Captain April's only real confidant, "Bones" Boyce considers himself the only realist aboard, measures each new landing in terms of relative annoyance, rather than excitement.

The First Lieutenant—The captain's right-hand man, the working level commander of all the ship's functions from manning the bridge to supervising the lowliest scrub detail. His name is "Mr. Spock." And the first view of him can be almost frightening—a face so heavy-lidded and satanic you might almost expect him to have a forked tail. Probably half Martian, he has a slightly reddish complexion and semi-pointed ears. But strangely—Mr. Spock's quiet temperament is in dramatic contrast to his satanic look. Of all the crew aboard, he is the nearest to Captain April's equal, physically and emotionally, as a commander of men. His primary weakness is an almost cat-like curiosity over anything the slightest "alien."

The Captain's Yeoman — Except for problems in naval parlance, "Colt" would be called a yeoman; blonde and with a shape even a uniform could not hide. She serves as Robert Aprils secretary, reporter, bookkeeper, and undoubtedly wishes she could also serve him in more personal departments. She is not dumb; she is very female, disturbingly so.

Excerpted from orders to Captain Robert M. April:

III. You are therefore posted, effective immediately, to command the following: The S.S. Yorktown

Cruiser Class — Gross 190,000 tons

Crew Complement — 203 persons

Drive — space-warp. (maximum velocity .73 of one light-year per hour)

Range — 18 years at galaxy patrol speeds

Registry — Earth, United Space Ship

IV. Nature and duration of command:

Galaxy exploration and Class M investigation: 5 years

V. You will patrol the ninth quadrant, beginning with Alpha Centauri and extending to the outer Pinial Galaxy limit.VI. You will conduct this patrol to accomplish primarily:

(a) Earth security, via exploration of intelligence and social systems capable of a galaxial threat, and

(b) Scientific investigation to add to the earth's body of knowledge of life forms and social systems, and

(c) Any required assistance to the several earth colonies in this quadrant, and the enforcement of appropriate statutes affecting such Federated commerce vessels and traders as you might contact in the course of your mission.

VII. Consistent with the equipment and limitations of your cruiser class vessel, you will confine your landings and contacts to planets approximating Earth-Mars conditions, life, and social orders.

Some format and budget considerations. . .

SETS. Our format is tailored to practical production and cost factors. Use of stage sets, backlot and other locations are simplified by Captain April's "Class M" orders. And our own "Parallel Worlds" concept. The majority of story premises listed can be accomplished on such common studio backlot locales and sets such as Early 1900 Street, Oriental Village, Cowtown, Border Fort, Victorian Drawing Room, Forest and Streamside.

STAGES. The remarkable story latitude inherent in the concept also serves practical considerations by permitting reasonably simple adaptation of stories to fit current studio construction. For example, interiors and exteriors temporarily available after an "Egyptian" motion picture, a "horror" epic, or even an unusual telefilm. . . could be used to meet the needs of a number of story premises listed here.

SET AND LOCALE CARRY-OVER. Where particularly advantageous set or location conditions occur, or where a particularly exciting "world" is created, STAR TREK may do three or four stories there.

THE CRUISER. The "S.S. Yorktown" is, of course, a standing set to be amortized over the life of the series. For economy, the basic set is designed so that all cabins, wardrooms, and passages can be redressed and doubled.

LANDINGS. The Cruiser will stay in space orbit, will rarely land on a planet. Landings are made via a small (and transportable) recon rocket vehicle. Generally, audience view of sightings and landings will be that of the control crew, i.e., through instruments or on a "telescreen" (permitting use of selected stock film). Also for economy, ship miniaturization footage will be planned for maximum use, also amortized over the life of the series.

CASTING. Although it would be foolish to state we will never do a "monster" episode, most casting will be fairly routine. Where required, "alien" variations will be obtained via padding, wigs, and simpler makeup devices. But again, our general format stays "Parallel Worlds" and (as always in quality drama) the most unusual, exotic, and shockingly exciting differences always come out of action and reaction.

LANGUAGE. We establish a "telecommunicator" device early in the series, little more complicated than a small transistor radio carried in a pocket. A simple "two-way scrambler", it appears to be converting all spoken language into English.

WEAPONRY. Equally basic and simplified. The Cruiser is armed with Laser Beams for self-protection only. Crew sidearms are rifles and pistols with an adjustment and will fire simple bullets, explosive projectiles, or hypodermic pellets which stun or tranquilize. Alien weaponry, because mineral, vegetation and gravity are similar to earth, will follow a general earth pattern. Ranges from spears, bows, swords and lances, to variations of firearms. Now and then, of course, we may spring a surprise variation, such as a fairly advanced civilization which clings to feudal armor and swords as a way of life.

COSTUME. Alien garments are basically recognizable, i.e., also following the parallel worlds concept. Pastoral, Indian or Viking types of alien would general clothe themselves close to that worn at similar periods in our own social evolution. Crew uniforms are 'naval' in general appearance, attractively simplified and utilitarian. Again, surprise variations are possible here too.

Specifics on the SS Yorktown. . . As with GUNSMOKE's Dodge City, KILDARE's Blair General Hospital, we may never get around to exploring every cabin, department and cranny of our cruiser. The point being — it is a whole community in which we can anytime take our camera down a passageway and find a guest star or secondary character (scientist, specialist, ordinary airman, passenger or stowaway) who can propel us into a story.

Now and then a story will take place exclusively aboard the Yorktown, i.e. such as the tale of a strange "intelligence" which has made its way aboard and is working to take over the minds of certain key crewmen. Or the transportation of a person or a material which poses a mounting jeopardy to the ship and our characters.

The interior construction is utilitarian rather than exotic with a few appropriate indications of advanced controls and instruments. There are galleys, recreation rooms, a library, a hospital unit, and scientific laboratories, in addition to expected items such as the bridge, communication room and crew quarters always with a slight naval flavor.

Other story springboards. . .

THE PERFECT WORLD. Landing on this particular planet, Captain April and the STAR TREK reconnaissance team find a civilization approximating earth circa 1964. But with some unusual exceptions—seeming perfect order, no crime, no social problems, no hunger or disease, a place of charming and completely adjusted people. In fact, so pleasant and well ordered that something has to be wrong. Investigation in this direction finds Robert April seized and subjected to incredible police barbarism, even more shocking by its contrast. Only slowly does it become apparent that our wanderers have stumbled upon an example similar to the novel "1984", but with all the rough edges removed, i.e. completely efficient, also completely despotic communism carried to its extreme.

MR. SOCRATES. The most unusual world in the universe, a society secretly in a telepathic contact with the earth for centuries, selecting and duplicating in intelligence, lifelike form, the most unusual intellects produced in mankind's history. On a single street one might meet such people as Julius Caesar, Napoleon, Florence Nightingale, Genghis Khan, Thomas Jefferson, Carry Nation and Adolf Hitler. What at first seems like pure fantasy to the STAR TREK principals, suddenly becomes a very real and very deadly game as they begin to realize this is a form of "Roman Coliseum", that the participants are all "Gladiators", the stakes are life and death, and the games are about to begin.

THE STRANGER. After taking off from a planet, the S.S. Yorktown proceeds toward another planet in the same solar system. Not until then does it become apparent that an alien intelligence has made its way aboard with the aim of taking over the minds of key crew members—purpose to use our Cruiser to attack a rival civilization on the other planet. Actually a "horror" tale, we emphasize the subtleness of this attack on intelligence, reaching a point where mutual suspicion is endangering the entire ship.

THE MAN TRAP. A desert trek story, taking members of our band from one point on a planet to another. But what appears to be a pleasant, totally earth-like and harmless world rapidly develops into a hundred miles of fear and suspicions as Captain April and crew begin to encounter strange apparitions. Actually more than apparitions, these are wish-fulfillment traps which become as real as flesh and blood. Whatever a man wants most will appear before him, i.e. water, food, a female, a long-dead parent, gold, or even a way to power. The traps become increasingly subtle to the point where our crew nearly destroys itself out of a total inability to separate the reality they must have from the apparitions which will destroy them.

CAMELOT REVISITED. A planet of Hermes II, an incredible social order which is thoroughly modern in many respects but retains the knighthood, armor and other trappings similar to our middle ages. A touch of "A Connecticut Yankee In King Arthur's Court." As our star wanderers stop briefly to investigate and then become increasingly embroiled in a web of archaic social practices, finally reaching the point where they too are engaged in lance and sword play to preserve their own skins.

100 A.B. Or, "A Century After the Bomb" — a terrifying parallel as we examine what might be our own world a few decades after an atomic holocaust.

KENTUCKY, KENTUCKY. An earth colony on a planet in the Sirius group is visited by the S.S. Yorktown fifty years after colonization. An attack by the Viking-like savages has destroyed and scattered the colonists, reducing them to a "frontier" log-fort life. Unwilling to risk the S.S. Yorktown, Captain Robert April attempts, with a small band, to regroup and lead the colonists in defense.

REASON. In the Isaac IV group, a world where intelligent life has died, leaving a perfectly functioning robot society. Long speculative problem on earth, this requires detailed investigation and analysis, even at the risk of the Cruiser's reconnaissance party pretending to be robots themselves. Can a robot be capable of emotional feeling? Can it be capable of reasoning in human terms? What happens when an efficient robot society discovers alien flesh and blood spies in its midst?

REASON II. An extension, possibly the second part of the previous tale, portraying the struggle of the last human survivors, aided by our Cruiser's reconnaissance party, outmatched and relatively defenseless as they attempt to retake possession of their planet. Can a man, ragged and miserable, still be master?

A MATTER OF CHOICE. Another entrapment story, i.e. a planet in which the intelligent life has achieved no great material success but instead, has learned the power to live and relive over and over again in different ways, any portion of their past life they choose. This is a starring vehicle for Captain Robert M. April as he is presented with the chance to do those certain things all over again.

THE RADIANT ONE. A love story, the passion of a crew member for an angelic female on a 'Garden of Eden' planet—the one hitch being her chemistry includes radium in lethal quantity. The man who became her lover would live six weeks to six months, no longer.

THE TRADER. Satunii, a planet of incredible oriental splendor mercilessly ruled as emperor by a space trader turned renegade. Like a visit to the court of Ghengis Khan.

A QUESTION OF CANNIBALISM. Visiting the earth colony on Regulus, April's sortie party became aware the cow-like creatures raised on the ranches there are actually intelligent beings. But the colonists, who have built their empire largely on the supply and sale of this meat, rebel at the attempt to free their "cattle."

THE MIRROR. Near collision with another Yorktown on an exact opposite course. Not only is it the same cruiser, it is manned by exactly the same crew. Could you face yourself after discovering survival depends on killing yourself?

TORX. The first major menace to Earth. An alien intelligence, claiming to be pure thought and no body, which "devours" intelligence, leaving behind a helpless idiot. Near starvation for eons, it has been frantically seeking precisely the type of "food" the Earth could supply in quantity.

THE PET SHOP. Exactly duplicating St. Louis, 1910, a city where women are so completely the masters that men have the status of pets. Something of a satire on "people and dogs", this story shows men treated in that fashion, caged in kennels, others clothed and perfumed and treated as lapdogs, as long as they continue to fawn, appreciate and selflessly love.

KONGO. The "Ole Plantation Days" of the South, with the slight exception of it being white savages who are shipped in and auctioned at the slave mart. Part of our crew is trapped, thought to be runaways, and sold as plantation and household hands.

THE VENUS PLANET. The social evolution process here centered on love—and the very human male members of our crew find what seems the ultimate in amorous wish-fulfillment in the perfectly developed arts of this place of credibly beautiful women. Until they begin to wonder what happened to all the men there. . .

INFECTION. A female crew member discovered to be pregnant, and the growing realization it could be the larvae of an alien, using her body like some insects plant their eggs in other living insects.

"Infection": sounds amazingly like the concept behind the 1979 movie ALIEN. It just shows how different people come up with similar ideas, especially when they've both read a lot of science fiction. Gene's initial version of STAR TREK, while bearing superficial similarities to what finally aired, was considerably rewritten along the way to change the names of nearly everyone and everything first conceived for the series in 1964. Several of these plots which Gene had thought up did ultimately find their way into the series in one form or another, and the basic themes and concepts of many of these ideas he would rework and explore time and again over the years. The too-often used "parallel world" or parallel society fixture in STAR TREK ("Bread And Circuses," "A Piece Of The Action," etc) was part of Gene's concept from the beginning. One story idea which wound up being reworked years later was "Pet Shop" which ultimately became the telemovie PLANET EARTH in which Dylan Hunt is taken captive by a society that treats men as pets. It should be noted that Gene's original concept for "Pet Shop" didn't comment on women per se, but on pet owners!

APPENDIX THREE

PRESS RELEASE OF January 6, 1978

HAILING FREQUENCIES OPEN:

Please forgive this being a duplicated letter as it answers many friends who are curious about the return of STAR TREK. The news is generally good. Let me begin with a short history on the background of STAR TREK's return.

It is well over two and one half years ago that I checked onto the Paramount lot to bring STAR TREK back. The plan was to make a medium cost film to be shown in motion picture theatres. Then the new STAR TREK sets, paid for by the motion picture, would make STAR TREK's return to television much easier and much less expensive. However, the movie script which I wrote was rejected. The return of STAR TREK went into limbo.

Very discouraging months followed. Paramount had second thoughts about how successful a ten-year-old television show would be as a motion picture film. It really wasn't a situation of "STAR TREK good guys versus Studio bad guys." In all fairness, the STAR TREK fan phenomenon was something motion picture people had never dealt with before. My own estimate was that STAR TREK fans alone would account for a minimum of 10 million movie ticket, but many studio executives sincerely believed that my estimates were impossibly optimistic.

At this point, STAR TREK's return came very near dying. But, as happened eight years before when NBC first tried to cancel the show, the fans not only knew what was happening but how to cope with it. Paramount received an unprecedented barrage of mail on the subject. Fans also sent letters to newspaper editors, entertainment columnists, gathered petitions, distributed bumper stickers and posters, made telephone calls. Fans arranged for STAR TREK conventions to be properly covered in news programs; Smithsonian Institution put the eleven-foot Enterprise model on permanent display; fans caused NASA's space shuttle to be named "Enterprise;" magazines commented on Trekkies and Trekkers; radio talk shows gave hundreds of hours to the subject. The fans prevailed—Paramount became convinced they would probably sell enough tickets to make a STAR TREK film a reasonable gamble.

The STAR TREK motion picture project was revived. An experienced motion picture executive was brought into the picture; I was to produce under his supervision; experienced motion picture writers and a director were selected. For awhile, the project seemed very alive again and included even a scouting trip to England to investigate studio facilities where a film called STAR WARS was then in production. But although the renewed STAR TREK film project had attracted a group of talented professionals, somehow the chemistry did not work; the motion picture professionals could not get a STAR TREK script going.

Again, STAR TREK's return was cancelled. But this time the Studio did not lose its enthusiasm for STAR TREK. Since they had found difficulty in making it into a motion picture for theatres, why not take it directly to television, beginning with a major two-hour television movie? At about this time, Paramount had become interested in starting a new television network, and it was decided to use STAR TREK as their "flagship show." I was appointed Executive Producer again and brought back much of the original team. The two-hour television movie script was put into work, plus a dozen other scripts for the one-hour episodes which would follow the television movie. Paramount committed a considerable amount of money to these scripts and to a staff to supervise their preparation. Even more money was spent to design and construct entirely new, larger and more sophisticated starship interiors on stage. Paramount also ordered the designing and making of new costumes, phasers, and other STAR TREK props and paraphernalia.

During all this, STAR WARS happened. And it was a real happening—both in audience excitement and theatre tickets sold. On top of this came news that another large science fiction film called CLOSE ENCOUNTERS OF THE THIRD KIND might be equally successful. Interest in STAR TREK started to snowball, and the Studio asked me to improve the quality of the two-hour television movie so that it could be shown in theatres in foreign countries where the fan phenomenon was also being felt strongly. Meanwhile, the sets for the STAR TREK television movie were almost ready, the costumes were being completed, the props were approved and under construction.

In October, the Studio became concerned that a made-for-television STAR TREK was bound to suffer in any comparison with the big-budget STAR WARS and CLOSE ENCOUNTERS. Paramount decided to commit the Studio's resources to making STAR TREK a major wide-screen motion picture to be shown in theatres all over the world. Unfortunately, rumors circulated that STAR TREK was merely being shelved again. But this time the rumors were wrong. Production was merely being delayed for the months necessary to let us make STAR TREK a top quality film event.

And so this is the situation as of the writing of this letter. We are awaiting the studio's final "go ahead." Since the Studio has already invested several million dollars, it looks like it will finally happen this time. On stage, first class STAR TREK sets, costumes and paraphernalia are ready for the motion picture, and will be standing there—beautiful and ready—for still further STAR TREK production. Will we make all your efforts and postage stamps and aggravation worthwhile? We can only promise that we will try.

—GENE RODDENBERRY

APPENDIX FOUR

EPISODE GUIDE:
HAVE GUN, WILL TRAVEL

NOTE: Due to a lawsuit recently settled which dragged in and out of courts for 30 years, HAVE GUN WILL TRAVEL may no longer be available in syndication.

First Network Telecast September 14, 1957
Last Network Telecast September 21, 1963
"The Ballad of Paladin" by Johnny Western, Richard Boone and Sam Rolfe. Vocals by Johnny Western.
Filmed in black and white.
Starring Richard Boone as Paladin
With Kam Tong as Hey Boy
Lisa Lu as Hey Girl

FIRST SEASON:
1. "Three Bells to Perdido" (9-14-57) w/ Janice Rule and Jack Lord
2. "The Outlaw" (9-21-57) w/ Charles Bronson and Grant Withers
3. "The Great Mojave Chase" (9-28-57)
4. "Winchester Quarantine" (10-5-57)
5. "A Matter of Ethics" (10-12-57) w/ Harold J. Stone, Roy Barcroft, Steven Terrell
6. "The Bride" (10-19-57) w/ Bruce Gordon, Michael Connors, Marian Seldes, Barry Cahill
7. "Strange Vendetta" (10-26-57) w/ June Vincent and Michael Pate
8. "High Wire" (11-2-57) w/ Strother Martin, John Dehner, Buddy Baer and Fay Spain
9. "Show of Force" (11-19-57) w/ Vic Perrin, Peter Coe, Rudolfo Acosta
10. "The Long Night" (11-16-57) w/ Kent Smith, James Best, and William Schallert
11. "The Colonel and the Lady" (11-23-57) w/ Robert F. Simon
12. "No Visitors" (11-30-57) w/ June Lockhart, Grant Withers, Peg Hillias, Whit Bissell, Ruth Storey, Johnny Western and John Anderson
13. "The Englishman" (12-7-57)
14. "The Yuma Treasure" (12-14-57) w/ Warren Stevens, Henry Brandon, Harry Landers
15. "The Hanging Cross" (12-21-57)
16. "Helen of Abajnian" (12-8-57) w/ Harold J. Stone, Lisa Gaye, Wright King, Vladimir Sokoloff, Nick Dennis, and Naomi Stevens
17. "Ella West" (1-4-58) w/ Norma Crane, Earle Hodgens, William Swan and Mike Mazurski
18. "The Reasonable Man" (1-11-58) w/ Barry Atwater
19. "The High Graders" (1-18-58) w/ Susann Cabot and Robert Steele
20. "The Last Laugh" (1-25-58) w/ Stuart Whitman, Jean Allison and Gil Borden
21. "The Bostonian" (2-1-58) w/ Harry Townes, Chris Alcaide, Constance Ford, Joe De Santis, Louis Gomez
22. "The Singer" (2-8-58)
23. "Bitter Wine" (2-15-58) w/ Eduoardo Cianelli, Richard Shannon and Rita Lynne
24. "The Girl From Piccadilly" (2-22-58) w/ Betsy Von Furstenberg and Fenton Meyler
25. "The O'Hare Story" (3-1-58) w/ Victor McLaglen, John Doucette, Herbert Rudley and Christine White
26. "Birds of a Feather" (3-8-58) w/ Robert H. Harris and James Craig
27. "The Teacher" (3-15-58) w/ Carl Benson and Marian Seldes

28. "Killer's Widow" (3-22-58) w/ Barbara Baxley
29. "Gun Shy" (3-29-58)
30. "The Prize Fight Story" (4-5-58) w/ Hal Baylor, Don Megowan, King Calder, George E. Stone and Gage Clarke
31. "Hey Boy's Revenge" (4-12-58), featuring Kam Tong
32. "The Five Books of Owen Beaver" (4-26-58) w/ Lurene Tuttle, James Olsen, Paul Lukather, Tyler McVey and Walter Barnes
33. "The Silver Queen" (5-3-58) w/ Lita Milan, Earle Hodgins and Whit Bissell
34. "Three Sons" (5-10-58) w/ Parker Fennelly, Paul Jasmin, Jacqueline Mayo, S. John Launer and Kevin Hagen
35. "Twenty-four Hours to North Fork" (5-17-58) w/ June Lockhart, Charles Aidman, Grant Withers and Johnny Western
36. "Deliver the Body" (5-24-58)
37. "Silver Convoy" (5-31-58) w/ Donald Randolph
38. "The Manhunter" (6-7-58) w/ James Franciscus, R.G. Armstrong and Robert Gist
39. "The Statue of San Sebastian" (6-14-58) w/ Judson Pratt, Bart Bradley, John Carradine and Simon Oakland

SECOND SEASON:

40. "In An Evil Time" (9-13-58) w/ Joseph Calleia, David Whorff, Steve Colt, Martin Newman and Roy Poole
41. "The Man Who Wouldn't Talk" (9-20-58) w/ Hank Patterson, William Stevens, Charles Horvath
42. "The Gentleman" (9-27-58) w/ Charles Bronson
43. "The Hanginig of Roy Carter" (10-4-58) w/ Scott Marlowe, Robert Armstrong, John Larch and Paul Birch
44. "Duel at Florence" (10-11-58) w/ Dean Harens
45. "The Protégé" (10-18-58) w/ Peter Breck, George Mitchell, Ken Mayer, William Meigs and Mel Welles
46. "The Road to Wickenberg" (10-25-58) w/ Christine White, Harry Carey Jr., Rayford Barnes and Ed Faulkner
47. "A Sense of Justice" (11-1-58) w/ Barrie Chase
48. "Young Gun" (11-8-58) w/ Paul Carr, Dick Foran, Robert Simon, Meg Wylie, Abby Dalton and Frederick Miller
49. "The Lady" (11-15-58) w/ Patricia Medina, Robert Karnes, George Richardson and Earl Parker
50. "A Share for Murder" (11-22-58) w/Λ Harry Morgan
51. "The Ballad of Oscar Wilde" (12-6-58) w/ John O'Malley, David Lewis, Chet Stratton, Richard Shannon, Roy Engel and Jack Hogan
52. "The Solid Gold Patrol" (12-13-58) w/ Sean McClory, Don Keefer, Michael Hagen, Robert Cabal, and Jim Kline
53. "Something To Live For" (12-20-58) w/ Rayford Barnes, John Anderson, Tom Brown, Vaughn Taylor, Don Megowan and Nancy Hadley
54. "The Moor's Revenge" (12-27-58) w/ Vincent Price, Patricia Morrison, Morey Amsterdam, Richard Shannon and Joe Perry
55. "The Wager" (1-3-59) w/ Denver Pyle, Jacqueline Scott, Steve Gravers and Ken Lynch
56. "The Taffeta Mayor" (1-10-59) w/ΛEdward Platt, Robert Karnes, Norma Crane and Jeanne Bates
57. "Lady on the Stagecoach" (1-17-59) w/ Dolores Vitina, Fay Baker, Raymond Bailey, Ward Wood and Mark Dana
58. "Treasure Trail" (1-24-59) w/ Henry Brandon, Bruce Gordon, Dean Stanton and Willard Sage
59. "Juliet" (1-31-59) w/ Miranda Jones, John Beradino, Allen Case, Earle Hodgins and Ronald Green
60. "The Man Who Lost" (alternate title: "The Avengers") (2-7-59) w/ Robert J. Wilke, James Drury, Madlyn Rue, Vic Rodman, Mark Tapscott and Ralph Reed

61. "The Scorched Feather" (2-14-59) w/ Lon Chaney Jr., Mario Alcalde, Sy Malis and Mike Steele
62. "The Return of the Lady" (2-21-59) w/ Patricia Medina, Gene Nelson. Theodore Marcuse and Pilar del Rey
63. "The Monster of Moon Ridge" (2-28-59) w/ Barney Phillips, Natalie Norwick, Walter Coy, Ralph Moody and Robert Forster
64. "The Long Hunt" (3-7-59) w/ Stephen Roberts, Lane Bradbury, Anne Barton and Anthony Caruso
65. "Death of a Gunfighter" (3-14-59) w/ Suzanne Pleshette, Russell Arms, Christopher Dark, I. Stanford Jolley, Joe Bassett, Larkin Ford and Tom Greenway
66. "Incident at Borasca Band" (3-21-59) w/ Jacques Aubuchon, Perry Cook, Ben Wright and Ted Markland
67. "Maggie O'Brien" (4-4-59) w/ Marion Marshall, Peggy Rea, Paul Sorenson, Mickey Simpson, George Cesar, and Don Haggerty
68. "The Chase" (4-11-59) w/ Olive Sturgess, Paul Birch, Adam Williams, Paul Richards and Wright King
69. "Alaska" (4-18-59) w/ Richard Shannon, Karl Swenson, Elizabeth York, Allen Case and Paye Roop
70. "Hunt The Man Down" [directed by Ida LupinO] (4-25-59) w/ Mort Mills, Ed Nelson, Rudolfo Acosta, Jack Elam and Marilyn Hanold
71. "The Return of Roy Cartwer" (5-2-59) w/ Clu Galager, Larry Blake, Brad Von Beltz, Diana Crawford and Craig Duncan
72. "The Sons of Aaron Murdoch" (5-9-59) w/ Philip Coolidge, Lee Kinsolving, Elizabeth York, Wesley Lau and Bill Shaw
73. "Commanche" (5-16-59) w/ Shirley O'Hara, Larry Pennell, Susan Cabot, Roy Barcroft and Robert Anderson
74. "Homecoming" (5-23-59) w/ Lewis Martin, Ed Nelson, Don Megowan, and Dick Rich
75. "The Fifth Man" (5-30-59) w/ John Emery, Ward Wood, Leo Gordon and Clarke Alexander
76. "Heritage of Anger" (6-6-59) w/ Carol Hill, Ricky Vera, Peter Coe, James Gavin, Carol Thurston and Roberto Contreras
77. "The Haunted Trees" (6-13-59) w/ Doris Dowling, Roy Barcroft, Jane Chang, Duane Grey and Brad Trumbull
78. "Gold and Brimstone" (6-20-59) w/ Eduoardo Cianelli, Philip Pine, Alan Reed and William Vaughn

THIRD SEASON:

79. "First, Catch a Tiger" (9-12-59) w/ Harry Bartel, John Anderson, King Calder, Don Megowan and Pmela Lincoln
80. "Episode in Laredo" (9-19-59) w/ Eugene Lyons, Norma Crane, J. Pat O'Malley, Johnny Eimen
81. "Les Girls" (9-26-59) w/ Roxanne Berard and Danielle De Metz
82. "The Posse" (10-3-59) w/ Perry Cook, Harry Carey Jr., Denver Pyle and Ken Curtis
83. "Shot By Request" (10-10-59) w/ John Abbott, Malcolm Atterbury, Sue Randall, John Holland, Robert Gist and Greg Dunne
84. "Pancho" (10-24-59) w/ Rafael Campos, Rico Alaniz, Luis Montell and Edward Colmans
85. "Fragile" (10-31-59) w/ Werner Klemperer, Jacqueline Scott and Alan Caillou
86. "The Unforgiven" (11-7-59) w/ David White, Hampton Fancher, Luiciana Paluzzi, William Phipps and Paul Burke
87. "The Black Handkerchief" (11-14-59) w/ Ed Nelson, Joe Perry, Terrence De Marney and Sven Grunveld
88. "The Gold Toad" (11-21-59) w/ Lorna Thayer, David White, Bill Wellman Jr., Kevin Hagen and Paul Sorenson
89. "Tiger" (11-28-59) w/ Parley Baer, Elsa Cardenas and Paul Clark
90. "Champagne Safari" (12-5-59) w/ Bill Mims, Patric Knowles, Valerie French, Lou Krugman, Gilmman Rankin and Vic Perrin

91. "Charley Red Dog" (12-12-59) w/ Scott Marlowe, Raymond Bailey, Kelton Garwood, Edmund Glover and William Bryant

92. "The Naked Gun" (12-19-59) w/ Robert J. Wilke, Ken Curtis, Lane Chandler, Dallas Mitchell and Hal Needham

93. "One Came Back" (12-26-59) w/ James Coburn, Tommy Cook, Strother Martin, George Matthews and Robert Dorough

94. "The Prophet" (1-2-60) w/ Sheppard Strudwick, Barney Phillips, Florence Martin, Lorna Thayer, Eddie Little Sky and Brad Von Beltz

95. "The Day of the Bad Man" (1-9-60) w/ William Joyce, Eleanor Audley, Harry Fleer, Norman Shelly, Sue Randall, Tony Haig and Hal Needham

96. "The Pledge" (1-16-60) w/ Robert Gist, Charles Gray, Brad Weston and Susan Davis

97. "Jenny" (1-23-60) w/ Ellen Clark, Peter Leeds, Phil Chambers, Quentin Sondergaard, Trevor Bardette, Ben Brogan, Olan Soule, Bud Osborne, and Hal Needham

98. "Return To Fort Benjamin" (1-30-60) w/ Anthony Caruso, Herbert Patterson, Charles Aidman and Robert J. Wilke

99. "The Night The Town Died" (2-6-60) w/ Barry Cahill, Robert J. Stevenson, Mary Gregory, Arthur Space, Barney Phillips, Sally Singer and Vic Perrin

100. "The Ledge" (2-13-60) w/ Richard Shannon, Don Beddoe, John Hoyt and Richard Rust

101. "The Lady on the Wall" (2-20-60) w/ Howard Petrie, Ralph Clanton, Hank Patterson, James Stone, Barry Ivins and William Bronson

102. "The Misguided Father" (2-27-60) w/ Harry Carey Jr., Douglas Kennedy, Hampton Fancher, Gregg Palmer and Lee Sands

103. "The Hatchet Man" (3-5-60) w/ Lisa Lu, Allen Jung, Nolan Leary, Benson Fong and Fuji

104. "Fight At Adobe Wells" (3-12-60) w/ Ken Lynch, Miranda Jones, Sandy Kenyon, Dorothy Dells, Brad Weston and Gregg Palmer

105. "The Gladiators" (3-19-60) w/ Dolores Donlon, Paul Cavanagh, George Neise, James Coburn and Chet Stratton

106. "Love and a Bad Woman" (3-26-60) w/ Geraldine Brooks, Lawrence Dobkin, Bob Hopkins, Ed Faulkner, Sherwood Keith, Edwin Mills, Harry Landers, Mitchell Kowal and Sherwood Keith

107. "An International Affair" (4-2-60) w/ Ziva Rodann, Fenton Meyler, David Janti, Harry Corden and Oscar Beregi

108. "Lady With A Gun" (4-9-60_ w/ Jack Weston, Paula Raymond, Jean Eager and Ron Soble

109. "Never Help The Devil" (4-16-60) w/ Jack Lambert, Kelton garwood, Lewis Martin, Bill Wellman Jr., Dick Rick

110. "Ambush" [directed by Richard Boone] (4-23-60) w/Alan Dexter, Michael Ferris, Natalie Norwick, George Macready, Dan Barton, Ed Nelson and Hal Needham

111. "Black Sheep" (4-30-60) w/ Pat Wayne, Stacy Harris, June Vincent, Suzanne Lloyd, Ed Faulkner and Ross Strulin

112. "Full Circle" (5-14-60) w/ Adam Williams, Barbara Baxley, Stewart Bradley, Raymond Hatton, Howard Dayton, Bobby Rose and Hal Needham

113. "The Twins" (5-21-60) w/ Brian Hutton, Jennifer Lea, Lane Chandler, Tony Reagan and Sonja Warren

114. "The Campaign of Billy Banjo" (5-28-60) w/ Jacques Aubuchon, rita Lynn, Charles Davis, Dorothy Dells, Stewart East, Brad Von Beltz, Vic Perrin, Chuck Robertson, Denise Myers, and Hal Needham

115. "Ransom" (6-4-60) w/ Valerie French, Gene Roth, Robert H. Harris, Denver Pyle, Tom Palmer and Alex Davion

116. "The Trial" (6-11-60) w/ Robert F. Simon, Bud Slater, Raymond Hatton, Hal Smith, John Thye, Harry Antrum, Tom Jackson, James Bell, Bill Hunt, Rick Silver and Angela Stevens

117. "The Search" (6-18-60) w/ Wright King, Earl Hodgins, Perry Cook, Peggy Rae, Tex Lambert, Charles Aidman and William Bronson

FOURTH SEASON:

118. "The Fatalist" (9-10-60) w/ Martin Gabel, Roxanne Berard, Regina Gleason, Robert Blake, John Close and Lee Sands

119. "Love's Young Dream" (9-17-60) w/ Ken Curtis, Lorna Thayer and Mike Mazurki

120. "A Head of Hair" ((-24-60) w/ Ben Johnson, George Kennedy and Donna Brooks

121. "Out At The Old Ball Park" (10-1-60) w/ John Larch, J. Pat O'Malley, Jack Albertson, Ted Hamilton, Sandy Kenyon, and Perry Cook

122. "Saturday Night" (10-8-6) w/ Martin Balsam, Joanne Linville, Wesley Lau, Denny Miller, Rudy Solari, Terence De Marney and Raoul De Leon

123. "The Calf" (10-15-60) w/ Denver Pyle, Parker Fennelly, Don Grady, Carl Henry and Hal Needham

124. "The Tender Gun" (10-22-60) w/ Jeanette Nolan, Don Keefer, Tony Reese, Herb Patterson and Lou Antonio

125. "The Shooting of Jesse May" (10-29-60) w/ Robert Blake, William Talman, Hari Rhodes, Rayford Barnes, Barney Phillips, and John Milford

126. "The Poker Friend" (11-12-60) w/ Jack Weston, Betsy Jones-Moreland, Warren Oates, Peter Falk, Brett Sommwers, Leo Penn, Tony Haig and James Boles

127. "Crowbait" (11-19-60) w/ Russell Collins, Jacqueline Scott, Gordon Polk and Eddie Little Sky

128. "The Marshall's Boy" (11-26-60) w/ Ken Lynch, Andrew Prine, Harry Carey, Jr., and Hal Needham

129. "Fogg Bound" (12-3-60) w/ Patric Knowlws, Peter Whitney, Arlene McQuade and Jon Silo

130. "The Legacy" (12-10-60) w/ George Kennedy, Harry Carey, Jr., Chuck Roberson and Harry Lauter

131. "The Prisoner" (12-17-60) w/ Buzz Martin, Barry Kelley, George Mitchell, Liam Sullivan, Narda Onyx and Howard McNear

132. "The Puppeteer" (12-24-60) w/ Crahan Denton, Natalie Norwick, Peter Boone and Denver Pyle

133. "Vernon Good" (12-31-60) w/ John Mauldin, James Anderson, Albert Salmi, Leo Gordon and Oscar Beregi

134. "A Quiet Night In Town, Part One" (1-7-61) w/ Robert Carricart, Robert Emhardt, Phyllis Love, James Best, Sydney Pollock, Fredd Wayne, Kevin Hagen and William Challee

135. "A Quiet Night In Town, Part Two" (1-14-61) w/ Robert Carricart, Robert Emhardt, Phyllis Love, James Best, Sydney Pollock, Fredd Wayne, Kevin Hagen and William Challee

136. "The Princess and the Gunfighter" 91-21-61) w/ Arline Sax, Ben Wright, Shirley O'Hara, Earl Parker and Barry Cahill

137. "Shadow of a Man" (1-28-61) w/ Kent Smith, Dianne Foster, Walter Burke, Mike Kellin and Robert Karnes

138. "Long Way Home" (2-4-61) w/ William Talman, Ivan Dixon, Rayford Barnes and John Milford

139. "The Tax Gatherer" (2-11-61) w/ Roy Barcroft, Harry Carey Jr., Raymond Hatton, Stewart East, John Hopkins, Bob Woodward and Hal Needham

140. "The Fatal Flaw" (2-25-61) w/ Allyn Jostlyn, Royal Dano, Jena Engstrom and Miguel de Anda

141. "Fandango" (3-4-61) w/ Robert Gist, Karl Swenson, Andrew Prine, Jerry Summers and Rudolfo Acosta

142. "The Last Judgement" (3-11-61) w/ James Anderson, Harold J. Stone, Donald Randolph, Leo Gordon, Robert J. Stevenson

143. "The Gold Bar" (3-18-61) w/ John Fiedler, Jena Engstrom, Val Avery and Chet Stratton

144. "Everyman" (3-25-61) w/ Barry Kelley, David White, Vic Perrin, June Vincent, Don Engel and Suzi Carnel

145. "The Siege" (4-1-61) w/ Mike Kellin, Perry Lopez, David J. Stewart, Brad Weston, Robert Karnes and Russ Bender

146. "The Long Weekend" (4-8-61) w/Roy Barcroft, Ralph Moody, Paige Adams, Clegg Hoyt, Stephen Roberts and Ned Glass

147. "El Paso Stage" (4-15-61) w/ Buddy Ebsen, Karl Swenson, Jeremy Slate, Hank Patterson and Mary Mundy

148. "Duke of Texas" (4-22-61) w/ Scott Marlowe, Eduard Franz, Robert Carricart, Albert Cavens, and Roberto Contreras

149. "Broken Image" (4-29-61) w/ Kenneth Tobey, June Vincent, Johnny Eiman, Bob Woodward, Rick Silver, Stewart East, Joan Dupuis and Hal Needham

150. "My Brother's Keeper" (5-6-61) w/ Wright King, Ben Wright, Karl Swenson, Betsy Jones-Moreland, Ed Nelson, Otto Waldis and Allen Wood

151. "Bear Bait" (5-13-61) w/ Judi Meredith, Richard Rust, Martin West, Ralph Reed, Stephen Roberts, Frank Ferguson, Ollie O'Toole and Jack Tesler

152. "The Cure" (5-20-61) w/ Norma Crane, Jerry Wayne, Jeanne Vaughn, Craig Duncan and Olan Soule

153. "The Road" (5-27-61) w/ Ben Wright, George Kennedy, Gene Lyons, Trevor Bardette, Perry Cook and Joel Crothers

154. "The Uneasy Grave" (6-3-61) w/ Pippa Scott, Werner Klemperer, Lillian Bronson, Steve Warren, Wolfe Barzell and Don Beddoe

155. "Soledad Crossing" (6-10-61) w/ Ed Faulkner, Ken Curtis, Natalie Norwick, Chuck Roberson and Walter Edminston

SEASON FIVE:

156. "The Vigil" (9-16-61) w/ Mary Fickett, George Kennedy and Dan Stafford

157. "The Education of Sara Jane" (9-23-61) w/ Jena Engstrom and Duane Eddy

158. "The Revenger" (9-30-61) w/ Anthony Caruso, Janet Lake, Russell Arms, Shug Fisher, Harry Carey Jr., and Rayford Barnes

159. "Odds For A Big Red" (10-7-61) w/ Richard Ney, Hope Holiday, Virginia Capers, Ollie O'Toole, Robert Karnes and Perry Cook

160. "A Proof of Love" (10-14-61) w/ Charles Bronson, George Kennedy, Shirley O'Hara and Chana Eden

161. "The Gospel Singer" (10-21-61) w/ Suzi Carnell, John McLiam, Ed Peck, Noah Keen, Brad Weston and Roy Engel

162. "The Race" (10-28-61) w/ Ben Johnson, Michael Pate and Stu East

163. "The Hanging of Aaron Gibbs" (11-4-61) w/ Rupert Crosse, Odetta, Barry Cahill, Ed Faulkner and Hal Needham

164. "The Piano" (11-11-61) w/ Keith Andes, Antoinette Bower, Richard Reeves, Gertrude Flynn and Arny Freeman

165. "Ben Jalisco" (11-18-61) w/ Charles Bronson, Coleen Gray, Chuck Roberson, Rick Silver, Lane Chandler, John Litel

166. "The Brothers" (11-25-61) w/ Buddy Ebsen, Paul Hartman, Stu East, Peggy Stewart, Edward Faulkner and Hal Needham

167. "A Drop of Blood" (12-2-61) w/ Martin Gabel, Roxanne Berard, Mike Kellin, Regina Gleason and Noah Keen

168. "A Knight To Remember" (12-9-61) w/ Hans Conreid, Robert Carricart, Dolores Donion, and Wright King

169. "Blind Circle" (12-16-61) w/ Susan Davis, Gerald Gordon, Hank Patterson, Ellen Atterbury, Harrison Lewis and Bob Jellison

170. "Squatter's Rights" [alternative title "The Kid"] (12-23-61) w/ Flip Mark, Jacques Aubuchon, Roy Engel and Eleanor Audley

171. "Justice In Hell" (1-6-62) w/ Strother Martin, Dabbs Greer, Chris Alcalde, L.Q. Jones, Gaylord Cavellero and Gerald Gordon

172. "The Mark of Cain" (1-13-62) w/ Betsy Hale, Don Beddoe, William Schallert, Alan Carney, John Alderson and Larry Brightman

173. "Lazarus" (1-20-62) w/ Phil Coolidge, Roy Barcroft, and Iphegenie Castiglioni

174. "The Exiles" (1-27-62) w/ Gerald Price, Jay Novello, Vivi Janiss, Richard Bermudez, Bob Hopkins and Joan Tabor

175. "The Hunt" (2-3-62) w/ Joan Elan, Hank Patterson, Edward Faulkner, John Mitchum and Leonid Kinskey

176. "Dream Girl" (2-10-62) w/ Peggy Ann Garner, Joseph Dimmitt, Fred Hakim, Chuck Couch and Hal Needham

177. "One, Two, Three" (2-17-62) w/ Robert F. Simon, Jack Elam, Lloyd Corrigan, Eve McVeagh, Barbara pepper, Dorothy Dells, William Woodson and Dean Smith

178. "The Waiting Room" (2-24-62) w/ James Griffith, Dean Stanton, Ceorge Cesar and Byron Foulger

179. "The Trap" (3-3-62) w/ Jeanette Nolan, Frank Sutton, Crahan Denton and Ed Peck

180. "Don't Shoot The Piano Player" (3-10-62) w/ George Kennedy, James Callahan, Fenton Meyler, Virginia Gregg and Mike Mazurki

181. "Alive" (3-17-62) w/ Jena Engstrom, Jeanette Nolan, Richard Shannon, Mary Gregory, William Stevens and Perry Cook

182. "The Man Who Struck Moonshine" (3-24-62) w/ William Conrad and Phyllis Avery

183. "Ailent Death" (3-31-62) w/ Robert Emhardt, John Holland and Michael Pate

184. "Hobson's Choice" (4-7-62) w/ Milton Selzer, Parley Baer, Olan Soule, Titus Moede, Harrison Lewis and Jan Peters

185. "Coming of the Tiger" (4-14-62) w/ Marc Marno, Teru Shimada, James Hong, Fuji, Bob Ozaki and Beulah Quo

186. "Darwin's Man" (4-21-62) w/ Kent Smith, Richard Rust, Buzz Martin and Bud Osbourne

187. "Invasion" (4-28-62) w/ Robert Gist, Lew Brown, Douglas Lambert, Roy Roberts, Robert Gibbons and Vicki Benet

188. "Cream Of The Jest" (5-5-62) w/ Stanley Adams, Jeff Davis, Catherine McLeod, Peter Brocco and Naomi Stevens

189. "Bandit" (5-12-62) w/ Natalie Norwick, Robert Adler, Charles Couch, Bob Woodward, Jerry gatlin and Hal Needham

190. "Pandora's Box" (5-19-62) w/ Martin West, Lorna Thyer, Ken Curtis, Lewis Martin, Mary Mundy, Robert J. Stevenson and Jamie Brothers

191. "The Jonah" (5-26-62) w/ Crahan Denton, Richard Shannon, Harry Carey Jr., and Dorothy Dells

192. "The Knight" (6-2-62) w/ Jay Novello, Will Corey, Charles Kuenstle and Jean Inness

SIXTH SEASON:

193. "Genesis" (9-15-62) Richard Boone plays three roles. W/ James Mitchum, William Conrad, Parley Baer and Ann Morrison

194. "Taylor's woman" (9-22-62) w/ Kathie Brown, Harry Carey Jr., Tom Hennessey, and Olan Soule

195. "The Fifth Bullett" (9-29-59) w/ Ben Johnson, Shug Fisher, Peter Boone and Dorothy Dells

196. "A Place For Abel Hix" (10-6-62) w/ Kevin Hagen, Robert Blake, Paul Tripp and Jean Engstrom

197. "Beau Geste" (10-13-62) w/ Paul Richards, Faith Domergue, Henry Beckman and Ray Guth

198. "The Bird of Time" (10-20-62) w/ George Mathews and John Hoyt

199. "Memories of Monica" (10-27-62) w/ Judi Meredith, Bing Russell, Larry Ward and Hal Needham

200. "The Predators" (11-3-62) w/ Richard Jaeckel, Ellen Willard and Lester Maxwell

201. "Shootout At Hogtooth" (11-10-62) w/ Patrick McVey, Les Damon and Doodles Weaver

202. "A Miracle For St. Francis" (11-17-62) w/ Rafael Campos, David Garner and Miriam Goldyn

203. "Marshal of Sweetwater" (11-24-62) w/ David White, Kathie Brown and Gordon Jones

204. "Man In An Hourglass" (12-1-62) w/ Edgar Buchanan, Jim Stacy, Morgan Woodward, Alan Baxter, Dan White and Jerry Gatlin

205. "Penelope" (12-8-62) w/ Joanna Barnes, Lawrence Dobkin, Ivan Bonar and Jack Doner

206. "Trial At Tablerock" (12-15-62) w/ Sherwood Price, Barry Kelley, William Mims, Gregg Palmer, John Damier and Joey Higgins

207. "Be Not Forgetful To Strangers" (12-22-62) w/ Duane Eddy, Josie lloyd, Roy Barcroft, Pat Newby, Robert J. Stevenson, Ed Faulkner and Hal Needham

208. "The Treasure" (12-29-62) w/ Jeanne Cooper, Jim Davis, DeForest Kelley, Lee Van Cleef and Bob Woodward

209. "Brotherhood" (1-5-63) w/ Charles Bronson, Michael Keep, Max Mellinger, Shug Fisher, Dawn Eiulesky and Warren Joslin

210. "Bob Wire" (1-12-63) w/ Woodrow Parfrey, Irish McCalla, Chris King, James Bell and Hal Baylor

211. "The Debutante" (1-19-63) w/ Robert Emhardt, Wayne Rogers, and Eleanor Audley

212. "Unforgiving Minute" (1-26-63) w/ Patricia Medina and Al Ruscio

213. "American Primitive" (2-2-63) w/ Harry Morgan, Robert J. Wilke, Pitt Herbert and Peggy Rea

214. "The Burning Tree" (2-9-63) w/ Elinor Donahue, Whit Bissell and Paul Fix

215. "Cage At McNaab" (2-16-63) w/ Lon Chaney Jr., Jacqueline Scott, Christopher Dark and John Harmon

216. "Caravan" (2-23-63) w/ Miriam Colon, Dolores Faith, John Alderson, Cliff Osmond and Hal Needham

217. "The Walking Years" (3-2-63) w/ Elen Willard, Jacqueline Wilson, Satenio Donigan, Fred Hakim, Stewart East and Hal Needham

218. "Sweet Lady Of The Moon" (3-9-63) w/ Crahan Denton, Richard Shannon, Dorothy dells, Harry Carey Jr., and Robert J. Stevenson

219. "The Savages" (3-16-63) w/ Patric Knowles, Judi Meredith and James Griffith

220. "The Eve of St. Elmo" (3-23-63) w/ Warren Stevens, Brett Sommers, George Kennedy, Chris Alcalde, and P.L. Smith

221. "The Lady of the Fifth Moon" (3-30-63) w/ Bethel Leslie and William Schallert

222. "Two Plus One" (4-6-63) w/ Susan Silo, Gail Kobe, Rex Holman and Ken Hudgins

223. "The Black Bull" (4-13-63) w/ Carlos Romero, Faith Domergue and Lita Marshall

224. "Face of a Shadow" (4-20-63) w/ Enid Jaynes, Lee Van Cleef, Nestor Paiva, Richard Reed, Harry Carey Jr., Rayford Barnes, Roy Barcroft, William Woodson and Laurindo Almeida

225. "The Sanctuary" (6-22-63) w/ Harry Carey Jr., Hank Patterson and Jerry Summers

226. "The Mountebank" (8-3-63) w/ Warren Stevens, Robert J. Stevenson, Natalie Norwick, Carlos Romero and Sandy Kenyon

APPENDIX FIVE

EPISODE GUIDE:
THE LIEUTENANT

First Network Telecast September 14, 1963
Last Network Telecast September 5, 1964
Filmed in black and white
Starring Gary Lockwood as 2nd Lieutenant Bill Rice
Robert Vaughn as Captain Raymond Rambridge
Carmen Phillips as Lily
Steve Franken as Lieutenant Samwell Panosian
Richard Anderson as Col. Hiland
Don Penny as Lt. Harris
John Milford as Sgt. Kagey

1. "A Million Miles From Clary" (9-14-63) w/ Bill Bixby, Russell Thorson and John Doucette
2. "Cool Of The Evening" (9-21-63) w/ Kathryn Hays, Norman Fell, Jack Albertson and Paul Mantee
3. "The Proud And The Angry" (9-28-63) w/ Rip Torn and Tim Connolly
4. "The Two-Star Giant" (10-5-63) w/ Neville Brand, Hal Gould, Richard Anderson and Linda Evans
5. "A Very Private Affair" (10-12-63) w/ James Gregory and Stuart Margolin
6. "To Take Up Serpents" (10-19-63) w/ John Alderman and Gregory "Pappy" Boyington
7. "A Touching Of Hands" (10-26-63) w/ Bqrbara Bain, David White, Ina Balin and June Vincent
8. "Captain Tomson" (11-2-63) w/ Ken Tobey, Paul Burke, and Jay Sheffield
9. "Instant Wedding" (11-9-63) w/ Jeremy Slate, Martin West and Marlyn Mason
10. "A Troubled Image" (11-16-63) w/ Pilar Seurat
11. "Fall From A White Horse" (11-30-63) w/ Andrew Prine and Katharine Ross
12. "Alert" (12-14-63) w/ Ted Bessell, Sharon Farrell, Steven Mailo, Charles McGraw and Chris Connelly
13. "The Aret of Discipline" (12-21-63) w/ John Considine and Anne Helm
14. "The Alien" (12-28-63) w/ Frank Maxwell, Danny Nagai and Madlyn Rhue
15. "O'Rourke" (1-4-64) w/ Eddie Albert, Wayne Heffley and Robert Diamond
16. "Gone The Sun" (1-18-64) w/ John Beal, Joan Tompkins, John Anderson, Ray Teal, Sherry Jackson and Strother Martin
17. "Between Music and Laughter" (1-25-64) w/ Patricia Crowley
18. "Interlude" (2-1-64) w/ Conrad Nagel, Joanna Moore and Arch Johnson
19. "Capp's Lady" (2-8-64) w/ Nita Talbot and James Gregory
20. "Green Water, Green Flag" (2-15-64) w/ Jan Marlen and Nancy Rennick
21. "To Set It Right" (2-22-64) w/ John Marshall, Woody Strode and Dennis Hopper
22. "In The Highest Tradition" (2-29-64) w/ Andrew Duggan, Leonard Nimoy and Martine Bartlett
23. "Tour Of Duty" (3-7-64) w/ Ricardo Montalban, Kelly Thorrison and Louis Nye
24. "Lament For A Dead Goldbrick" (3-14-64) w/ Joseph Campanella, Robert Duvall and John Zaremba
25. "Man With An Edge" (3-21-64) w/ Chad Everett and Joan O'Brien
26. "Operation: Actress" (3-28-64) w/ Leora Dana and Leslie Parrish
27. "Mother Enemy" (4-4-64) w/ Neva Patterson and Walter Koenig
28. "The War Called Peace" (4-11-64) w/ Lloyd Bochner and Denver Pyle
29. "To Kill A Man" (4-18-64) w/ James Shigeta

APPENDIX SIX

Episode Guide
CLASSIC STAR TREK

First Network Telecast September 8, 1966
Last Network Telecast September 2, 1969
Filmed in color

FIRST SEASON

(1966-67)
1. "The Man Trap"; written by George Clayton Johnson; directed by Marc Daniels
2. "Charlie X"; written by Dorothy Fontana and Gene Roddenberry; directed by Lawrence Dobkin
3. "Where No One Has Gone Before"; written by Samuel A. Peeples; directed by James Goldstone
4. "The Naked Time"; written by John D.F. Black; directed by Mark Daniels
5. "The Enemy Within"; written by Richard Matheson; directed by Leo Penn
6. "Mudd's Women"; written by Gene Roddenberry and Stephen Kandel; directed by Harvey Hart
7. "What Are Little Girls Made Of?"; written by Robert Bloch; directed by James Goldstone
8. "Miri"; written by Adrian Spies; directed by Vincent McEveety
9. "Dagger of the Mind"; written by S. Bar David (Simon Wincleberg); directed by Vincent McEveety
10. "The Corbomite Maneuver"; written by Jerry Sohl; directed by Joseph Sargent
11. "The Menagerie, Part One"; written by Gene Roddenberry; directed by Marc Daniels
12. "The Menagerie, Part Two"; written by Gene Roddenberry; directed by Robert Butler
13. "The Conscience of the King"; written by Barry Trivers; directed by Gerd Oswald
14. "Balance of Terror"; written by Paul Scneider; directed by Vincent McEveety
15. "Shore Leave; written by Theodore Sturgeon; directed by Robert Sparr
16. "The Galileo Seven"; written by Oliver Crawford and S. Bar David; directed by Robert Gist
17. "The Squire of Gothos"; written by Paul Schneider; directed by Don McDougall
18. "Arena"; written by Gene L. Coon, from the story by Fredric Brown; directed by Joseph Pevney
19. "Tomorrow Is Yesterday"; written by Dorothy Fontana; directed by Michael O'Herlihy
20. "Court Martial"; written by Don M. Mankiewics and Stephen W. Carabatsos; directed by Marc Daniels
21. "The Return of the Archons'; written by Gene Roddenberry and Boris Sobelman; directed by Joseph Pevney
22. "Space Seed"; written by Gene L. Coon and Carel Wilbur; directed by Marc Daniels
23. "A Taste of Armageddon"; written by Robert Hammer and Gene L. Coon ; directed by Joseph Pevney
24. "This Side of Paradise"; written by Nathan Butler and D.C. Fontana; directed by Ralph Senesky
25. "The Devil In The Dark"; written by Gene L. Coon; directed by [?]
26. "Errand of Mercy"; written by Gene L. Coon; directed by John Newlam
27. "The Alternative Factor"; written by Don Ingalls; directed by Gerd Oswald
28. "The City On The Edge of Forever"; written by Harlan Ellison; directed by Joseph Pevney

29. "Operation: Annihilate"; written by Stephen W. Carabatsos; directed by Herschel Daugherty

SECOND SEASON

(1967-68)

30. "Amok Time"; written by Theodore Sturgeon; directed by Joseph Pevney
31. "Who Mourns For Adonis?"; written by Gilbert Ralston and Gene L. Coon; directed by Marc Daniels
32. "The Changeling"; written by John Meredyth Lucas; directed by Marc Daniels
33. "Mirror, Mirror"; written by Jerome Bixby; directed by Joseph Pevney
34. "The Apple"; written by Max Erlich; directed by Joseph Pevney
35. "The Doomsday Machine"; written by Norman Spinrad; directed by Marc Daniels
36. "Catspaw"; written by Robert Bloch; directed by Joseph Pevney
37. "I, Mudd"; written by Stephen Kandel; directed by Marc Daniels
38. "Metamorphosis"; written by Gene L. Coon; directed by Ralph Senesky
39. "Journey To Babel"; written by D.C. Fontana; directed by Joseph Pevney
40. "Friday's Child"; written by D.C. Fontana; directed by Joseph Pevney
41. "The Deadly Years"; written by David P. Harmon; directed by Joseph Pevney
42. "Obsession"; written by Art Wallace; directed by Ralph Senesky
43. "Wolf In The Fold"; written by Robert Bloch; directed by Joseph Pevney
44. "The Trouble With Tribbles"; written by David Gerrold; directed by Joseph Pevney
45. "The Gamesters of Triskelion"; written by Margaret Armen; directed by [?]
46. "A Piece of the Action"; written by David Harmon and Gene L. Coon; directed by James Komack
47. "The Immunity Syndrome"; written by Robert Sabaroff; directed by Joseph Pevney
48. "A Private Little War"; written by Judd Crucis and Gene Roddenberry; directed by Marc Daniels
49. "Return To Tomorrow"; written by John Kingsbridge; directed by Ralph Senesky
50. "Patterns of Force"; written by John Meredyth Lucas; directed by [?]
51. "By Any Other Name"; written by Jerome Bixby and D.C. Fontana; directed by Marc Daniels
52. "Omega Glory"; written by Gene Roddenberry; directed by Vincent McEveety
53. "The Ultimate Computer"; written by Lawrence Wolfe and D.C. Fontana; directed by John Meredyth Lucas
54. "Bread And Circuses"; written by John Kneubel and Gene Roddenberry; directed by Ralph Senesky
55. "Assignment: Earth"; written by Art Wallace and Gene Roddenberry; directed by Marc Daniels

THIRD SEASON

(1968-69)

56. "Spock's Brain"; written by Lee Cronin; directed by Marc Daniels
57. "The Enterprise Incident"; written by D.C. Fontana; directed by [?]
58. "The Paradise Syndrome"; written by Margaret Armen; directed by Judd Taylor
59. "And The Children Shall Lead"; written by Edward J. Lasko; directed by Marvin Chomsky
60. "Is There In Truth No Beauty?"; written by Jean Lisette Aroests; directed by Ralph Senesky
61. "The Spectre of the Gun"; written by Lee Cronin (pseudonyn for Gene L. Coon); directed by Vincent McEveety
62. "Day of the Dove"; written by Jerome Bixby; directed by Marvin Chomsky
63. "For The World Is Hollow And I Have Touched The Sky"; written by Rick Vollaerts; directed by Tony Leader
64. "The Tholian Web"; written by Judy Barnes; directed by Herb Wallerstein

65. "Plato's Stepchildren"; written by Meyer Dolinsky; directed by David Alexander

66. "The Wink of An Eye"; written by Arthur Neineman and Lee Cronin; directed by Jud Taylor

67. "The Empath"; written by Joyce Muscat; directed by John Erman

68. "Elaan of Troyius"; written and directed by John Meredyth Lucas

69."Whom Gods Destroy"; written by Lee Erwin and Jerry Sohl; directed by Herb Wallerstein

70. "Let That Be Your Last Battlefield"; written by Lee Cronin and Oliver Crawford; directed by Jud Taylor

71. "The Mark of Gideon"; written by George Slavin and Stanley Adams; directed by Jud Taylor

72. "That Which Survives"; written by D.C. Fontana and George Meredyth Lucas; directed by Michael Richards

73. "The Lights of Zetar"; written by Shari Lewis and Jerry Tarcher; directed by Herb Wallerstein

74. "Requiem For Methuselah"; written by Jerome Bixby; directed by Murray Golden

75. "The Way To Eden"; written by Michael Richards and Arthur Heineman; directed by David Alexander

76. "The Cloud Minders"; written by Oliver Crawford, Margaret Armen and David Gerrold; directed by Jud Taylor

77. "The Savage Curtain"; written by Gene Roddenberry and Arthur Heinemann; directed by Herschel Daugherty

78. "All Our Yesterdays"; written by Jean Lisette Aroeste; directed by Marvin Chomsky

79. "Turnabout Intruder"; written by Gene Roddenberry and Arthur Heinemann; directed by Herb Wallerstein

(80) "The Cage"; written by Gene Roddenberry: Although incorporated into the two-part episode "The Menagerie," the original first pilot, "The Cage," has been released complete and uncut on Paramount Home Video. This uncut version of "The Cage" was never broadcast on television

APPENDIX SEVEN

BIBLIOGRAPHY

(Special thanks to Audrey Anderson for research items.)

THE MAKING OF STAR TREK by Stephen E. Whitfield (Ballantine, 1968)

SAN FRANCISCO EXAMINER-CHRONICLE (3/10/68) "Star Trek—Cause of the Greatest Public Uprising" by John Stanley

FLORIDA TIMES UNION (3/17/68) "Fans Launch Star Trek Into Another Season's Orbit" by Gene Roddenberry

LOS ANGELES TIMES (8/13/68) "Enterprising Star Trek Taps TV's Potential" by Don Page

ST. PAUL DISPATCH (8/16/68) "Tarzan Movie Will Play It by Book" by Bill Diehl

ERB-dom #26 (1969) Letter from Gene Roddenberry (re: Tarzan)

SAN DIEGO UNION (8/1/72) Roddenberry interviewed by Don Freeman

SHOW (Jan. 1973) "New High, TV Sci-Fi" by R.A.L.

CLEVELAND PLAIN DEALER (3/19/73) "TV Science Fiction Booming" by Jerry Buck

THE MIAMI NEWS (3/30/73) "Star Trek Creator's Back" by Jay Sharbutt

LOS ANGELES TIMES (3/5/74) "When The World Ran Out Of Gas" by Cecil Smith

COLUMBUS CITIZEN JOURNAL (4/13/74) "Trek creator may have new series" by David Drake

TRAPEZE (10/8/74) "Talking With Roddenberry" by Kevin Turcotte

STAR TREK LIVES! (Bantam, 1975) by Jacqueline Lichtenberg, Sondra Marshak and Joan Winston

CHROMAKEY (CAPA-ALPHA, April 1975) "Gene Roddenberry Press Conference at Fla. State Univ." by Marc Wielage (Featuring Mike Clark)

ROCKET'S BLAST COMICOLLECTOR #118 (April 1975) "An Evening With Gene Roddenberry" by James Van Hise

THE COMMUNICATOR #4/5 (Fall 1975) "Gene Roddenberry at Marquette University" by Louise Kleba

LONG ISLAND ENTERTAINER (October 1975) "Star Trek Comes to the Big Screen" by Donna Gould

MONTREAL STAR (4/8/76) "Star Trek Creator No Guru"

ENTERPRISE INCIDENTS #1 (Feb. 1976) "An Interview With Gene Roddenberry"

PENTHOUSE (March 1976) "Star Trek's Gene Roddenberry" by Linda Merinoff

ENTERPRISE INCIDENTS #2 (July 1976) "An Interview With DeForest Kelley" by Joe Gulick

MEDIA SPOTLIGHT #3 (March 1977) "The Roddenberry Tapes"

TREK #8 (June 1977) "An Evening With Gene Roddenberry"

STAR TREK MAGAZINE #4 (1977) "Gene Roddenberry—An Exclusive Interview" by Richard Clabaugh

ERB-dom #89 (1977) "How I'd Film Tarzan" by Gene Roddenberry

STARLOG #12 (March 1978) "The Making of Star Trek II—A Conversation With Gene Roddenberry" by Susan Sackett

STARLOG #17 (October 1978) "All Systems Are Finally Go On. . . Star Trek The Motion Picture" by Joe Bonham

ROCKET'S BLAST COMICOLLECTOR #147 (Feb. 1979) "An Interview With George Clayton Johnson" by Dennis Fischer

ENTERPRISE INCIDENTS #7 (Nov. 1979) "Gene Roddenberry Phone Call—August Party August 3, 1979" by Rich Kolker

ST. LOUIS POST DISPATCH (12/9/79) "End of a Long Trek for Gene Roddenberry" by Desmond Ryan

THE MAKING OF STAR TREK THE MOTION PICTURE (1980) by Susan Sackett

STARLOG #40 (November 1980) "An Interview With Gene Roddenberry The Man Behind The Myth" by Karen E. Willson

THE MONTREAL GAZETTE (5/26/81) "Star Trek creator's lectures are much in demand" by Bettelou Peterson

STARLOG #51 (October 1981) "Gene Roddenberry—The Years Between, The Years Ahead" by Jeff Szalay

LINGUACODE IV (1982) "An Interview With Gene Roddenberry" by Cathy Conrad

ENTERPRISE INCIDENTS #10 (1982) "Gene Roddenberry—His 1968 Speech At Berkeley" (Transcribed by Dennis Fischer)

ENTERPRISE INCIDENTS SUMMER SPECIAL (1983) "Gene Roddenberry—Looking Ahead From 1983"

SAN FRANCISCO CHRONICLE (4/16/84) "It's the only police force in the country where it helps to have an agent" by William Overend

ENTERPRISE INCIDENTS (Sept. 1984) "The Creator of Star Trek Takes Stock" by Stanley Wiater

DAILY VARIETY (11/2/84) "Roddenberry First Writer Nominated For H'Wood Star" by Will Tusher

THE FUTURIST (February 1985) "Mr. Spock and Gaan—Alen Perspectives on the Future" by Gene Roddenberry

STARLOG #100 (November 1985) "Inside Gene Roddenberry's Head" by Kerry O'Quinn

ST. PAUL DISPATCH (4/18/86) "Star Trek Creator On New Enterprises" by Rick Shefchik

STARLOG #108 (July 1986) "Gene Roddenberry" by Ian Spelling

THE BOSTON HERALD (11/28/86) "Roddenberry still at helm" by Daniel M. Kimmel

NEWSWEEK (12/22/86) "Star Trek's Nine Lives" by Charles Leerhsen, Peter McAlevey, Janet Huck, David Gates and Peter McKillop

CINEFANTASTIQUE (March 1987) "Star Trek's 20th Anniversary" by Ben Herndon, Allen Malmquist, Hans Siden

THE STAR TREK INTERVIEW BOOK by Allan Asherman (Pocket, 1988)

CINEFANTASTIQUE (March 1989) "The Next Generation—Behind The Scenes" by Mark Dawidziak and Mark Altman

UNTOLD TALES OF THE NEXT GENERATION (1989) by Ed Gross

THE MAKING OF STAR TREK V (1989) by Lisabeth Shatner

CINEFANTASTIQUE (September 1990) "Star Trek—The Next Generation" by Mark Altman

THE HUMANIST (March/April 1991) "Gene Roddenberry—Writer, Producer, Philosopher, Humanist" by David Alexander

THE MAKING OF THE TREK FILMS (August 1991) by Ed Gross, Kay Anderson, Wendy Rathbone, Ron Magid and Sheldon Teitelbaum

FEAR magazine #24 (October 1991) "Star Trek: From Here To Eternity" (uncredited)

CINEFANTASTIQUE (October 1991) "Star Trek: The Next Generation" by Mark Altman

CINEFANTASTIQUE (December 1991) "Star Trek: The 25th Anniversary" by Sheldon Teitelbaum